LEARNING FROM THE FIELD

LEARNING FROM THE FIELD
A Guide from Experience

William Foote Whyte
with the collaboration of Kathleen King Whyte

 SAGE PUBLICATIONS Beverly Hills London New Delhi

For information address:

SAGE Publications, Inc.
275 South Beverly Drive
Beverly Hills, California 90212

SAGE Publications India Pvt. Ltd.
C-236 Defence Colony
New Delhi 110 024, India

SAGE Publications Ltd
28 Banner Street
London EC1Y 8QE, England

Printed in the United States of America

Library of Congress Cataloging in Publication Data

Whyte, William Foote, 1914-
  Learning from the field.

  Bibliography: p.
  1. Social sciences—Field work. 2. Sociology—Field
work. 3. Participant observation. 4. Interviewing.
I. Whyte, Kathleen King. II. Title.
H62.W455 1984   300'.723   84-15942
ISBN 0-8039-2161-6

FIRST PRINTING

CONTENTS

PREFACE

This book has been a much bigger job than I anticipated when I started on it. At that time I was thinking that over the years I had published a number of articles and chapters in books on field research methods, so I would just need to pull this material together, do some minor revisions, add a point or two here and there, and I would have the book. The further I got into the task, the more I realized that this would not do justice to what I should be able to contribute. Over the last fifty years, more or less, I have had an extraordinarily wide range of experience in field work with a variety of methods and in a variety of settings. That should make me especially qualified to write on the subject. Therefore I buckled down to do substantial rethinking and rewriting, and to add many pages on topics on which I had not written before.

I have tried to make this book both personal and professional: personal in conveying the thoughts and feelings behind the process of doing field work and then figuring out what you have learned; professional in providing broad coverage of topics that should be of concern to any field worker.

For helpful criticisms and suggestions on parts of this manuscript, I am indebted to Giorgio Alberti, Max Elden, Davydd Greenwood, Peter Lazes, Christopher Meek, Robert J. Thomas, Martin King Whyte, and Lawrence K. Williams.

As in nearly all of my previous work, I have spent many hours in discussing the ideas in this book with Kathleen King Whyte. Her detailed and comprehensive editing of the book has greatly improved its style and clarified its ideas. Since she has contributed so much in the shaping of this book over the years, it is fitting that she be recognized formally as a collaborator.

For typing the various drafts of this book, I am indebted to Melissa Harrington. I am fortunate in having a secretary who is not only tireless and efficient but also very much interested in my work.

—William Foote Whyte
Ithaca, New York

1

Purpose and Focus
of This Book

My aim in this book is to report what I have learned about doing research from field work over about a half a century and in a wide variety of social settings. This is not a textbook; I don't attempt to cover every topic of potential importance to those doing field research nor to present summaries and interpretations of all the significant writing done on this topic. However, I do present and interpret a wide range of personal experience in field work and in the analysis of data. Insofar as can be done in writing, I hope to take readers with me into the field so that they can get a sense of what field work is like. While this is only one researcher's view, in some cases I point out parallels to my own experience in the work of others. This suggests that my experience may be useful to other field workers in the future.

This is not simply a success story. Though I have been reasonably satisfied with much of the work I have done, I have made serious mistakes in various projects, and I have also failed to grasp some of the opportunities that now seem apparent to me as I say to myself that common refrain, "If I had only known then what I know now." I think it important to own up to my errors, and not simply because confession is good for the soul. It is important to recognize that explorations in the field are bound to confront one with confusing situations and conflicting pressures, so that some errors are almost inevitable, but few errors are serious enough to abort a project. We can and do learn from the mistakes we make, and it will help readers to see field work as a more human process if I lay out my own errors.

In this book I concentrate upon the field methods with which I am most closely identified, semistructured interviewing and participant observation and other forms of observation. For convenience, I will call them "anthropological" methods, recognizing of course that they are used by many sociologists beside myself. I am not trying to tell students how to do a questionnaire or survey (the method most characteristic of sociologists), but I shall discuss how surveys and anthropological field methods can be integrated to produce results not likely to be had when either is used alone. Similarly, I will not try to tell readers how to study history, but I will report from experience in one program how I came to appreciate the importance of historical research. Finally, I will discuss how I have tried to use theory to guide my field work and how learning from the field has advanced my theoretical ideas.

PERSONAL BACKGROUND FOR
AN INTERPRETATION FROM EXPERIENCE

In the chapters that follow I will be using case material gathered over the years, from the street corners of Boston to the rural highlands of Peru, from northern Quebec to the Basque country of Spain, and in a wide variety of industrial settings at home and abroad. Since I will draw from different periods of this experience, let me first sketch my career in field work in chronological order.

In a sense, I began sociological and social anthropological field work long before I knew what those terms meant. In my senior year in high school, I covered the school for the *Bronxville Press,* the village paper that came out twice a week. I also wrote a weekly column called "The Whyte Line."

I was able to get far enough ahead in some of my subjects so that I had a good deal of free time during school hours. My parents had moved to Bronxville because it was supposed to have the best public school system within commuting range of New York City, where my father taught German in the city college system. I liked Bronxville High School, but I came to recognize that regents' examinations and state education requirements limited its flexibility, which suggested that the more creative and interesting educational activities were going on in the elementary school. Without permission from the school administration, I spent several hours a week observing until I had covered one class in each grade from kindergarten through sixth.

As I recall, I did ask each teacher for permission to visit her class, and then I just sat in the back of the room trying to figure out what was going on. After the school day was over or when the teacher had some free time, I did my first field interviewing, asking the teacher to tell me what she was trying to accomplish and how what I had observed fitted into the general course of study.

As he told me later, School Superintendent Willard W. Beatty (later commissioner of Indian education), was apprehensive when he first learned that Bill Whyte was on the prowl in the elementary school. When the series was done, however, he told me it was the best interpretation of the new elementary education he had seen and arranged to put the columns together in my first publication beyond the newspaper, in a bulletin entitled "Bill Whyte Visits the Elementary School" (1931). Of course, winning approval from the chief executive of the organization we study provides no certification of the quality of that study, but this field experience prepared me for sociological research far better than anything I studied in college.

My father had a sabbatical year in Germany, so my entry into Swarthmore College was delayed a year. The editor did not want to lose his columnist, so he asked me to write a weekly column, "Personally Conducted," from Europe. Capitalizing on my local reputation, I proposed a 25 percent raise in pay, from 8 to 10 cents an inch. On that basis I began reporting weekly from Europe on anything that came my way. Much of this involved interviewing. For example, I got personal stories of experience from young people of my generation who had grown up in the bleak years for Germany of the 1920s and early 1930s.

I was fascinated with the rise of Adolf Hitler. When I left home, the newspapers were reporting news about Hitler, but no one seemed to take him seriously enough to write in any depth about his personal background and career. I read about him and his movement, and I interviewed Germans who were both for and against Hitler. I also took on the role of participant observer, particularly during a two-month period when I attended school in Partenkierchen, Bavaria. Since I was there simply to learn the language and was not seeking any advanced educational credits, I was free to savor the experience and reflect upon it. At that time, the faculty were so sharply divided politically that there was an informal agreement not to discuss politics within the school, but outside I was free to interview on political issues. This experience did not make me sympathetic to the Nazi leader, but it did provide good experience in understanding people whose views and values differed sharply from my own.

During my years in Swarthmore College (1932-1936) there was no department of sociology or anthropology, so I remained innocent of these disciplines. I majored in economics, but the professors who particularly attracted me were those who had strong social concerns in the

Quaker tradition. From my reading I had already developed an interest in slum districts, and during one intense weekend experience in Philadelphia, in a program arranged by a settlement house, I got a brief and superficial exposure to what a slum was like.

During my college years the closest I got to sociological field work was through a term paper in a seminar on social economics. The assignment was to write on some topic of public finance. I asked Professor Clair Wilcox if I could do my paper on financing New York City. He told me that I could proceed at my own risk on this, since he knew of only one book on the topic. Taking off early for Christmas vacation, I spent most of that period in the municipal library, digging out the data, but I also interviewed a few city career officials. Wilcox thought enough of the paper to advise me to develop it for publication. Thus my first social science publication was a study in economics (1935).

As a junior fellow at Harvard (1936-1940), I had the extraordinary opportunity to be supported for a three-year period (later extended to a fourth year) with full freedom to do research. All the facilities of Harvard, from its magnificent library to the classrooms and seminars, were open to me, with but one restriction. At the time, junior fellows were not allowed to take courses for credit. I shall always be grateful for that restriction. Coming from an academic family and with a strong undergraduate record behind me, if I had been allowed to work for graduate degrees, I might well have thought that I must concentrate on acquiring those credits.

For four years I was free to find what I really wanted to do—and to find myself in the process. I knew at the outset that I wanted to study a slum district, but at first I thought I was undertaking a study of the economics of slums and housing.

Two main influences moved me gradually out of economics and into sociology or anthropology. In the first place, from an early age, I had been interested in writing—and not just newspaper writing, although I recognized that it had been an extraordinarily valuable experience. I wanted to write novels or plays, but I felt limited by my own background, growing up in a well-protected but not affluent upper-middle-class family. I recognized that I could only hope to write good fiction out of my own experience, and I realized that that experience was severely limited.

It was a desire to extend my social experience, as well as a commitment to social reform, that led me into the slum district. Still, I gradually came to realize that I could not be satisfied just learning about slum housing, rents, land values, taxation, and so on. I needed to know the people. It was at this point that I came under the influence of another junior fellow, social anthropologist Conrad M. Arensberg, who had recently returned from a field study in rural Ireland. He took an interest in my work and guided me into the methods of interviewing and observation that I used in *Street Corner Society*. On the one hand, all that he was teaching me was new, but on the other, it seemed to build naturally upon my journalistic field experience in Bronxville and in Europe.

When I moved to Chicago to begin formal graduate work in 1940, I was still in the process of working out my disciplinary identity. When I abandoned the notion of becoming an economist, for some months I described myself as a social anthropologist. I went to Chicago particularly to study under W. Lloyd Warner, the social anthropologist who had directed the path-breaking Yankee City Project.

Since Warner had joint appointments in sociology and anthropology, I could study under him in either department. I also noted that the subfield of social anthropology largely overlapped with what was called "social organization" in the department of sociology. As I studied the catalog for degree requirements, I came to the conclusion that these disciplines contained about an equal amount of material in which I was not interested, but in anthropology that material seemed harder to learn—physical anthropology and archaeology, for example. I also assumed that there were more college jobs available in sociology than in anthropology—although I was not so sure later, when my first job offer was the only one I received. In any case, for such considerations of expediency, I opted for the doctorate in sociology, but I minored in social anthropology, and for many years I was active in the Society for Applied Anthropology.

In Chicago I studied with Warner and Everett C. Hughes. I did pass statistics courses with William F. Ogburn and Samuel Stouffer, but I had forgotten all the statistics I learned in graduate work by the time I became involved in surveys.

At the University of Oklahoma (1942-1943), to encourage me to get some research started, Sociology Department Chairman W. B. Bizzell arranged my teaching schedule so that I could spend Tuesdays and Thursdays in the field. He told me that there were 42 Indian tribes represented within Oklahoma, and he assumed that I would want to study Indians. I had been interested in reading about Indians, but we were now involved in World War II, and it seemed to me that the oil industry would have more practical relevance. My first study in industry was with Phillips Petroleum Company in Oklahoma City. In 1943, as I was leaving Oklahoma for a teaching and research job at Harvard, I came down with polio and so spent most of the next eleven months in

Massachusetts General Hospital and Georgia Warm Springs Foundation. It was in this period that *Street Corner Society* was published.

In May 1944 I went back to the University of Chicago as a research associate to join the Committee on Human Relations in Industry, formed a year earlier by Lloyd Warner and Burleigh G. Gardner. This was an exciting time to be at Chicago and working with this particular group. We were not the first in this country to study what we then called "human relations in industry," but the Harvard-Western Electric program had come to an end years earlier, and the Harvard people had turned to other pursuits. A project to study human relations in the restaurant industry brought me to Chicago, and that project led into an action-research project in a large hotel. In this period I was also becoming involved in factory studies, focusing particularly on worker participation and union-management cooperation.

The next move—which turned out to be permanent—was to Cornell University in 1948 to join the faculty of the New York State School of Industrial and Labor Relations, founded in 1945. As in the last two years at Chicago, my appointment was for half-time teaching and half-time research, which gave me two days a week to participate in field work with graduate students in plants in nearby Elmira and Corning.

As I was beginning to see patterns in my work in U.S. industry, I became increasingly curious about whether my conclusions had general significance for organizational behavior everywhere or whether patterns of organizational behavior in other countries with quite different cultures would differ markedly from what I had found at home. My first opportunity for research abroad came with a sabbatical year, 1954-1955, with Creole Petroleum Company in Venezuela.

Kathleen King Whyte had been with me for two years in the street corner study, and she and our four children joined me in this first foreign field project. With three research assistants, I was studying the relations of Venezuelan workers and first-line supervisors with U.S. management people, and the evolution of company-community relations in a situation of built-in paternalism. The company had initially provided all the community infrastructure needed to support its operations in what had been practically an unsettled area.

A year later, during the summer of 1956, I directed a study of relations between workers and management, and French-Canadians and English-Canadians, in the Aluminum Company of Canada's installations in Arvida, Northern Quebec. My three research assistants, young French professors from Laval University, concentrated on interviewing the French-Canadian workers and supervisors, while I limited my field efforts to English-Canadians, with one exception. With careful advance preparation to phrase the questions I wanted to ask, I did manage one interview with a union leader who did not speak English.

Intellectually rewarding as these two first international projects were, they still left me with unanswered questions regarding the nature of worker-management relations in another culture, since in both cases those relations were compounded by the fact that managers were predominantly of one ethnic or nationality group and workers of another.

In the period between sabbatical years (1955-1961) I was so occupied with editing *Human Organization* (the journal for the Society for Applied Anthropology) and directing Cornell University's Social Science Research Center that I had no further opportunity to involve myself personally in field work and had to content myself with consulting with students.

Beginning in 1961, Kathleen and I were involved in a second foreign research experience, this one lasting far longer. Starting with fourteen months in Lima, I continued research in Peru until 1976. I assumed at the outset that I would be concentrating on studies of organizational behavior in industry, and learning about rural life from social anthropologist Allen Holmberg and others who were engaged in rural studies. However, as I became more interested in Peruvian politics and problems, I found myself lured into surveys of the values and attitudes of high school students, and then into a long-range program of surveys and anthropological studies of Peruvian villages. Thus in a sense I found myself back where I started, doing community studies, but this time in a very different setting.

Toward the end of the long period of Peruvian studies, I gradually shifted into two lines of research that had their origins in Peru and that involved me in further rural and industrial studies. At Cornell I was invited to join the Program for Policies for Science and Technology in Developing Nations, in our Center for International Studies. As I became active in this program, I saw the possibilities of building on my knowledge of peasant communities and small farmers to examine the agricultural research and development organizations that were trying to increase agricultural production and enhance rural welfare.

In the village studies extension agents and agricultural researchers were simply there in the background. To the very limited extent that they had any impact upon the villages I was studying, I had to take that impact into account, but I did not focus attention on the agricultural professionals. By 1975 I was putting villages in the background and concentrating on these agricultural professionals. In field trips lasting from several weeks to months, in Colombia, Costa Rica, Honduras,

Guatemala, and Mexico, I observed and interviewed the agricultural professionals, and, in some cases, the farmers with whom they were working. In contrast to the Peruvian program, where I had been working at first with four research assistants and then, from 1964 to 1976, with students and Peruvian professors of sociology and anthropology, in this new line of research I was working on my own most of the time—but not always (Gostyla and Whyte, 1980). I was picking up information here and there, learning enough so that I could venture conclusions on the basis of much more limited evidence than could be secured by more intensive study over a longer period of time. I hoped that, if I found similar patterns emerging in the various countries where I was doing field work, these diagnostic studies might ultimately lead to more definitive conclusions (see Whyte and Boynton, 1983).

In 1970 those who called themselves the "Revolutionary Government of the Armed Forces" in Peru decreed the Industrial Community Law, which required private companies to give their employees shares of stock and representation on company boards of directors. Although I was not optimistic enough to believe that this drastic measure would achieve the power sharing, increased productivity, and worker commitment to companies that the government rhetoric promised, the change seemed striking enough to deserve study. With Giorgio Alberti, who had become a key figure in our Peruvian program, I began a study of the progress of the industrial community. At Cornell I joined a discussion and action group brought together by economist Jaroslav Vanek, a leading authority on the Yugoslavian system of self-management. This led me to realize that I had unconsciously treated ownership as a constant rather than a variable. Like most other behavioral scientists, I was assuming that, practically speaking, private stockholder or government ownership were the only possible forms. Since those studying government bureaucracies were finding no greater promise for the democratic management of work than we were finding in private firms, we had simply concentrated on the interrelations of variables within private firms.

Having heard about the extraordinary complex of worker industrial cooperatives in association with other types of cooperative organizations in the Basque country of Spain, in spring 1975 I managed to arrange a trip to Mondragón to get a firsthand look (Gutíerrez-Johnson and Whyte, 1977). That visit hooked me on Mondragón. I was fascinated with the discovery of people who had learned how to create economically viable and thoroughly democratically managed worker cooperatives, thus demonstrating the potentialities of a form of organization and control that social scientists had looked upon as simply a utopian idea that could not survive competition with private companies.

Putting together what I was learning about Mondragón and about the industrial community in Peru with my reading of the literature on power sharing and democratic management, in fall 1975 I gave a course, "Systems of Labor Participation in Management." In collaboration with Tove Hammer and Robert Stern and students in my Department of Organizational Behavior, I put together what we called the New Systems of Work and Participation program. With support from NIMH's Center for Work and Mental Health, from 1976 on we carried out studies of new patterns of labor-management cooperation in private industry and of the emergence of employee ownership in the United States, particularly as it arose out of impending plant shutdowns. I kept in touch with Mondragón through the doctoral thesis project of Ana Gutierrez-Johnson until I could return to Mondragón for three weeks in 1983.

FINDING MY WAY

Over this half century of field work at home and abroad in community and organizational studies, I was grappling with general problems underlying my whole research career. Since these are problems faced by many other field researchers, what I have learned from experience may be helpful to students and colleagues.

(1) Scientific research versus social reform. In my early experience in family and community, I developed a strong commitment to whatever reform I thought might improve the lot of poor people. This commitment to the underdog was strong enough to be reflected even in such trivial matters as my choice of teams to root for in professional sports.

In my research I was always hoping that what I found could be of some use to people less fortunately situated than I. But while in the Harvard Society of Fellows, I was conditioned to believe that if research was to be truly scientific, researchers' values must be set aside. In general I tried to follow that maxim in my street corner years, though my urge to do good at times led me to backslide. When I organized a march on city hall to protest the lack of hot water and towels in the public bathhouse, I told myself that I might learn something from this experience, but I knew that that was not the real reason. On the other hand, when I intervened with the director of a settlement house to persuade him to appoint Doc, my most valued informant and collaborator, as director of a storefront recreation center, that move did open up valuable lines of research.

These deviations from "pure research" were more or less spontaneous, at least in the sense that they were not initially planned as part of the project. As I gained experience in a wider range of research situations, I found myself gradually abandoning the idea that there must be a strict separation between scientific research and action projects. Through the rest of my career, I have been exploring how research can be integrated with action in ways that will advance science and enhance human progress at the same time. In Chapter 10 I discuss how I arrived at this reconciliation.

(2) One set of methods versus the integration of methods. I began my research career committed to what I call the anthropological methods of interviewing and observation. In the early years (1936-1948) I had no use for the questionnaire or survey method. From 1948 on, working with students on surveys, I came to recognize that, while the method had limitations, it also had important strengths. Many years later, in the course of our research program in Peru, I became convinced not only of the importance of integrating surveys with anthropological methods but also that the study of local history could enrich our knowledge far beyond what I had originally imagined. I discuss this integration and enrichment process in Chapters 8 and 9.

(3) How do you think about thinking? "Research has to be opportunistic because you don't know what you are going to discover. The things you discover may not be what you set out to do" (New York Times, January 9, 1984). I quote here Dr. Joshua Lederberg, a distinguished biomedical scientist and president of Rockefeller University, and the same idea has been expressed in various ways by other natural scientists. This suggests that it is a good idea to be flexible and open to new opportunities, but it doesn't tell us how to strike a balance between following an initial research design and exploiting unexpected opportunities. Nor does it tell us how to get or recognize a good idea.

I am convinced that good ideas do not arise simply out of following mechanically the rules of field research and data analysis, but, on the other hand, neither do I believe that good ideas are immaculate conceptions, created simply by sheer brain power. Without claiming that I have discovered some general rules for thinking about thinking, in the final chapters of this book I trace out as best I can the process whereby I arrived at certain ideas that seemed good to me—and even, in some cases, seemed good to others reading my work. Perhaps if other behavioral scientists reflect upon their own idea-generation process, all of us can learn more about ways to make that vital move from data to ideas.

In tracing my own thought processes, I deal first with concrete problems in particular studies (Chapter 12) and then move on to reflections on the way my own field experience has changed my theoretical orientation to the nature of society and organizational behavior (Chapter 13).

(4) Theory on what level? I recognized early in my career that I had no talent for the kind of grand theory represented by Talcott Parsons or by Karl Marx. Nor did such theorists awaken in me an urge to do grand theory. As I struggled through the complex ideas and impenetrable style of Parsons, I found very little I could use. With Marx, my reaction was somewhat different. While I have found his overall theoretical framework—to the limited extent that I understand it—of little value, I have increasingly recognized in recent years the value of some of his insights and orientations.

Any behavioral scientist would like to be considered a good theorist by his or her colleagues, but what kind of theory can one develop—or to what existing body of theory can one contribute? I have found myself focusing on the concrete behavior of individuals, groups, and organizations, striving to arrive at what Robert Merton has called "middle range theory." To avoid argument as to what constitutes a theory, let me say that I have been seeking some kind of conceptual framework that will strengthen my power of understanding and interpreting behavior and organizations across a wide range of social situations.

Without denying the chance factors guiding my career, from the street corner to the farm, from the factory floor to management offices, I have been concerned with figuring out how the total human resources of the organization, including the brain power of those on the lower levels of society, can be utilized to advance the welfare of the underdog and to build more socially satisfying and economically efficient organizations. Whatever theoretical integration I am achieving revolves around understanding the processes of worker or peasant participation in the decision-making process. In the final chapters, I try to show how widely separated fields of interest and an apparent scattering of my field work over projects generally considered in separate intellectual categories has led to my current conception of what social theory means to Bill Whyte. This is a story of how working through changes in conceptual schemes may help one to pull together seemingly disparate bodies of data.

2

Participant Observation
Rationale and Roles

Participant observation offers learning opportunities that cannot be duplicated by any other method. On the other hand, the method is not suitable for everyone and has its own limitations.

First, let us consider the types of information and ideas that can come from participant observation and that are exceedingly unlikely to arise with any other method. My *Street Corner Society* experience provides a number of examples.

When I first began associating with the Norton Street Gang, I thought I was simply joining the group in order to gain better access to the community, thus learning things that had little direct relationship with the men I was getting to know. As I spent time with the thirteen men, day after day, I became fascinated by the patterns of their activities and interactions. As I became aware that this informal group had a marked and stable structure of leadership and followership, I set about making systematic observations so as to build up data on group struc-ture. Only as a participant would I have been able to associate closely enough with these men to work out the structure of the group. If my information had been limited to personal interviews, this would not have been possible. When I asked one or another of them who their leader was—as I did from time to time—the answer was always the same: "We have no leader. We are all equal."

As I bowled with these men at the time of the final match for money prizes, I became aware of the close relationship between position in the group structure and performance at the bowling alleys. O. J. Harvey and Muzafer Sherif (1953) reported that it was my accidental discovery that led them to design their experimental studies to verify this relationship between position in the informal group and athletic performance.

I also encountered a relationship between mental health and changes in interactions and activities. This happened when the man I called Doc, the leader of the Nortons, confided to me that Long John had been suffering from recurrent nightmares and insomnia. When the Nortons had been intact, Long John had associated particularly with Doc, and with Mike and Danny, who shared the top leadership positions with Doc. I had noted even in this period that Long John was not respected by the followers in the gang. They appeared to think he did not deserve his high position and that he was there simply because he was under the protection of the three top men.

During the preceding months, Mike and Danny had drifted away from the corner, and Doc had begun associating with Spongi, who ran a horse-betting establishment a block away. When I had been on the Norton Street corner in this period, along with the remainder of the gang, I had noted that when Long John appeared, he was treated with more overt disrespect than in the earlier period when he was supported by Doc, Mike, and Danny. Long John was now spending much of his time in Spongi's betting parlor but was accorded no special attention there.

In spite of the declining frequency of the presence of Doc, Mike, and Danny on the street corner, the Nortons continued their Saturday-night bowling sessions. Long John was now performing poorly, and the followers in the group were razzing him unmercifully. It seemed that the razzing he had previously encountered had been muted by his acceptance among the group's leaders.

My analysis suggested a therapy. There was no means of reestablishing the Norton Street Gang in its previous form, but if Long John could be accepted into the inner circle at Spongi's, this might provide him with the kind of social support he had enjoyed earlier. I had no idea how this could be done, but Doc assured me that it would be easy.

By this time, Doc had become a member of Spongi's inner circle. Now, whenever Doc entered Spongi's, he would ask Spongi and others whether they had seen Long John, and soon he had them asking each other. Then, when Long John would appear, Doc would greet him with a great show of interest and attention. In just a couple of weeks, Long John was admitted into Spongi's inner circle. Whenever Spongi went out for "coffee ands" with his closest friends, he would invite Long John to come along.

The results of this brief social therapy manifested themselves dramatically in the final session of the season, when we were again bowling for money. Long John was back in his old form—in fact, he bowled better than ever and won the first prize. After this, Doc heard no more about nightmares and insomnia from Long John.

Donald Roy's important contributions (1953, 1964) to organizational behavior grew largely out of his wide-ranging and intense experience as a participant observer on industrial jobs. Roy was not the first social scientist to note the frictions and frustrations associated with working on piece rates, but he was the first to discover how satisfactions on the job were related to the ease or difficulty of making the informal standard of piece rate payoff established by the workers (Roy, 1953).

At one extreme were jobs so difficult that it was impossible to make bonus and at the other extreme there were jobs so easy that one could have gone far beyond the informally established norm. Let us say, to simplify matters, that performance rated at 100 percent would give a worker a piece rate pay exactly equaling the guaranteed hourly pay. Assume, then, that 140 percent had come to be the norm established by workers on their assumption that performance beyond this level would lead management to reexamine the job and look for ways to cut the rate. On jobs where even his best effort would not yield much more than 100 percent, like his fellow workers, Roy would hold back to keep his performance at 80 percent or below. On jobs where it was easy to reach 140 percent, Roy found himelf holding back so as not to go over this quota. The fun jobs were those in between the two extremes. On those, Roy could work up a steady rhythm. At intervals he would check the time against the number of pieces he had run in order to see whether he was ahead or behind the informal quota for that fraction of the hour. If he was ahead, he would relax and slow the pace. If he was behind, he would step up the pace until he checked his score at the next time interval. Working in this range of jobs came to mean playing a game against the clock.

Furthermore, playing the game had important physical as well as psychological impacts. When Roy had a run of jobs in this midrange throughout the day, he found the time passing swiftly, and, at the end of the day, he still felt physically fresh. On jobs at either of the other extremes, he found the time passing very slowly, and he would feel exhausted and emotionally drained at the end of the day. Having observed these reactions in himself, Roy then talked with other workers and discovered that they had the same experience.

In one of his most cited articles, "Banana Time" (Roy, 1964), Roy discovered how social rituals relieved the boredom of a highly repetitive unskilled job on the clicking machine. "Banana time" was the most prominent of these—a ritual initiated by one worker's announcement that it was time for the banana, this being followed by a brief break in which all the workers peeled and ate their bananas.

After this ritual had been played out regularly for some weeks, a conflict arose within the work group, and banana time came to an end. Now the workers kept steadily at their clicking job. Throughout Roy's time, this department had been on a ten-hour day. There was no difference in the ease or difficulty of the work, and yet Roy recalled that during the banana time period, he had ended the day in good spirits and only moderately tired. After the end of banana time, he was ending the day exhausted and depressed.

In *The High Valley,* a study of a tribe in New Guinea, Kenneth Read (1965: 180-208) provides us with a further example. In this tribe, it was customary for young women to be sought in marriage by men from a different clan. Since the tribe was patrilocal in its culture, the woman left her native clan to move to the clan of her husband. It was customary for the women of the prospective bride's clan to express their sense of loss with a ceremonial show of resistance against the men who were to take her away. On this occasion the resistance went far beyond ceremonial bounds, with the women striking out with solid blows and the men reeling back with shouts of outrage and then charging in to enforce the marriage agreement.

How to explain this deviation from custom? Tarova, the prospective bride, had not yet reached the age of menstruation and the women considered her too young to marry. Some of Tarova's male relatives were reluctant to agree to the marriage, but the suitor was from a neighboring clan that had provided several brides to Tarova's clan. Besides, the suitor and his fellow clansmen were persistent, and also offered an attractive bride price. By custom, only the men could decide these matters, and they had finally agreed to an arrangement they did not consider entirely proper.

If the anthropologist had relied exclusively upon interviewing, he would have come away with a deceptive picture of a culture with rigid rules that were invariably honored in practice. He learned through observation that the rules regarding appropriate ages for marriage partners could be violated (as they were in this case) but that the violation could precipitate certain consequences, as happened when the women of the clan vented their outrage on the men.

These cases illustrate the potential of participant observation to enable the field worker to place individuals in a group context and gain a realistic picture of the dynamics of individual and group behavior.

Furthermore, the observation of one particular event can lead the field worker toward a generalization that would not otherwise have arisen.

Participant observation offers the advantage of serendipity: siginificant discoveries that were unanticipated. In contrast to the survey, which is planned on the basis of what the researcher expects to find, participant observation opens up possibilities for encountering the completely unexpected phenomenon that may be more significant than anything the field worker could have foreseen, suggesting important hypotheses worthy of further study.

Valuable as it is, participant observation is not an all-purpose method. Unless the field worker can quanitfy some of the findings—which is possible in some cases, as we will note later—readers may naturally question to what extent the reports are colored by the researcher's personality and values.

All of us face the problem of maintaining perspective in any situation in which we participate intimately over a considerable period of time. When we begin our research in a community or organization quite different from anything else we have previously experienced, nearly everything seems new and different. We do not understand what is going on, but, to counterbalance this deficiency, we open our minds to seek explanations. As we learn to adjust to the local culture and social practices, we begin to take more and more behavior for granted. As Everett C. Hughes has commented, "The most important things about any people are those that they take for granted." Therefore, the participant observer must periodically question the dynamics of behavior taken for granted. It is useful to leave the field every few weeks and report what you have been learning to people unfamiliar with the scene. Of course, if you are studying a primitive tribe and for many months have no contacts with outsiders, it is impossible to follow this advice. The best you can do is use field notes to ask yourself more questions than come naturally.

Another important limitation of participant observation is the high cost in time. The researcher avoids expenses for elaborate equipment and data processing, but has to devote full time to the enterprise over an extended period. The first days or weeks in the field generally yield little data of lasting value. It takes time to fit into the scene, adjust to people, gain acceptance, and begin to understand what is going on.

Also, we should not assume that all roles the participant observer may play in a community or organization can be equally rewarding. Some roles can be highly confining, while others can offer the field worker rich opportunities to gain a broad range of experiences and observations as well as considerable depth.

PARTICIPANT OBSERVER ROLES

The participation of the researcher in the activities of the people being studied will be shaped in part by the degrees of difference in cultural background, race, or ethnic identification between the field worker and the study subjects. Where these differences are minimal, the researcher may be accepted almost as a native. Where the differences are large, participation opportunities will be more limited, but we can hope to be accepted as friendly and sympathetic observers.

In the early decades of social anthropological studies, field work was confined almost exclusively to primitive tribes. Since the field site was usually far removed from so-called civilized communities, the anthropologist lived among members of the tribe. Such studies generally involved an extended period of time in the field. In one classic case, Bronislaw Malinowski (generally regarded, along with A. Radcliffe-Brown, as the father of modern social anthropology) spent four years among the Trobriand Islanders in the Southwest Pacific (Malinowski, 1922). As a Pole coming from territory occupied by Germany at the time of World War I, Malinowski was interned by the British throughout the war. That lengthy period provided a gifted and dedicated researcher with an unparalleled opportunity to gain an intimate knowledge of the culture of a primitive tribe.

The systematic and intimate nature of behavior reported by Malinowski make it evident that he was well accepted by the tribe. Nevertheless, it is nearly impossible for outsiders who come from a drastically different culture to participate fully in the lives of the people they study. This limitation has mixed effects. On the negative side, researchers cannot fully experience what it is like to play some of the important roles in the community. On the positive side, field workers avoid dilemmas about how closely their behavior should conform to that of the people being studied—a topic we will discuss later. Also, field workers are not so likely to become completely immersed in the life of the community as to lose the detachment that helps to preserve objectivity. That total immersion imposes problems is illustrated by the experience of Robert Johnson, a young black sociologist, when he was studying the black community of Elmira, New York. He put it this way: "I began as a non-participating observer and ended up as a non-observing participant."

Some of the most valuable studies of organizational behavior have been made by participant observers such as Donald Roy, Orvis Collins, and Melville Dalton. These men all took regular jobs in the factories they were studying. This made it unnecessary to explain to fellow workers what they were doing, but in each case the researchers let their fellows know that they were involved in some sort of college or university educational program. Since working one's way through college is a well-recognized and respected activity, the outside connection could be viewed favorably by fellow workers. This educational connection could also legitimate the researcher's curiosity. The researcher can justify asking questions simply by telling people that he or she is trying to take advantage of work experience to further his or her education.

The roles of participant observer in community research and in industrial studies can differ markedly in freedom of movement. Even a blundering field worker is rarely ejected physically from the community. Of course, lack of skill in gaining entry may severely limit access to information. The situation can be markedly different when the participant observer has a full-time job. No matter what social skills the field worker may have, the nature of the job will, to a considerable extent, determine access to interviewing and observational opportunities.

At one extreme is Donald Roy's clicking machine job. In this department, each worker operated a separate machine, and there were no work-related group tasks. At the other extreme is Melville Dalton's job as checker on the incentive or piece-rate system in a large maintenance department in a steel mill. The fairness of the piece rates was often a matter of dispute between union and management, but this was no problem for Dalton because he had no responsibility for setting the rates. His only responsibility was clerical: to check the number of pieces produced by each worker on a given job against the time spent on that job, in order to calculate piece-rate earnings. The job required Dalton to move freely around a department of up to 300 workers. The job did not fully occupy his time throughout an eight-hour day, so he was free to observe and talk with workers. As long as he got the job done, his superiors had no need to check up on how he was spending his time.

Dalton needed supplies and equipment, which were provided in an office area adjoining the maintenance department. There he was thrown into contact with time-study men, foremen, and even some middle-level management people. Dalton participated freely with his office mates at coffee and lunch breaks and other informal activities. Using this physical and organizational base, Dalton was able to establish contacts that enabled him to interview four or five levels of authority above the shop floor. For these interviews he engaged in one minor deception. Since managers in this company did not recognize any difference between sociology and socialism, Dalton told them that he was studying industrial psychology.

Through contacts on the shop floor or in the office area, Dalton got to know stewards and higher-level union officials. With both union and management contacts, he was able to explore in some depth the formal and informal relations between the two organizations.

Finally, Dalton's job provided him with an opportunity, unusual for a participant observer, to gather and tabulate precise quantitative data. This made it possible for him to carry out his unique studies of piece-rate earnings in relation to informal work group norms and of the informal relations among workers that separated "rate busters" from those who abided by the norms.

If the participant observer wishes to study workers, then clearly assuming a management position is not appropriate. On the other hand, one particularly concerned with studying management may well learn through performing a managerial role some things unlikely to be learned through interviewing alone.

Few field workers will have the opportunity to pick and choose in order to secure the ideal job. On the other hand, anyone who hopes to combine research with paid work must consider whether the nature of the job available will provide a base for the kind of research the applicant hopes to do.

OVERT OR COVERT RESEARCH?

It is important to distinguish among overt, semiovert, and covert researcher roles. In the overt role, you let people know you are doing a study. They may have only a vague idea of the nature of the study and judge it primarily in terms of their evaluation of you personally, but still you are prepared to explain what you are doing to anyone who asks.

In the semiovert role, you combine a regular job in the organization with your study of that organization. Since you appear to be earning your living like everyone else, full explanations of your research are not necessary. However, if you wish to go beyond casual work relations in order to ask questions that would not be expected from other workers, it will be helpful to let some people know of your research interests.

In a community study, maintaining a covert role is generally out of the question. People will not put up with interviews and observations for which no purpose is explained. If you are to hold a regular position in an organization, then it is possible (within certain limits) to maintain a fully covert role in the study of that organization. (The ethical questions regarding such a deceptive role will be discussed in Chapter 11.)

Air force Lieutenant Morton Sullivan, who had a master's degree in sociology, proposed to Stuart Queen that he get himself inducted into that service as a recruit in order to make a study of the USAF training process. This required Queen to work out administrative arrangements with several Air Force officials. On the airbase, no one but the commanding officer and the chaplain knew of the deception.

FROM PARTICIPATION TO RESEARCH

So far I have focused on participant observer roles in which the field worker is consciously carrying out research while participating. There is another, lesser known, type in which the writer bases the research report on a role played earlier simply as a participant.

José Moreno, a student who was then a Catholic priest, set out from Cornell University to do his doctoral research in the Dominican Republic on a study of intervillage systems. Shortly after he arrived in Santo Domingo, an armed struggle broke out, and rebel forces took control of the city. Moreno's sympathies were with the rebels, and he volunteered to serve in a noncombatant role. His dedication and abilities in organizing the supply of food and medical and health services for the people of the beleaguered city led him into a close working relationship with the rebel leaders.

Moreno returned to Cornell without even having begun the study outlined in his initial research design. However, he did not come back empty-handed. Faculty members on his committee agreed that a study of intervillage systems could always be done, while major rebellions aimed at overthrowing a government were relatively rare events. So far as we knew, this was the only rebellion within which a sociologist had played a participant observer role. José Moreno's thesis on the Dominican uprising led to a fascinating book appropriately titled *Barrios in Arms* (1970).

Without being aware of it at the time, Tom Germano began work on his doctoral thesis when he was employed full time in the U.S. Post Office in New York City. Germano worked through a period of rising labor discontent, which culminated in the only extensive strike in the history of the Post Office.

Germano did not plan to become one of the principal strike leaders, but he was gregarious, articulate, and well respected by members of his informal group within the post office. In a mass meeting, members of Germano's informal group pushed him onto the platform to speak for them. His statement was greeted with such enthusiasm that he was projected immediately into the forefront of insurgent leaders, combatting both the federal government and the established officers of their national union. Germano remained active in the strike leadership and in subsequent negotiations and collective bargaining between the federal government and the union for a number of months.

This intense experience stimulated Germano's interest in studies of labor relations and led him into formal graduate work in sociology. His doctoral thesis examined the postal workers' strike in the context of the changing nature of labor relations in that service over a period of years. We should not assume that the participant observer in this mode of research is entirely dependent upon memory. If that were the case, the scientific basis for such studies would be weak. Obviously, to a considerable extent both Moreno and Germano had to rely upon their memories. Nevertheless, the participant observer inside the revolution returned home with copies of some of the essential documents necessary for him to provide an accurate report on the popular mobilization of the citizens of Santo Domingo during the months of the struggle. Resistance was organized on a block-by-block basis, and Moreno secured records showing how each neighborhood was organized, as well as how the neighborhoods were related to the central revolutionary command.

As he became immersed in the intense activities of the strike, Germano sensed the importance of the events and the significance of his central role. This led him to begin to collect records of formal meetings and to make notes on informal discussions. Over a period of years after he had left the postal service to take a position in the Extension Division of the New York State School of Industrial and Labor Relations at Cornell, Germano shifted his role from one of unplanned participant observation to one of increasingly guided and planned investigation. He maintained contact with members of his former informal group and with those who had arisen as insurgent leaders in other districts of the postal service in New York City, which had been the center of strike activity throughout the nation. He was able to fill in gaps in his data through interviews and also to track down significant documents that he had not gathered at the time.

While we may acknowledge that restrospective participant observation does not meet the ideals of scientific methodology, when it comes to important unpredictable events, we must consider ourselves fortunate when a sociologist or potential sociologist is on the scene and is resourceful and insightful enough to give us a solid description and analysis.

3

Planning the Project and Entering the Field

Using anthropological methods, unless we are entering an organization or community well known to us from previous research, the initial phase of the project should be considered a social exploration. We learn what we can in advance about this relatively unknown territory, but once we are there, the first requirement is to gain some initial familiarity with the local scene and establish a social base from which we can continue our exploration until we are able to study some parts of that territory systematically.

This style of research has both positive and negative aspects. Like the explorer of physical terrain, you run the risk of getting lost and never coming out with a coherent map of the territory. On the other hand, the flexibility of the methods offer the possibility of making discoveries far more valuable than you could have anticipated.

The planning process is begun but not completed before the researcher enters the field. I am not proposing that we enter with blank minds, leaving it to subsequent observations and experience to shape research plans. Striving for such a state of unconsciousness would be folly, but it is important to avoid the other extreme of becoming so fixated on a previously prepared and detailed research design as to miss opportunities to gather data about problems that may turn out to be more important.

Author's Note: Parts of this chapter are from W. F. Whyte, *Street Corner Society,* © 1981 University of Chicago Press. Used by permission.

In *Barrios in Arms,* the researcher ended up with a more valuable study than that originally planned. However, José Moreno did not have to choose between following his original research design or studying an attempted revolution. The decision was made for him by events.

The more difficult problem arises when there is a choice: It is possible to carry out the project as initially planned, but the researcher encounters a new problem and perhaps also a new set of data that could lead to a more important study.

That was Wesley Craig's problem in his study in the Convención Valley on the eastern slopes of the Andes in Peru. Craig set out to make a study of intervillage systems. Here a peasant movement had recently accomplished an extraordinary social and economic transformation, overcoming the domination of the large landholders and establishing independent and autonomous villages. Craig was aware of this before he entered the field, but he had decided to focus on the current scene rather than upon a reconstruction of the dynamics of the peasant movement. On a visit to the provincial capital city of Cuzco, he accidentally discovered a storehouse of documents in an unguarded garage. In discarded cardboard boxes were files of grievances against the landlords of the haciendas by the workers who, at the beginning of the protest period, had been subjected to conditions close to serfdom. These were documents presented to the provincial labor authorities in Cuzco, and they appeared to be complete from the first grievance filed years earlier through an increasing flow of grievances culminating in the peasant movement. Each grievance identified the landlord and gave the name of the hacienda and the names of the complainants. With this set of documents, Craig was in a position to trace the process of peasant organization through time and in its geographical spread. The documentation of the names of the grievers, of those representing them, and of the landlords also provided rich data that could readily lead the researcher to key informants for their accounts of particular cases and of the process of peasant mobilization.

When I received Craig's letter informing me of his find, my first impulse was to urge him to forget about intervillage systems and concentrate on reconstructing the peasant movement. However, I was only a minor committeeman on his thesis. I therefore consulted with Frank Young, who was not only chairman of Craig's doctoral thesis committee but also the inventor of the theory and methodology underlying studies of intervillage systems. Young assured me that he would approve the change, and I passed on this recommendation to Craig. He replied that he had decided against abandoning the intervillage systems study and would do both projects at the same time. The intervillage study was well done, but it hardly made an important contribution to the research literature.

Of course, it is never possible to prove what might have been, but the Craig thesis (1969) did not fully exploit the potential values of the peasant movement project.

Several years later, Eduardo Fioravanti (1974), a young Spanish sociologist, entered the Convención Valley to spend a full year devoted entirely to field work on the peasant movement. In general Fioravanti's analysis supported the interpretation earlier presented by Craig, while pointing out some errors on minor points, but Fioravanti had been able to document the case in much richer detail. Thus it was not Craig but Fioravanti who published the definitive study of this peasant movement. The moral of this case? When the field situation reveals opportunities to do a more valuable study by changing the research design, seize the opportunity—and don't compromise by making the dubious assumption that you can exploit the new opportunity fully and at the same time pursue your original research design.

ENTERING THE COMMUNITY

The entry process differs according to whether one studies a formal organization or a community. The organization has official gatekeepers who control access. The community has unofficial gatekeepers who can either facilitate entry and encourage access to information or see to it that the researcher never penetrates beyond superficial acquaintance and the formal portrait of themselves the people would like to give to the outside world.

Entry strategy depends in part upon whether you plan to study a whole community with all of its social classes, ethnic groups, associations, neighborhoods, and so on, or whether the study is more narrowly focused to gain a more intimate view of a particular segment of that community.

If you aim to study a whole community, the most open points of entry are among those who share your social class background. Since university-based researchers come from upper- or upper-middle-class backgrounds, or are moving into the upper middle class through higher education, this means that contacts will be established most readily with business and professional people. But not all contacts at a given level are of equal value. The researcher at an early stage tries to identify those in leadership positions in the hope that they will provide useful contacts and even informal sponsorship.

Having gained the acceptance of some key people, the researcher then attempts to participate in ways that establish an acceptable personal identity, making it possible to move beyond the limits of the initial sponsorship. The researcher then faces the question of deciding between broad and necessarily somewhat superficial coverage of the community and a narrower but more intensive study of one or more of its segments. (Chapter 12 contains a discussion of the depth verses breadth issue.) How much time the researcher can devote to the project and how many field workers are involved will determine to what extent it is possible to achieve both depth and breadth.

The Middletown Studies

In their pioneering study *Middletown* (1929), Robert S. and Helen Merrill Lynd moved to Muncie, Indiana, a city of about 38,000 population, opened an office, and lived there from January 1924 until June 1925. Their secretary worked with them for the entire period, and they had two assistants, one for a year, the other for five months. For the restudy (Lynd and Lynd, 1937), Robert Lynd returned to Muncie in June 1935 with five assistants for "less than a tenth of the man-days of research time" (p. 4) of the original study, which suggests that the later field period was about ten weeks. Of course, the first study had provided a baseline and a wealth of information, which made it possible to work more rapidly and efficiently in 1935.

Before entering the field in their initial study, the Lynds (1929: 4) had determined the broad outlines of the project:

getting a living
making a home
training the young
using leisure in various forms of play, art, and so on
engaging in religious practices
engaging in community activities

The six parts of the first Middletown book faithfully reflect the initial study outline. Since they aimed to cover all social classes and ethnic groups under each of these six headings, this necessarily limited their depth of penetration for any segment of the community. Even though their field time in the restudy was much shorter, they achieved much greater depth on one element with their chapter, "The X Family: A Pattern of Business Class Control" (pp. 74-101). It is interesting to note that it was local informants who guided them in this direction. "Since *Middletown* was published, some local people have criticized it for underplaying the role of the X family in the city's life" (p. 74). If they had begun research in a more open, exploratory manner, they might have recognized the dominance of the X family in the first study.

Yankee City

W. Lloyd Warner did his first field study on a primitive tribe (Warner, 1958), but, as he reported later:

> My fundamental purpose in studying primitive man was to know modern man better; . . . some day I proposed to investigate (just how I did not then know) the social life of modern man with the hope of ultimately placing the researches in a larger framework of comparison which would include the other societies of the world [Warner and Lunt, 1941: 3-4].

This suggested a more intensive analysis of kinship, social structure, and formal and informal organizations than the Lynds had undertaken. The community chosen, "Yankee City" (Newburyport, MA), with about 17,000 population, was less than half the size of Muncie, but still the attempt to achieve substantial depth and breadth was a formidable undertaking.

After describing the process of acquiring background information on the city, Warner gives this description on his interpersonal entry strategy:

> It seemed highly advisable to secure the consent and cooperation of the more important men in the community lest we later find it impossible to obtain certain vital information. We finally selected one prominent and, it later developed, much-trusted individual who we knew was important in the town and who, we believed, might be interested in the work we proposed doing. We obtained introductions to him, told him in general what we wanted to do, and asked his cooperation. After asking us a number of questions and showing a decided interest in our work, he agreed to help us in any way he could. We then asked him to introduce us to some of his friends who were leaders in the city's activities. This he did, and from his friends we received other introductions which shortly spread our sources of information from the top to the bottom of the city [Warner and Lunt, 1941: 41-42].

Warner does not tell us how he obtained the initial introduction, but it is not hard to imagine how this was done. Newburyport is not far from Harvard, where the research program was based, and many of the leading citizens of the city were Harvard graduates. There must have been a number of potential social bridges from Harvard into the Newburyport elite.

Warner does not tell us how coworkers went from one contact to another "from the top to the bottom of the city." However, this was a research program extending over several years, with 25 people participating in field work. At the time, this was the most exciting program within Harvard's anthropology department—so exciting that it seemed a threat to some senior professors. (Conrad Arensberg reports that Professor A. M. Tozzer warned him, "There are no jobs in social anthropology. Stick to archaeology, and you can get a job in a museum.")

So broad was the appeal of the Yankee City program that Warner was able to attract some of the best students in the department. He thus could find people able and willing to overcome the barriers of ethnic and social class differences to observe and interview far below the elite.

Deep South

Burleigh B. Gardner wrote me (January 27, 1984) this account of the launching of *Deep South* (Davis et al., 1941):

> After the Yankee City study was well under way, Lloyd Warner, with the support of Elton Mayo, began seeking ways to expand his dream of similar studies in other communities. One goal was to conduct a study of an old southern community for comparison with the findings in Yankee City. In 1932 the Committee on Industrial Physiology at Harvard obtained funding for the project, and, with this assured, Warner took the following steps.
>
> He decided on criteria for the study location and selected a number of communities that seemed appropriate, in terms of size and background. He then made a survey trip through the Old South to examine the communities. On this trip he met with a few leaders in each place, both to get information and to establish contacts if the community was to be used. His final choice was Natchez.
>
> Because of the strong caste system, he thought it advisable to have both a Negro and a white who could be accepted. The opportunity was offered to Allison Davis and to Burleigh Gardner, who, with their wives, would make up the research team. Allison, having been raised in Virginia, and Burleigh Gardner, from Texas, were knowledgeable about appropriate behavior in the caste system.
>
> In his survey trip, Warner had become acquainted with the mayor of Natchez, had discussed the survey with him, and had gained the promise of cooperation.
>
> It had been suggested that the study include a more rural community still dominated by the plantation system. Through someone he met in

Natchez, Warner was referred to the publisher of a local paper in Woodville, Mississippi, a small town about thirty miles from Natchez. When the Gardners were ready to start the study, they first moved to Woodville, where they were cordially received by the publisher. He and his family soon introduced them to the leading planters and businessmen. Of course, everyone was curious about "what the Gardners were doing," and they explained that they were studying the community and its historical background.

Through people in Woodville, the Gardners were introduced to people in Natchez, especially the editor of the Natchez newspaper and some of the prominent families. They also called on the mayor to tell him when they expected to move the study to Natchez.

After two or three months in Woodville, the Gardners moved to Natchez. Through the mayor, Burleigh met the chief of police, the sheriff, and other city and county officials.

A month or so later the Davises arrived in Natchez and took rooms with the leading Negro doctor. Gardner informed the mayor and the chief of police of this, with the implication that the Davises were helping with the study of the Negro community. It was necessary that the officials have an acceptable understanding of why the Davises had come to Natchez and what they were up to.

The Gardners were quickly accepted socially into the upper- and upper-middle-class white society, and had no difficulty interviewing those people. However, contacts with the lower-class whites ("po' whites" especially) were more difficult, so Mary Gardner volunteered with the local Emergency Relief Program, which dispensed aid to the needy. She requested a caseload of white families and was given the very poorest. She had to call on her "cases" regularly, and was able to make friends and interview them extensively. Once she was accepted as someone who liked to listen to their problems and their life stories, she had no difficulty in getting the desired information.

Gardner added later,

As you can see, the use of two research teams in the caste situation added some complications. I had to gain the acceptance of the mayor, sheriff, and police in order to protect the Davises in case of some unexpected suspicion of them. From the beginning, I spent a lot of time at the jail getting acquainted with the policemen. They may never have quite understood what I was doing, but I seemed innocuous, and I tried to see that any questions about the Davises would come to me.

Living with the leading Negro doctor must have provided the Davises with an entrée to the elite of Negro society. I have no information on how they managed to establish effective research relations with lower-class Negroes.

For access and for their own protection, it was necessary for Gardner to inform certain key officials that the project included research in the Negro as well as the white community, but this was not generally known in Natchez. In fact, the two couples avoided contact with each other in Natchez, meeting for discussion and planning sessions at out-of-town sites.

Street Corner Society

In fall 1936, I set out to study an Italian-American slum district, the North End of Boston. After abortive attempts at entry through a housing survey and a bar on the edge of the district (Whyte, 1981: 289-290), I sought help from social workers in a settlement house. Here was I, the son of middle-class parents, seeking to make contact with lower-class people through association with middle-class social workers, none of whom, furthermore, was of Italian-American extraction. I now look upon this as like trying to get to know a foreign country by making entrance through the American Embassy and its immediate social circles. Fortunately, I recognized that this road into the community was bound to be a dead end, and I was also fortunate enough to meet a social worker who helped me to shift my point of entry. None of the other social workers expressed interest in my study, beyond giving me their definitive interpretations of the community, but somehow, in spite of the vagueness of my own explanations, the head of girls' work in the Norton Street House understood what I needed. She began describing Doc to me. He was, she said, a very intelligent and talented person who had at one time been fairly active in the house but had dropped out, so that he hardly ever came in any more. Perhaps he could understand what I wanted, and he must have the contacts that I needed. If I wished, she would make an appointment for me to see him in the house one evening. This at last seemed right. I jumped at the chance. As I came into the district that evening, it was with a feeling that here I had my big chance to get started. Somehow Doc must accept me and be willing to work with me.

In a sense, my study began on the evening of February 4, 1937, when the social worker called me in to meet Doc. She showed us into her office and then left so that we could talk. Doc waited quietly for me to begin, as he sank down into a chair. I found him a man of medium height and spare build. His hair was a light brown, quite a contrast to the more typical black Italian hair. It was thinning around the temples. His cheeks were sunken. His eyes were a light blue and seemed to have a penetrating gaze.

I began by asking him if the social worker had told him about what I was trying to do.

"No, she just told me that you wanted to meet me and that I should like to meet you."

Then I went into a long explanation which, unfortunately, I omitted from my notes. As I remember it, I said that I had been interested in congested city districts but had felt very remote from them. I hoped to study the problems in such a district. I felt I could do very little as an outsider. Only if I could get to know the people and learn their problems first hand would I be able to gain the understanding I needed.

Doc heard me out without any change of expression, so that I had no way of predicting his reaction. When I was finsihed, he asked: "Do you want to see the high life or the low life?"

"I want to see all that I can. I want to get as complete a picture of the community as possible."

"Well, any nights you want to see anything, I'll take you around. I can take you to the joints—gambling joints—I can take you around the street corners. Just remember that you're my friend. That's all they need to know. I know these places, and, if I tell them that you're my friend, nobody will bother you. You just tell me what you want to see, and we'll arrange it."

The proposal was so perfect that I was at a loss for a moment as to how to respond to it. We talked a while longer, as I sought to get some pointers as to how I should behave in his company. He warned me that I might have to take the risk of getting arrested in a raid on a gambling joint but added that this was not serious. I only had to give a false name and then would get bailed out by the man that ran the place, paying only a five-dollar fine. I agreed to take this chance. I asked him whether I should gamble with the others in the gambling joints. He said it was unnecessary and, for a greenhorn like myself, very inadvisable.

At last I was able to express my appreciation. "You know, the first steps of getting to know a community are the hardest. I could see things going with you that I wouldn't see for years otherwise."

"That's right. You tell me what you want to see, and we'll arrange it. When you want some information, I'll ask for it, and you listen. When you want to find out their philosophy of life, I'll start an argument and get it for you. If there's something else you want to get, I'll stage an act for you. Not a scrap, you know, but just tell me what you want, and I'll get it for you."

"That's swell. I couldn't ask for anything better. Now I'm going to try to fit in all right, but, if at any time you see I'm getting off on the wrong foot, I want you to tell me about it."

"Now we're being too dramatic. You won't have any trouble. You come in as my friend. When you come in like that, at first everybody will treat you with respect. You can take a lot of liberties, and nobody will kick. After a while when they get to know you they will treat you like anybody else—you know, they say familiarity breeds contempt. But you'll never have any trouble. There's just one thing to watch out for. Don't spring [treat] people. Don't be too free with your money."

"You mean they'll think I'm a sucker?"

"Yes, and you don't want to buy your way in."

We talked a little about how and when we might get together. Then he asked me a question. "You want to write something about this?"

"Yes, eventually."

"Do you want to change things?"

"Well—yes. I don't see how anybody could come down here where it is so crowded, people haven't got any money or any work to do, and not want to have some things changed. But I think a fellow should do the thing he is best fitted for. I don't want to be a reformer, and I'm not cut out to be a politician. I just want to understand these things as best I can and write them up, and if that has any influence . . ."

"I think you can change things that way. Mostly that is the way things are changed, by writing about them."

That was our beginning. At the time I found it hard to believe that I could move in as easily as Doc had said with his sponsorship. But that indeed was the way it turned out.

While I was taking my first steps with Doc, I was also finding a place to live in Cornerville. My fellowship provided a very comfortable bedroom, living room, and bath at Harvard. I had been attempting to commute from these quarters to my Cornerville study. Technically that was possible, but socially I became more and more convinced that it was impossible. I realized that I would always be a stranger to the community if I did not live there. Then, also, I found myself having difficulty putting in the time that I knew was required to establish close relations on Cornerville. Life in Cornerville did not proceed on the basis of formal appointments. To meet people, to get to know them, to fit into their activities, required spending time with them—a lot of time day after day. Commuting to Cornerville, you might come in on a particular afternoon and evening only to discover that the people you intended to see did not happen to be around at the time. Or, even if you did see them, you might find the time passing entirely uneventfully. You might just be standing around with people whose only occupation was talking or walking about to try to keep themselves from being bored.

On several afternoons and evenings at Harvard, I found myself considering a trip to Cornerville and then rationalizing my way out of it. How did I know I would find the people whom I meant to see? Even if I did so, how could I be sure that I would learn anything today? Instead of going off on a wild-goose chase to Cornerville, I could profitably spend my time reading books and articles to fill in my woeful ignorance of sociology and social anthropology. Then, too, I had to admit that I felt more comfortable among these familiar surroundings than wandering around Cornerville and spending time with people in whose presence I felt distinctly uncomfortable at first.

When I found myself rationalizing in this way, I realized that I would have to make the break. Only if I lived in Cornerville would I ever be able to understand it and be accepted by it. Finding a place, however, was not easy. In such an overcrowded district a spare room was practically nonexistent. I might have been able to take a room in the Norton Street Settlement House, but I realized that I must do better than this if possible.

I got my best lead from the editor of a weekly English-language newspaper published for the Italian-American colony. I had talked to him before about my study and had found him sympathetic. Now I came to ask him for help in finding a room. He directed me to the Martinis, a family which operated a small restaurant. I went there for lunch and later consulted the son of the family. He was sympathetic but said that they had no place for any additional person. Still, I liked the place and enjoyed the food. I came back several times just to eat. On one occasion I met the editor, and he invited me to his table. At first he asked me some searching questions about my study: what I was after, what my connection with Harvard was, what they had expected to get out of this, and so on. After I had answered him in a manner that I unfortunately failed to record in my notes, he told me that he was satisfied and, in fact, had already spoken in my behalf to people who were suspicious that I might be coming in to "criticize our people."

We discussed my rooming problem again. I mentioned the possibility of living at the Norton Street House. He nodded but added: "It would be much better if you could be in a family. You would pick up the language much quicker, and you would get to know the people. But you want a nice family, an educated family. You don't want to get in with any low types. You want a real good family."

At this he turned to the son of the family with whom I had spoken and asked: "Can't you make some place for Mr. Whyte in the house here?"

Al Martini paused a moment and then said: "Maybe we can fix it up. I'll talk to Mama again."

So he did talk to Mama again, and they did find a place. In fact, he turned over to me his own room and moved in to share a double bed with the son of the cook. I protested mildly at this imposition, but everything had been decided—except for the money. They did not know what to charge me, and I did not know what to offer. Finally, after some fencing, I offered fifteen dollars a month, and they settled for twelve.

The room was simple but adequate to my purposes. It was not heated, but, when I began to type my notes there, I got myself a small oil-burner. There was no bathtub in the house, but I had to go out to Harvard now and then anyway, so I used the facilities of the great university (the room of my friend, Henry Guerlac) for an occasional tub or shower.

Physically, the place was livable, and it provided me with more than just a physical base. I had been with the Martinis for only a week when I discovered that I was much more than a roomer to them. I had been taking many of my meals in the restaurant and sometimes stopping in to chat with the family before I went to bed at night. Then one afternoon I was out at Harvard and found myself coming down with a bad cold. Since I still had my Harvard room, it seemed the sensible thing to do to stay overnight there. I did not think to tell the Martinis of my plan.

The next day when I was back in the restaurant for lunch, Al Martini greeted me warmly and then said that they had all been worried when I did not come home the night before. Mama had stayed up until two o'clock waiting for me. As I was just a young stranger in the city, she could visualize all sorts of things happening to me. Al told me that Mama had come to look upon me as one of the family. I was free to come and go as I pleased, but she wouldn't worry so much if she knew of my plans.

I was very touched by this plea and resolved thereafter to be as good a son as I could to the Martinis.

At first I communicated with Mama and Papa primarily in smiles and gestures. Papa knew no English at all, and Mama's knowledge was limited to one sentence which she would use when some of the young boys on the street were making noise below her window when she was trying to get her afternoon nap. She would then poke her head out of the window and shout: "Goddam-sonumabitcha! Geroutahere!"

Some weeks earlier, in anticipation of moving into the district, I had begun working on the Italian lanugage with the aid of a Linguaphone. One morning now Papa Martini came by when I was talking to the phonograph record. He listened for a few moments in the hall trying to make sense out of this peculiar conversation. Then he burst in upon me with fascinated exclamations. We sat down together while I demonstrated the machine and the method to him. After that he delighted in working with me, and I called him my language professor. In a short time we reached a stage where I could carry on simple conversations, and, thanks to the Linguaphone and Papa Martini, the Italian that came out apparently sounded authentic. He liked to try to pass me off to his friends as *paesano mio*—a man from his own home town in Italy. When I was careful to keep my remarks within the limits of my vocalbulary, I could sometimes pass as an immigrant from the village of Viareggio in the province of Tuscany.

Since my research developed so that I was concentrating almost exclusively upon the younger, English-speaking generation, my knowledge of Italian proved unnecessary for research purposes. Nevertheless, I feel certain that it was important in establishing my social position in Cornerville—even with that younger generation. There were schoolteachers and social workers who had worked in Cornerville for as much as twenty years and yet had made no effort to learn Italian. My effort to learn the language probably did more to establish the sincerity of my interest in the people than anything I could have told them of myself and my work. How could a researcher be planning to "criticize our people" if he went to the lengths of learning the language? With language comes understanding, and surely it is easier to criticize people if you do not understand them.

My days with the Martinis would pass in this manner. I would get up in the morning around nine o'clock and go out to breakfast. Al Martini told me I could have breakfast in the restaurant, but, for all my desire to fit in, I never could take their breakfast of coffee with milk and bread.

After breakfast, I returned to my room and spent the rest of the morning, or most of it, typing up my notes regarding the previous day's events. I had lunch in the restaurant and then set out for the street corner. Usually I was back for dinner in the restaurant and then out again for the evening.

Usually I came home again between eleven and twelve o'clock, at a time when the restaurant was empty except perhaps for a few family friends. Then I might join Papa in the kitchen to talk as I helped him dry the dishes, or pull up a chair into a family conversation around one of the tables next to the kitchen. There I had a glass of wine to sip, and I could sit back and mostly listen but occasionally try out my growing Italian on them.

The pattern was different on Sunday, when the restaurant was closed at two o'clock, and Al's two brothers and his sister and the wives, husband, and children would come in for a big Sunday dinner. They insisted that I eat with them at this time and as a member of the family, not paying for my meal. It was always more than I could eat, but it was delicious, and I washed it down with two tumblers of Zinfandel wine. Whatever strain there had been in my work in the preceding week would pass away now as I ate and drank and then went to my room for an afternoon nap of an hour or two that brought me back completely refreshed and ready to set forth again for the corners of Cornerville.

Though I made several useful contacts in the restaurant or through the family, it was not for this that the Martinis were important to me. There is a strain to doing such field work. The strain is greatest when you are a stranger and are constantly wondering whether people are going to accept you. Much as you enjoy your work, as long as you are observing and interviewing, you have a role to play, and you are not completely relaxed. It was a wonderful feeling at the end of a day's work to be able to come home to relax and enjoy myself with the family. Probably it would have been impossible for me to carry on such a concentrated study of Cornerville if I had not had such a home from which to go out and to which I might return. (I lived with the Martinis for eighteen months until I married Kathleen King and we moved into our own flat.)

I can still remember my first outing with Doc. We met one evening at the Norton Street House and set out from there to a gambling place a couple of blocks away. I followed Doc anxiously down the long, dark hallway at the back of a tenement building. I was not worried about the possibility of a police raid. I was thinking about how I would fit in and be accepted. The door opened into a small kitchen almost bare of furnishings and with the paint peeling off the walls. As soon as we went in the door, I took off my hat and began looking around for a place to hang it. There was no place. I looked around, and here I learned my first lesson in participant observation in Cornerville: Don't take off your hat in the house—at least not when you are among men. It may be permissible, but certainly not required, to take your hat off when women are around.

Doc introduced me as "my friend Bill" to Chichi, who ran the place, and to Chichi's friends and customers. I stayed there with Doc part of the time in the kitchen, where several men would sit around and talk, and part of the time in the other room watching the crap game.

There was talk about gambling, horse races, sex, and other matters. Mostly I just listened and tried to act friendly and interested. We had wine and coffee with anisette in it, with the fellows chipping in to pay for the refreshments. (Doc would not let me pay my share on this first occasion.) As Doc had predicted, no one asked me about myself, but he told me later that, when I went to the toilet, there was an excited burst of conversation in Italian and that he had to assure them that I was not a G-man. He said he told them flatly that I was a friend of his, and they agreed to let it go at that.

We went several times together at Chichi's gambling joint, and then the time came when I dared to go in alone. When I was greeted in a natural and friendly manner, I felt that I was now beginning to find a place for myself in Cornerville.

When Doc did not go off to the gambling joint, he spent his time hanging around Norton Street, and I began hanging with him. At first, Norton Street meant only a place to wait until I could go somewhere else. Gradually, as I got to know the men better, I found myself becoming one of the Norton Street gang.

Then the Italian Community Club was formed in the Norton Street Settlement, and Doc was invited to be a member. Doc maneuvered to get me into the club, and I was glad to join, as I could see that it represented something distinctly different from the corner gangs I was meeting.

As I began to meet the men of Cornerville, I also met a few of the girls. One girl I took to a church dance. The next morning the fellows on the street corner were asking me: "How's your steady girl?" This brought me up short. I learned that going to the girl's house was something that you just did not do unless you hoped to marry her. Fortunately, the girl and her family knew that I did not know the local customs, so they did not assume that I was thus committed. However, this was a useful warning. After this time, even though I found some Cornerville girls exceedingly attractive, I never went out with them except on a group basis, and I did not make any more home visits either.

As I went along, I found that life in Cornerville was not nearly so interesting and pleasant for the girls as it was for the men. A young man had complete freedom to wander and hang around. The girls could not hang on street corners. They had to divide their time between their own homes, the homes of girl friends and relatives, and a job, if they had one. Many of them had a dream that went like this: some young man, from outside of Cornerville, with a little money, a good job, and a good education would come and woo them and take them out of the district. I could hardly afford to fill this role.

Joining a political organization seemed the best way to study local politics, but I hesitated to make a commitment to one faction. That problem solved itself with a special election for a vacant seat in Congress. State Senator Joseph Ravello was the only Italian-American running, so the other North End politicians all had endorsed him—rather reluctantly. I signed up as a campaign worker. The candidate had no idea how to use me, but I suggested that I take notes on meetngs of the campaign workers and write them up later so that no good ideas would be lost. I am sure the candidate never made any use of those notes, but carbon paper enabled me to document the campaign for my own purposes. I never did penetrate the high-level strategy sessions in which Ravello met with political leaders in other wards of the congressional district, but I did get a picture of politics at the grass-roots level.

Many months had passed before I had an opportunity to approach a study of the rackets organization. This was frustrating because I could look out my window to the store across the street where the man who was said to be the racket boss for all New England sometimes dropped in to see old friends.

In fact, I once got up my courage, crossed the street, and told the proprietor I would like to talk to Joe Lombardi. Naturally, he wanted to know why. I told him, "I am collecting for the United Fund, and I would like to see him about a contribution." The reply: "He already gave at the office." I was tempted to ask, "And where is the office?" but I could not think of a plausible reason for the question.

My opening finally came when the eldest son in the family with which I had been living was grumbling to me about a pair of banquet tickets he had had to buy from a local policeman. His wife did not want to go to the banquet, and he asked if I would like to accompany him. I asked what the occasion was. He told me that the banquet was in honor of the son of the local police lieutenant. The young man had just passed his bar examinations and was starting out on his legal career. I thought a moment. It was perfectly obvious what sorts of people would be present at the banquet: mainly policeman, politicians, and racketeers. I decided that this might be an opportunity for me.

My friend knew Tony Cataldo, a middle-level operator in the numbers racket, and we sat at his table and went bowling later with him and a business associate. Luckily for me, Tony lived with his family within a block of the flat where Kathleen and I lived; the small store he owned was just as close to us. Tony was not there much of the time, but his older brother conducted legitimate business while the numbers operation was carried on in a back room. After this promising beginning, however, I was unable to develop the relationship so as to lead me deeper into the racket organization.

Would it have been possible for me to carry out an intensive study of the racket organization? Taking advantage of the fact that a major "crime family" has some of its second- and third-generation members established in legitimate businesses and professions and in politics, years later Francis Ianni (1972) built on a chance meeting with a young lawyer in what he calls the Lupollo family to build a friendship that led him into family social gatherings. He became so much a part of the Lupollo social cricle that, without formal interviewing, he was able to gather a wealth of data, not only on the family organization, but also on the racket operations.

But note that Ianni did his study over a period of years, picking up data as opportunities arose. Throughout his field work period he was engaged full time in other activities. Such a study does not lend itself to concentrated and systematically planned field work.

Other students made their initial entries into inner-city slums by pathways somewhat different from mine. Elliot Liebow, Elijah Anderson, and Ruth Horowitz all began by finding a place to hang around, but followed up on initial chance contacts by finding a key informant and gatekeeper and establishing a firm social base through this relationship.

Tally's Corner

Liebow (1967: 236) had originally planned to do a series of urban studies,

> a neighborhood study, then moving on say, to a construction laborer's union, then a bootleg joint, and perhaps rounding these out with a series of genealogies and life histories.

> I was going to give myself about a month or so of poking around town, getting the feel of things, before committing myself to any firm plan of action.

> In taking up the director's [Hylan Lewis's] suggestion that this would be "a good place to get your feet wet," I went in so deep that I was completely submerged and my plan to do three or four separate

studies, each with its own neat, clean boundaries, dropped forever out of sight. My initial excursions into the street—to poke around, get the feel of things, and to lay out the lines of field work—seldom carried me more than a block or two from the corner where I started. From the very first weeks or even days, I found myself in the middle of things; the principal lines of my field work were laid out, almost without my being aware of it. For the next year or so, and intermittently thereafter, my base of operations was the corner Carry-out across the street from my starting point.

Liebow began by simply hanging around a street corner, picking up casual conversations until he was able to extend them into more intimate and friendly discussions. In the early days of his study, these contacts led him to Tally Jackson, around whom much of the life of the neighborhood revolved. Tally then filled the role for Liebow that Doc had played for me.

Elliot Liebow did his field work before the height of black militancy, when Afro-American intellectuals were attacking white social scientists for studying black communities instead of concentrating on the white neighborhoods and organizations oppressing minority people.

Would it have been impossible for Liebow to study a black slum neighborhood in the more militant later period? I doubt it. In the first place, black middle-class intellectuals don't control access to black slum neighborhoods. Furthermore, during the height of the black power militancy, I heard a black sociologist pause in his argument to say that he was specifically exempting Elliot Liebow.

A Place on the Corner

For his study in and around Jelly's Bar in a black neighborhood, Elijah Anderson (1978) had neither the color difference to overcome nor a major gap in social status between himself and those he studied. Nevertheless, there was a difference both in social class and culture as well as a major difference in levels of education. In a session at the 1981 meeting of the American Sociological Association, he gave this interpretation of himself:

> I grew up in a home situation in which my father worked in a factory and my mother worked for a while as a domestic. Later, they bought and operated a grocery store that served the local black community. What we call "middle-class" values were emphasized in my home situation—decency, hard work, neatness, personal hygiene, punctuality, delayed gratification. Having been raised in a black American

milieu and having attended integrated schools, I became bilingual: I spoke what linquists are beginning to call "Black English Vernacular" and standard English, and I, like so many black Americans, speak either, often depending on the social situation. With this ability and other related cultural skills, I was able to fit in with the social environment of Jelly's in ways that other researchers might not have been able to. My past cultural experience undoubtedly helped me as I began to negotiate my way into that setting.

What became *A Place on the Corner* (Anderson, 1978) began as a term paper project in graduate work at the University of Chicago.

Even the finding of Jelly's was affected by certain presuppositions that I held about such places. When Jerry Suttles told members of the seminar to go out and find sites to study, I remember driving along and up and down the ghetto streets of the Southside as well as the Westside, looking for a suitable place to study. I checked out a number of taverns, some of which were very tough looking and some of which seemed mild. Although I have a great love for social science, I do care about my physical safety, and that was a consideration. Somehow Jelly's as a place felt good to me. When I walked in, took a seat, and began drinking and talking with people, something clicked. The ambience, the hospitality, which the people maybe didn't know they were offering—it just felt good, and I sincerely wanted to get to know the people. And I think this fact was very important for the success of my study.

Before he met his principal guide and informant, Anderson had already put in enough time at Jelly's to become a familiar figure, while still remaining on the fringes of any social group.

After about four weeks into the setting, I met Herman. He became my main informant, sort of like Doc was for you, I guess. Herman seemed to take a liking to me right away. I was very straight and up front with him, or at least as straight as I could be at the time. You see, I wasn't certain in the beginning how this whole thing would work out. I didn't know it would work out to be anything more than a seminar paper, and I certainly didn't know the work would become a dissertation, let alone a book. As we talked, Herman and I became friendly. I told him that I was a student at the University of Chicago, and he thought that was very nice and decent, and he told me as much. As he got to know me and found me trustworthy, he warmed up to me considerably. When I went to Jelly's, I dressed the way the others dressed—in jeans,

army jackets, sneakers and boots. Herman believed me and I believed
myself at that point, and I thought I was simply writing a paper for a
class and I felt it wasn't worth it to formalize things by saying, "I want to
do a study of your group, can I do it?" And I didn't say that then, but
after a couple of months when I was clearly becoming increasingly
involved and sensing that this project was much more than a seminar
paper, I broached the subject with Herman. And he became very
supportive and said, "Yea, sure, do it." Then the next day, Herman
told the men, "Al' right, ya'll, do somethin'. Eli's studyin' ya'll. Do
somethin'." It seemed clear to him that our friendship was much more
important than any paper coming out of this work.

It was Herman who vouched for Anderson and brought him into the
inner circle at Jelly's.

Honor and the American Dream

Ruth Horowitz's (1983) study of a Chicano neighborhood is
noteworthy in two respects. In the first place, Horowitz carried out her
study in two time periods, 1971 to 1974 and 1977, thus enabling her to
follow her people over a six-year period. In the second place, Horowitz
was able to present apparently equally intimate accounts of the lives of
Chicano teenagers and young adults of both sexes. I had assumed that
it would have been impossible for me to study young Italian-American
women as a participant observer, and indeed that was probably the
case. While they often passed the street corner, it was not customary for
"good girls"—or for any females, for that matter—to spend time on the
corners. Pursuing them into their homes would hardly have led me into
the kind of relaxed, informal situation conducive to good participant
observation.

Horowtiz was fluent in Spanish, a practical asset for communication
with the older generation and no doubt an advantage with the younger
generation as it suggested a sincere interest in people in their ethnic
background. Beyond that, as she described herself,

> I am Jewish, educated, small, fairly dark, a woman, dressed slightly
> sloppily but not *too* sloppily, and only a few years older than most of
> those I observed.

> I had little choice but to acknowledge publicly the reasons for my
> presence on 32nd Street; not only do I differ in background from the
> 32nd Street residents but I had to violate many local expectations to
> gather the data I needed. For example, women do not spend time

alone with male gangs as I did. Because I was an outsider I had to ask a lot of "stupid" questions—"Who are the guys in the black and red sweaters?" or "Why do you fight?" As anything but an acknowledged outsider I would have had a difficult time asking them. Moreover, while my appearance allowed me to blend into a youthful crowd, I sounded and looked sufficiently different so that most people who did not know me realized that I was not from the neighborhood [Horowitz, 1983: 6].

Here she describes the initial encounter with the first group she studied:

I chose to sit on a bench in a park where many youths gathered from noon until midnight. On the third afternoon of sitting on the bench, as I dropped a softball that had rolled toward me, a young man came over and said, "You can't catch" (which I acknowledged) and "You're not from the hood [neighborhood], are you?" This was a statement, not a question. He was Gilberto, the Lions' president. When I told him I wanted to write a book on Chicano youth, he said I should meet the other young men and took me over to shake hands with eight members of the Lions.

The park became my hangout every day after that, but it was several months, several bottles of Boone's Farm Strawberry Wine, and a number of rumors about my being a narcotics agent before gang members would give me intimate information about their girlfriends, families, and feelings about themselves and the future [pp. 7-8].

Though she writes that "my relationship with the male gang members never was easy" (p. 9), Horowitz was able to build on her acceptance with the Lions to establish relations with other neighborhood gangs. Her openings to groups of young women came in the fourth week of field work and through their friendships with members of the Lions. Her contacts with upwardly mobile youth began about a month later when two young women approached her to strike up a conversation. After they had satisfied their curiosity, they and their friends informally became her protectors in the neighborhood.

That night and many nights during the first year, they and a group of their friends walked me the five blocks to the bus stop. By the third time I saw them at the park they invited me to their homes to meet their families and to eat. In one family I was immediately adopted and included in all the family celebrations and holiday dinners [p. 10].

Regarding the problems of building effective research relations with both the young men and the young women, she writes:

> I did have to be extremely careful not to develop a sexual identity. My lack of care with appearance, which both males and females continually remarked upon, helped, but I was very careful not to spend too much time alone with any one male and not to dance with them at the many parties and dances I attended [p. 10].

ENTERING THE WORKPLACE

Where jobs are available, becoming a worker participant observer presents no problems of access in our own society. Gatekeepers in the employment office can consider you just another worker. However, access as a participant observer can present formidable problems in a culture and society foreign to the researcher.

Participant Observer in Japan

In a 1981 panel discussion at the American Sociological Association meeting, Robert Cole described how he started his research in Japanese industry:

> I thought I wrote a wonderful dissertation prospectus on the applicability of Max Weber to Japanese industrialization, but in fact my heart was set on trying to get into a Japanese factory. I was discouraged heavily by most folks I came into contact with, and for a long time I thought I was going to write my dissertation on what we can learn about Japanese society without getting in to work there.
>
> The access was extremely difficult in Japan compared to what I think one would experience in the U.S. for a Westerner for a number of reasons. First, there is very little tradition of doing participant observation in Japan by scholars. They were much more into the philosophical tradition, in terms of social science, and so that was fairly novel. There are cases of journalists doing what we would call participant observation, but strictly for journalistic purposes. Since that tradition is not well established in Japan, you simply have trouble explaining what you are about. Second, Japan is a pretty closed society. They don't have the mix of ethnic groups that we are accustomed to, that would make it understandable why a Westerner would want to work in a Japanese factory. They have a tradition of exploiting Koreans and some other marginal groups. Most Westerners were therefore excluded from employment in major firms. Most Westerners, to the

extent that they get involved in a Japanese factory, would be "technical experts" who came for a short period to impart information.

I didn't come to impart information, so I had a lot of trouble. I thought I
had fully explained that as much as possible I wanted to be treated as a
"normal" worker. I demanded pay, to give credibility to my venture,
but still when I showed up that first day they didn't really understand
that I expected to work. I made an ordinary request of a Western field
worker that no special treatment be given, for all sorts of the usual
reasons since with special treatment one runs the risk of discrediting
yourself in the eyes of the workers. I had a lot of trouble with that
because, in the context of Japan, no special treatment, to management and to the union, meant that I was being extraordinarily cocky. It
was as if I was telling them I knew all I had to know and I could take
care of myself. For them it was patently obvious that I didn't know a
damn thing about Japan, and no one could ever understand us, the
Japanese, so that was a real problem. In fact, at one company where I
was turned down, that was given as the reason. In this particular case,
I answered a newspaper ad and that blew everyone away. They were
having interviews, and I remember showing up, and a woman who
was taking applications just got all shook and turned to me and said in
the most blatant racist terms, "We don't hire foreigners." They hadn't
learned the sophistication of Westerners in terms of how racism gets
used to keep people out of jobs. But my application was so unprece-
dented that she hadn't really learned how to deal with it.

I finally made some contacts through a union in one company and
through a former employee of a major company, and they both
arranged for me to get into subcontract firms. That was not accidental
because the larger firms were concerned about me causing disruption,
and they felt safer if I went into a smaller subcontract firm where
anything that happened wouldn't embarrass the "parent" firm.

There was a lot of testing of me. The workers were involved in a rather
ferocious struggle. The plant had a militant union, and the struggle
was between the communists and the socialists. In the beginning, the
workers were feeding me information to see if it got back to management. Not that it made any sense for me to be a management spy.
Japanese management didn't need an illiterate foreigner as a management spy. It also took time to build the trust necessary to do my
work.

Initially, there were a couple of workers that befriended me. One of
them was a worker who had rather menial jobs in the plant, but he
took it upon himself to tell me like it was. If there was a fight going on in
the other section, he would come in to me and say, "Hey, you better

get over there and see what's going on." He really educated me in many ways. One of the factional leaders in the union also took me under his wing. These individuals became points of entry.

When I went into the Japanese factory, I went in "as an American student who was writing a paper." It was made very clear to me by Japanese scholars and other people that if I had come in as a professor, particularly in the context of Japan with all the status implications, I could not have developed the necessary rapport with workers that I needed to understand factory life. At least for some kinds of participative observation studies, there may be some age grading involved in the sense that one's age impacts on the kind of research you can do. When I began my work in the factory I was 28 years old. At the diecast company I was working at, this was the average age of workers as well, and it matched the ages of those in my work group. Consequently, a lot of the ice-breaking could be around similar kinds of life experiences. I had a good deal more difficulty developing rapport in my second job in an auto parts factory where those in work group were in their late teens and early 20s and just off the farm.

Studying Phillips Petroleum Co.

When I began my first industrial study in 1942, such research was unknown in Oklahoma and little known elsewhere. To break into this new field, as a novice I had to gain entry through people who had not the vaguest idea of what such a study might be like.

The head of the University of Oklahoma Sociology Department, W. B. Bizzell, was most helpful. He had previously been president of the university and had been bumped back to head of the department in a clash with the regents. As president he had become very well acquainted with Frank Phillips, founder and chairman of Phillips Petroleum, one of the great industrial entrepreneurs. The business was then only about 25 years old but already moving up to become one of the major oil companies.

The basis of Bizzell's friendship with Phillips was Phillips's interest in archaeology. Previously it had been believed that Oklahoma's early Indian tribes had been very primitive. Then some archeologists discovered the Spiro mound, which revealed an enormous quantity of elaborate pots and other artifacts that excited archaeologists and made Oklahomans swell with pride. So Bizzell would arrange for a fly-in dig for Frank Phillips. He would come in his private plane, the university archaeologist would lead him to the appropriate spot, Phillips would hand his coat to his pilot, the archaeologist would hand him a shovel,

Phillips would dig, and up would come a pot. Then, while Phillips posed with Bizzell and the pot, the university photographer would take pictures. Phillips would then climb into his plane with the pot and fly back to his headquarters in Bartlesville.

In November 1942 I arrived at Bartlesville with a letter from Bizzell. Phillips greeted me: "I can give you two minutes. Then I have to meet with my Board of Directors." I tried to give my two-minute introduction, presenting the study I wanted to do, interviewing and observing human relations among workers and management.

He asked me two questions: "What experience have you had in the oil industry?" None. "Are you a lawyer?" No. He raised his eyes to the ceiling. There was a pause while I tried to claim that I understood working people and would fit in somehow. He called in Warren Felton, his manager of employee relations. Phillips left me with Felton without apparent instructions. Felton took me to his office. We talked, and he certainly was puzzled too, as to what to do with me, but he introduced me to his assistant. I learned that his assistant was about to take off for Oklahoma City, a three-hour train ride, so I arranged to go back with him and had a good chance to get acquainted. He promised to explain the study to Division Manager Al Wenzel, and it would be up to him to decide.

When I encountered Wenzel and Jeff Franklin, the personnel manager, they had been briefed by Felton's assistant. They said that the study was a dandy idea but not right at that time. The CIO was then organizing, and they were facing a representation election. If I would just wait until that was over, whichever way it went, then it would be fine for me to come in. I asked when it would take place. "Maybe in a couple of weeks," they said, "but we're not sure." I knew nothing about industrial relations, but I knew enough not to accept that guess. This was November, the election took place in mid-April, and, as it turned out, I left Oklahoma in May.

I had to scramble for another approach. I explained that I knew practically nothing about the oil industry, so it would be very valuable if I could sit in the office and go over their personnel records. They couldn't think of a way to say no to that, so, for what must have been three to four weeks, two days a week I engaged in some of the dullest work of my career. I sat in the office with big sheets of paper, going through personnel records and marking things down, accumulating an enormous pile of data which I subsequently destroyed, but it gave me an excuse to be there.

Fortunately the headquarters of the division was on the edge of Oklahoma City. There were no restaurants nearby, so for lunch they would bring in sandwiches. We would sit and talk, and I would try to be as charming and nonthreatening as possible.

After this went on for some time, they figured they would never get me out of the office if they didn't think of something. They told me that a staff man in the personnel department was going into the field to do a job description, and I could go along and help him.

And so we went out to the Capok plant that was making aviation gasoline from natural gas. I met the plant superintendent and the foreman, and then I followed the staff man around as he interviewed workers. I made notes and I began to learn something about the nature of the work. But the next week the staff man was pulled off onto something more urgent. The superintendent was sympathetic and said if I wanted to continue with the job description that it was okay with him.

However, I was engaged in doing the first job description I had ever heard of, so it seemed rather implausible to continue. I had no recourse but to level with the men as to what I was really up to. I told them that I was a professor at the University of Oklahoma. They were naturally suspicious. Was I a company man? Well, I was on the payroll, but for only the $25 a month that the company was giving me for field expenses. I even showed my paycheck to the men, assuming that they wouldn't think a college professor would sell his soul that cheaply.

This turned out to be an ideal setting for a study because the work consisted of watching the dials and charts, running brief tests about once every hour, and making occasional adjustments, except in emergencies. The men were bored and were glad to talk to somebody new. I was happy to listen to them, and gradually they began talking more and more freely. Thus I was able to view from the inside the struggle between the CIO and management to win the hearts and minds of the workers—a project on which I wrote an unpublishable book (see Chapter 11).

Studying Restaurants

In 1944, when I began the restaurant projects, social research in industry was still such an unfamiliar phenomenon as to pose formidable problems of access. But since Vernon Stouffer was a member of the National Restaurant Association committee, which was sponsoring the project, he could hardly bar the way when I decided to make the Chicago Loop Stouffers our first case study.

Margaret Chandler wormed her way into a cafeteria where she had been having some of her meals and where she had already become personally acquainted with the owner. She then combined interviewing and observation with helping out as cashier and doing other odd jobs. Edith Lentz began her field work as a waitress.

Beyond these beginnings, I found the access problems were getting no easier. When I tried to sell the study to restaurant owners or managers, I was confronted with two equal and opposite rejections. One restaurateur would say, "Things are going so smoothly now that I don't want to take any chances letting an outsider in." The next restaurateur would say, "We have so many problems and things are so tense right now that letting an outsider in might cause a blow-up." In vain I tried to explain that the research methods we used did not "put ideas into people's heads" and that the catharsis of talking to a friendly outsider could have a calming effect.

Frustrated in this direct approach, I adopted a different strategy. After an initial explanation of the nature of the study, I asked the restaurateur to tell me how things were going in his or her restaurant and what problems should be given special attention in our study. As the discussion proceeded, with the restaurateur doing most of the talking, I would find openings to relate similar problems or experiences from other restaurants we were studying. Without pressing the point, I would add that we were then considering further restaurants for case studies and had a number of possibilities in mind.

On my first try with this strategy, the restaurateur asked if we would be willing to study his establishment. After a moment of apparent indecision, I agreed.

Although I have not used this strategy in experimentally controlled situations, it makes theoretical sense to me. If you approach the gatekeeper with the idea that you are determined to study his or her organization, your eagerness tends to build up his or her defenses. If you go in with the assumption that this is only one of a number of organizations that might be appropriate to your study, you can carry on a much more relaxed discussion, leading to a mutual exploration of the advantages and disadvantages for both parties of making this firm one of your cases. Nor does this strategy need to be considered simply a diplomatic maneuver. There can be cases in which the gatekeeper eventually expresses willingness to grant access, but the course of the conversation suggests to you that it would be better to carry on the study elsewhere. Over the years, as gatekeepers became more familiar with social research in industry, I found it much easier to negotiate my entry.

ACCESS ROUTES

The routes to access are somewhat different according to whether we are studying a community or a work organization (factory, government agency, hospital, and so on). For the work organization, access routes also differ according to whether you enter as an employee participant observer or as a recognized researcher. In the former case, in our own society, if a job is open, entry may require nothing more than going through the procedures open to any applicant. As Robert Cole found in Japan, this route may not be open in another country with a markedly different culture. For a recognized researcher, entry is impossible without permission from an *official* gatekeeper. The problem then is how to explain our purposes in a way that satisfies the gatekeeper and yet does not distort or unduly limit the nature of the study.

In a community-based study, social acceptance must be negotiated with gatekeepers. If we plan to study the total community, then it makes sense (as in Muncie, Newburyport, and Natchez) to approach first the key officials of local government and/or leading citizens. Students or professors should find that their upper-middle-class status and their university involvement provide a presumption of legitimacy to the research role in the eyes of such gatekeepers.

If we aim to gain an intimate view of lower class people beyond the boundaries of social agencies, access routes are much less clearly marked. Gatekeeping functions are less centralized, and public officials, social workers, or leading citizens are likely to be uninformed or misinformed regarding the identity of gatekeepers to informal groups or formal associations. The researcher has to plunge into unmapped territory to discover gatekeepers without outside help (as in the case of Liebow, Anderson, and Horowitz) or, as in my case, with just a single (but indispensable) bit of guidance from a social worker.

As I reflect upon the experience of the four of us who engaged in extended and intimate participant observation in lower class neighborhoods, I find important elements in common. The same conclusions may apply in broader community studies that include intensive studies within such neighborhoods.

(1) At the outset, we did not know what we were looking for. We did not enter the field with blank minds, yet our original formulations proved to have little relation to the studies that eventually evolved. We set out on the frontiers of our personal knowledge and began exploring beyond those frontiers.

(2) Such an exploration demands an investment of many weeks' time in getting familiar with the social terrain and gaining acceptance by local people. Participant observation is not for the researcher who aims to get firm answers quickly.

(3) Though far from our customary social circles, we do not operate alone. The successful participant observer finds local guides to join in the exploration and to vouch for the credibility and sincerity of the researcher.

(4) Full-time participant observation over an extended period of time tends to be an age-graded phenomenon. Such studies are most likely to be done by young people, in our student years. When we are established professionals, with teaching or other professional responsibilities, we are unlikely to have the time and the motivation to make such a full commitment. Nevertheless, the techniques we learn in full-time participant observation can be adapted to later studies where such immersion in the field is not possible.

4

Field Relations

Now that you are in, what do you do?

A witness in court is required to swear to tell "the truth, the whole truth, and nothing but the truth." In general, it is advisable to adhere to the first and third of those admonitions in field work, but the second requires some modification, as we will note later.

In discussing his classic study, "The Dynamics of Bureaucracy," Peter Blau (1964: 28) draws the following conclusion:

> The feelings of insecurity that the bureaucratic field situation tends to evoke in the observer, particularly the inexperienced one, are generally a major source of blunders. This is the fundamental pragmatic reason, quite aside from considerations of professional ethics, why the observer, in my opinion, should not resort to concealment and deception. It is difficult to simulate a role successfully over long periods of time, and if concern over detection adds to the observer's other worries he is not likely to be effective in discharging his research responsibilities. I explained quite openly what I was doing and the aims of my study to any respondent who was interested, the major exception being that I never called it a study of "bureaucracy." (Refraining from deception does not imply, of course, revealing one's hypotheses to respondents, since proper research procedure may require these to remain concealed.)

If you have a formal position in the organization—as in the case of Lieutenant Sullivan as a participant observer inducted into the Air Force—then it may be possible to maintain a covert research role. Otherwise the risks are too great, since discovery of the deception ends the field study.

To what extent do you have to behave like other people in order to be accepted in a group, organization, or community? This question is misleading in the implicit assumption that other people in the situation being studied are all behaving in the same way. Beyond the small group, in a complex society people of different ages, sexes, statuses, or organizational memberships and personal values will behave quite differently. If the researcher aims to participate in more than a single small group, it is obviously impossible to make major changes in behavior in moving from one group to another. However, apart from the research situation, it is quite normal for people to make some adjustments of behavior in moving from group to group and from situation to situation.

Even if we are concerned only with acceptance within a small group, it does not necessarily follow that the participant observer should seek to behave just like other members. I learned this lesson as I was trying to fit into the Norton Street gang.

> One evening as I was walking down the street with the Nortons, . . . I cut loose with a string of obscenities and profanity. The walk came to a momentary halt as they all stopped to look at me in surprise. Doc shook his head and said: "Bill, you're not supposed to talk like that. That doesn't sound like you."
>
> I tried to explain that I was only using terms that were common on the street corner. Doc insisted, however, that I was different and that they wanted me to be that way.
>
> This lesson went far beyond the use of obscenity and profanity. I learned that people did not expect me to be just like them; in fact, they were interested and pleased to find me different, just so long as I took a friendly interest in them [Whyte, 1981: 304].

Later on, in violating Doc's advice, I made the most serious mistake of all my time in Cornerville—a mistake that could have brought my study to an abrupt end. It happened when I was acting as a participant observer in the campaign for Congress of State Senator George Revello.

> When I got home, I began hearing alarming reports from the home ward of the Irish politician who was Ravello's chief rival. He was said to have a fleet of taxicabs cruising about his ward so that each of his repeaters would be able to vote in every precinct of the ward. It became clear that, if we did not steal the election ourselves, this low character would steal it from us.
>
> Around five o'clock one of the senator's chief lieutenants rushed up to a group of us who were hanging on the corner across the street from

my home polling place. He told us that Joseph Maloney's section of our ward was wide open for repeaters, that the cars were ready to transport them, and that all he needed were a few men to get to work. At the moment the organization was handicapped by a shortage of manpower to accomplish this important task. The senator's lieutenant did not ask for volunteers; he simply directed us to get into the cars to go to the polling places where the work could be done. I hesitated a moment, but I did not refuse.

Before the polls had closed that night, I had voted three more times for George Ravello—really not much of a feat, since another novice who had started off at the same time as I managed to produce nine votes in the same period of time [Whyte, 1981: 313-314].

When I went in to vote the second time in my home precinct, I was challenged, and, for a few agonizing seconds, I thought I was going to be arrested. In fact, a year later when I was out of town someone voted in my name and *was* arrested.

If I had been arrested, could my political friends have got me free? More important, could I have kept secret my identity as junior fellow at Harvard University? As I have reflected on these events over the years, I find myself encountering imaginary headlines: "Harvard Fellow Arrested for Repeating." Obviously, that would have been a newsworthy story, and the publicity could have ended my field work.

Beyond the legal penalities, I was at least as much concerned with my conception of myself as with other people's perception of me. I had regarded myself as committed to high principles—had my election day performance revealed my true character? Apart from the ethical issue, I learned that it is even more important for the field worker to be able to live with himself than to live with other people.

When I confessed my crime to Doc, his reaction confirmed what I had suspected. He and his friends disapproved of repeating and would not have engaged in it themselves. My experience reinforced this general conclusion: In studying a complex community with many groups, the researcher who seeks to conform fully to the standards of behavior of each group with which he or she associates becomes involved in insoluble problems of ethics and self-concept.

FORMALIZING FIELD METHODS

The participant observer role can pave the way for asking questions and even for conducting formal interviews. However, in the early stages of the project, when the researcher is still consolidating a social base, it is not advisable to formalize one's methodology.

Peter Blau spent three months in each of two governmental organizations. In both cases, he was able to do formal interviewing and observation, but, in his first study, he made the mistake of formalizing his methods before he was completely accepted. Blau had a desk that enabled him to observe all the agents whenever they were working in the office. Early on, he set out to record systematically who was interacting with whom and who initiated the interactions. He came to recognize that some of the agents assumed that he had deceived them about his true purposes and was really some kind of efficiency expert, studying who was wasting how much time.

> The continual observation to which keeping such a record subjects respondents makes them self-conscious and is irritating. Evidently I should have waited until my rapport was much better before using this technique (as I did, of course, in the second study). Why did I make the blunder of using it prematurely?
>
> I think the answer is not simply that lack of experience prevented me from knowing how much resistance this method of observing interaction would create in a group not yet fully reconciled to my presence. Common sense should have told me so, had not irrational factors prevented me from realizing it. I was a lone observer in the midst of an integrated group of officials who were initially suspicious of and even somewhat hostile to me and my research. While they were part of the bureaucratic structure, my position was not anchored in it. My anxiety engendered by this insecure position was undoubtedly intensified by the pressure I felt to progress with my observations, since I was not sure whether I could achieve my research aims in the limited time available. It seems (and I use the tentative wording advisedly because I am now reconstructing mental processes of which I was then not fully aware) that I tried to cope with this anxiety by imposing a rigid structure on my research activities. This emotional reaction may have prompted my decision to turn so early from more exploratory observations to the precisely circumscribed and fairly routine task of recording interaction frequencies [Blau, 1964: 28].

Within the first few days in the North End study, I made an error that could have been serious if Doc had not had such a strong position in the group in question.

> I learned this lesson one night in the early months when I was with Doc in Chichi's gambling joint. A man from another part of the city was regaling us with a tale of the organization of gambling activity. I had been told that he had once been a very big gambling operator, and he talked knowingly about many interesting matters. He did most of the

talking, but the others asked questions and threw in comments, so at length I began to feel that I must say something in order to be part of the group. I said: "I suppose the cops were all paid off?"

The gambler's jaw dropped. He glared at me. Then he denied vehemently that any policeman had been paid off and immediately switched the conversation to another subject. For the rest of that evening I felt very uncomfortable.

The next day Doc explained the lesson of the previous evening. "Go easy on that 'who,' 'what,' 'why,' 'when,' 'where' stuff, Bill. You ask those questions, and people will clam up on you. If people accept you, you can just hang around, and you'll learn the answer in the long run without even having to ask the questions."

I found that this was true. As I sat and listened, I learned the answers to questions that I would not even have had the sense to ask if I had been getting my information solely on an interviewing basis. I did not abandon questioning altogether, of course. I simply learned to judge the sensitiveness of the question and my relationship to the people so that I only asked a question in a sensitive area when I was sure that my relationship to the people involved was very solid.

When I had established my position on the street corner, the data simply came to me without very active efforts on my part. It was only now and then, when I was concerned with a particular problem and felt I needed more information from a certain individual, that I would seek an opportunity to get the man alone and carry on a more formal interview [Whyte, 1981: 303-304].

Such self-restraint may not come easy. The first few days or even the first few weeks of a study may bring in only superficial information, along with bits of data that either do not seem to make sense or do not fit together. One who has become accustomed to measuring progress in terms of pages read or written, naturally finds this beginning stage frustrating. Unless obviously dramatic events are unfolding before our eyes, it may seem that nothing is happening, that the situation is the same everyday. If we insist on asking people what is going on and why they are acting as they do, at best we get formalized explanations—the interpretations people give to outsiders.

If we are successful in establishing a social base, we may find quite suddenly that we have broken through the superficial level, that we begin to see patterns and movement which were not evident before, and at last we begin to get a vision of what it is we are really studying.

The questions is not whether to use formal interviews or observational methods, but when and under what circumstances. In the later stages of my first study, I did some formal interviewing. Even then, I found that people I had known well on the street corner seemed uncomfortable with this change in our relationship. Before, I had nearly always associated with them on a group basis (except for many hours I spent with Doc) and now for the first time I was separating informants from the group situation for interviews. However, this presented no serious problems, as by this time my relationships with individuals and the group had been solidly established.

CONFLICTING GROUP IDENTIFICATIONS

If you are accepted into one group, does this block or limit your access to other groups? In general, that depends upon the depth of cleavages within the community or organization.

Of course, regardless of social cleavages, the researcher must spend a certain amount of time with a group to be fully accepted; thus, there is a limit to the number of groups that one can be accepted into at the same time. To some extent this limitation can be overcome by studying different groups at different times, but even this poses its problems. For example, toward the end of my period in Cornerville, I was involved in a softball league, playing with a group that I called the Cornerville S&A Club. This presented no problems until there was a game scheduled between the Cornerville S&A Club and the Nortons, my original North End gang. When the Nortons discovered that I planned to play for the rival team, they were outraged. To preserve the lingering relationship I had with the Nortons, I felt obliged to make the supreme sacrifice—to remain on the sidelines.

Political organizations may present more formidable limitations. Except for one period, I avoided involvement with any political organization. Because his chief rival was an Irishman from Charlestown, across the river, working for George Ravello posed no problems in my relations with others in the district.

In his study entitled *Blue Collar Community,* Kornblum (1974: 240) did become active in one political organization:

> The pressure to become committed to other people is a general characteristic of community life in South Chicago, but during the time I lived in the community this pressure was probably as great as it had ever been. This was a time when the community was involved in sorting out the leadership of its most central institutions. For this reason all my friends and informants found themselves in one way or another drawn into competition between aggregations of community groups. It seemed that only the most financially secure or socially marginal people could afford not to take sides. This same spirit of

partisanship also affected me. I began to feel that I could not remain aloof from political commitment when all the people I cared for had so much more at stake than I did. Aside from the personal aspect of this decision, there are very real limitations to what one can learn about political proceses through informants. If one wishes actually to watch decisions being made in a competitive political system, it is often necessary to become part of the decision-making body itself. I did this by taking highly partisan, although "behind the scenes" roles in most of the political campaigns reported in this study.

The liabilities of this strategy are numerous and deserve some attention. First, it is obvious that the more committed one is to a particular faction, the less one can learn, at first hand, about others. This may not be quite so true in higher levels of political competition where political expertise is more rationally calculated and more often bought and sold, but it is certainly the case in community politics. Even though the competition is highly institutionalized, when neighbors and workmates compete against each other, careful attention is payed to one's affiliations, and trust is easily jeopardized. In consequence of this, whenever I committed myself to a given faction I attempted to function as much as possible in capacities which would require little public exposure. In order to keep up with events in opposing factions I attempted to explain my affiliations as frankly as possible to friends on opposite sides, in much the same terms as any other resident of the community would. In this way it was possible to act as a partisan and still communicate with friends in opposing factions who acted as my informants. Here the amount of time spent in fieldwork was extremely important. I did not become actively committed until the third year of my research. By that time I had friends throughout the community who could understand, if not always agree with my partisanship.

In *Stateville,* Jacobs (1977) was able to maintain good relations with rival black gangs, but, after an initial period of apparent acceptance, he found himself rejected by white inmates, who were in the minority:

> Despite careful explanation of my purposes within the prison, white inmates imputed to me a sentiment of racial solidarity with whites and a motive to work on *their* behalf to improve *their* position. When they concluded that I was unwilling to be their advocate and that I would continue to maintain my relations with black gang members, our rapport deteriorated rapidly, culminating with the following note:
>
> > Mr. Jacobs: Hey, you Super Liberal Piece of Shit. So far this week two white guys have been jumped on and beaten by groups of Afro-Americans.* The next time you go over to "B" house lock-up to let some jackoff ripoff artist know who told on him for rapping some white kid so he can get even later on why

don't you tell him about yourself too. Also instead of doing your
bull shit research from an armchair, why didn't you come in as
an inmate so you could find out what it's all about, you phoney
cock sucker.

*human nigger scum.

What had been a shaky working agreement between this faction of the
prison community and myself had utterly dissolved. Now I was rede-
fined as a "nigger lover" and racial traitor. No longer was there
enough common agreement on social identities and social tasks to
support more than the most superficial communication. Perhaps this
demonstrates that neutrality itself is a role enactment subject to interpretation [Jacobs, 1977: 223]?

Dalton frequently heard claims that in order to get ahead in management in the steel mill, you had to join the Masons. As the surrounding community was predominantly Catholic, this was a touchy subject.
One informant, Mason himself, then suggested that Dalton would learn
a lot more if he joined the order. Dalton managed to avoid this commitment, thus maintaining his friendly relations with non-Masons but also
somewhat limiting his access to information about the Masons. However, the main point he was trying to establish was how many and which
managers were members of the order. By this time he had solid enough
relations with individual Masons to be able to follow up in interviews.

Since the Masons were distributed among numerous lodges, to confirm membership I eventually had to submit lists of doubtful officers to
seventeen intimates among the Masons. I felt obliged to give each a
general explanation adapted to his personal tendencies as I saw them
[in Hammond, 1964: 68].

Apparently these informants did not get together to check the somewhat diverse explanations Dalton had given.

To what extent the researcher should avoid a strong identification
with a particular group or organization depends upon the purposes of
the project. If the field worker is studying a particular political organization, it may be advisable for him or her to become an active member of
that organization, even though this will limit his or her access to those
outside of it.

PASSIVE INFORMANT OR ACTIVE COLLABORATOR?

In filling out a questionnaire, the subject is necessarily a passive
respondent. In semistructured field methods, the subjects of study can

be treated as passive respondents, but the researcher who does so fails to exploit the possibilities of this methodology.

A union steward opened my eyes to the possibility of gaining an active participant even within a single interview. The interview took place in a steel fabricating plant to which I had returned for a brief visit after completing an intensive study there several years earlier. At that time I had given particular attention to a foreman I called Joe Walker, who had played a critical role in a key department in enabling management and the union to break out of a bitter conflict and develop an extraordinarily harmonious relationship. When I returned I was surprised to learn that Joe Walker had been demoted to foreman of a smaller and much less important department. My main purpose in interviewing the steward in Walker's former department was to discover what had happened to make this apparently highly successful foreman a failure. For about three-quarters of an hour, the steward seemed to be talking freely and frankly, and he expressed himself well. Nevertheless, my questions were getting nowhere.

Finally, I said something like this: "When I was here before, I had the impression that Joe Walker was highly regarded by management and union leaders and got along very well with the workers. I understand that management became very dissatisfied with Joe Walker, and the union leaders and the workers were having serious problems with him. Now, either I am mistaken about how he was getting along before or else I simply don't understand what happened to bring about such a drastic change."

The steward smiled and nodded his head as if to say, "Oh, so that's what you wanted to know. Why didn't you tell me?" Then for the next ten or fifteen minutes, the steward told me that my earlier impression of Walker's situation and reputation was correct, and that certain important changes had taken place. With a good deal of intelligence and sensitivity, the steward systematically explained the various changes that had undermined Walker's position (Whyte, 1969: 331-345). In other words, when I stopped trying to get at the causes indirectly and asked him point-blank, he told me.

Here I was not disregarding Blau's advice in revealing a research hypothesis to an informant. Nothing so grandiose was involved. I was simply trying to learn what had caused such a drastic change in the relations of the foreman to management, the workers, and the union. For this purpose, the sensible procedure would have been simply to tell the steward frankly what I was trying to figure out and ask him to help me, which I finally did, but only after three-quarters of an hour of beating about the bush.

If it can be useful even in a single interview to seek the informant's active help, then it should be obvious that developing intensive collaborative relations with a few key informants can enormously enrich the data and deepen the analysis. The most effective field workers don't treat people in the field study simply as passive respondents. In *Street Corner Society,* almost from the time of our initial meeting, I regarded Doc as a participant in the study. We spent many hours discussing what I was trying to find out. As he came to understand, even as I was learning myself, what the nature of the study was, he served as an alternate observer when I was not present. He would say, "Bill, you should've been around last night. Here is what happened." Then he would give me a detailed report, covering all the points that I would have liked to have observed had I been present—and probably some additional points that I would not have been sensitive enough to notice. Doc was helpful in more ways than simply in providing data. We spent so much of our time together jointly analyzing the data that I can no longer tell which ideas were his and which were mine.

Through Doc and through my own observations, I was able to work out the informal group structure of what I called the Norton Street gang, but I could hardly generalize on informal group structures on the basis of a single case study. Here again I gained invaluable assistance from Doc, as I followed him into the storefront recreation center he was directing. There I met Sam Franco (Ralph Orlandella), the leader of a corner gang in another part of the district. We worked together over many months, observing and analyzing his own gang and several others in his neighborhood. On one occasion, I got Doc and Sam working together, through observation alone, to pick the leader of each gang that came into the recreation center.

Here we had the great advantage of having two sharp observers checking each other on the same groups. I was reassured to find that they were in complete agreement on the top-leadership structure of every gang—with one exception. This one exception did trouble me until the explanation presented itself.

I had spent part of one afternoon listening to Doc and Sam argue over the leadership of one gang. Doc claimed that Carl was the man; Sam argued that it was Tommy. Each man presented incidents that he had observed in support of his point of view. The following morning Sam rushed up to our flat with this bulletin: "You know what happened last night? Carl and Tommy nearly had it out. They got into a big argument, and now the gang is split into two parts with some of them going with Carl and the rest going with Tommy." So their conflicting views turned out to be an accurate representation of what was taking place in the gang [Whyte, 1981: 327].

Years later in a study of union-management cooperation, I developed a collaborative relationship with Sidney Garfield, international representative of the International Chemical Workers Union. The collaboration went beyond the case study of S. Buchsbaum and Company (Whyte et al., 1946).

As we worked together, Garfield from time to time would throw in anecdotes regarding his experiences in other cases. I found him a shrewd analyst of the dynamics of collective bargaining. This led me to propose a collaborative writing project, which was later published as a series of four articles on the collective bargaining process (Garfield and Whyte, 1950-1951). I did all the writing, but the cases were all drawn from Garfield's experience, and he contributed much of the analysis.

In my study, "Human Aspects of Industrial Development in Peru," I developed a similar collaborative relationship with Robert R. Braun, who was acting director of IPAE, the Peruvian equivalent of the American Management Association. Braun had been born in Austria and had come to Peru after high school, 29 years before we met. He had a wide range of experience in management, working for German, American, and Peruvian companies as well as for the accounting and consulting firm, Price Waterhouse. Braun was trilingual and an extraordinarily sensitive observer of intercultural differences in behavior and attitudes.

When I explained my study, Braun immediately took a strong interest, and in fact volunteered to serve as my informal and unpaid associate. He became my principal guide to Peruvian culture and to the nature of its industrial organizations. Braun made his first important contribution in revising the statement I had drafted to explain my project to Peruvian management. By this time, I was fairly fluent in Spanish, but I never sent out anything I wrote, beyond letters to personal friends, without having the text gone over by a native speaker. The project secretary could correct grammatical errors, but this was not good enough for Braun. He went over the text and explained how certain changes in wording would make it more acceptable, without changing the meaning.

Braun helped me to set up an advisory group, suggested how to present my project to them, observed me in group meetings, and criticized my performance later. For example, when I had described what I had done to the group, I outlined the next steps I was planning. Unconsciously conforming to my own cultural background, I stopped to ask the group's advice on which company would be the logical next site for the study. Up to this point, the meeting had seemed to go very well, but now it deteriorated. I got no clear answers, and I sensed an uneasiness among group members, which I certainly shared. Braun explained to me later that they had considered me an expert in my field, but my question conveyed the sense that I didn't really know what I was doing. He argued that I should have proposed one particular company and asked them how to make the approach. If they had thought of some solid reason that company would not be appropriate, they might have told me, but otherwise they would have expected simply to help me arrange it. In other words, my attempt to be participative was counterproductive.

Working with Braun further sensitized me to the cultural implications of the Spanish language, as spoken by management people in Peru. Here I found it was an advantage not to be bilingual. Had I grown up speaking Spanish as well as English, the problems of translating from one language to the other would have been buried in my subconscious. As it was, I had gone well beyond the beginner's stage, but now I became concerned with the difficulties of expressing in Spanish certain concepts important in our own culture (*achievement*, for example). As I consulted Braun, I learned that sometimes the problem was not my language deficiency but real difficulty in devising an exact translation. As we explored these problems further, Braun and I worked together on the joint article, "On Language and Culture" (Whyte and Braun, 1968).

In *Stateville*, a study of a large Illinois penitentiary, James Jacobs (1977: 221) describes how he was able to penetrate the gang organizations among prisoners only as he developed collaborative relations with key gang leaders:

> Skilled informants were able to provide far more information privately when less sophisticated inmates were not present to misinterpret what was being said. CN, clerk for the assistant warden and articulate spokesman for the Latin Kings, quickly understood that my research posed no threat either to the Kings or to the other organizations. He met me at the gate each morning and personally undertook to orient me to Stateville. Over many weeks he gradually revealed to me the complex power relationships and social structures of the inmate organization. While GB, the younger and far less sophisticated leader of the Disciples, initially refused to enter into a relationship based upon his role as a gang leader, he eventually became an outstanding informant, providing deep insight into the organization and activities of Disciples and his own leadership position. What accounted for his acceptance of an informant role was his growing understanding of this

new role set, increased confidence in my integrity, and especially my expanding knowledge about inmate society. In the early weeks, off brand inmates had been extremely helpful in describing the extent and type of power the gangs held within the prison. Gang leaders soon realized that I knew far more about the underlife at Stateville than any staff member. Once I was credited with being an insider, the amount of information to which I was exposed increased exponentially.

In the plant where he worked for the longest period, Melville Dalton cultivated an extraordinarily large number of confidants. He lists a total of 81: "11 workmen, including three grievers (stewards), 24 first line foreman, 14 general foremen, 6 line superintendents, 8 staff heads or assistants, and 18 staff supervisors. 4 confidants among secretaries should be included (Blau, 1964: 65).

He explained that his duties

> allowed much unquestioned movement about the firms and required considerable functional interaction. I did what I could to expand my existing circle of intimates and to develop confidential exchanges with acquaintances. To this end, I gave every legitimate service and possible courtesy and went beyond what was normal in giving personal aid.

> From this group of personnel I selected, over a period of about three years, as *intimates* those who (1) trusted me; (2) freely gave me information about their problems and fears and frankly tried to explain their own motivations; (3) had shown repeatedly that they would be counted on not to jeopardize the study; (4) accepted what I was able to tell them and refrained from prying into the information I was getting from others; and (5) gave me knowledge and aid (warnings, guidance, "tips") of a kind that, if known, would have endangered their careers [pp. 64-65].

How far this quasi-spying went is illustrated by Dalton's relationship with a secretary in the payroll department. Dalton (1959: 65-66) was seeking information on the salaries of management people:

> She indicated, as I knew, that these were confidential and that it would be dangerous to try to get them. Then, without saying whether she would try or not, she told me she had been wanting to talk with me about a specialist I knew and with whom she had had two dates. She "hoped he was interested" in her. But she felt that his superior education and more prominent family might be obstacles. Knowing of my training in sociology, she "had thought" I might counsel her. My training had not included courtship and marriage, but the possibility

of getting data on salaries enabled me to adopt a counseling manner. I suggested some tactics and promised to learn what I could about the specialist, his family, and his plans for the future. After her next date, she called me for a conference and gave me the first group of salaries she had obtained. The conferences continued with the dating and the flow of data and after discontinuance of data brought on by a chance change of personnel. (Despite the counseling, the secretary married the specialist within a year.)

Dalton (1959: 67) concludes with this observation on the value of "intimates":

> Some intimates were invaluable not only as sources of information but also for help in research situations. Especially at Milo and Fruhling they occasionally served as what chemists would call "catalytic agents," because they accelerated reactions. In effect, they sometimes initiated and pushed uncontrolled experiments for me. In the staff groups, particularly, as well as in any situation where discussion was taking place and I knew in advance that I could be present and seemingly occupied with work, they introduced agreed-on topics and questions into the conversation. These stimuli were typically on issues in the problem areas. Usually "busy" over in a corner of the room, I was observing and taking notes on the remarks and other behavior of one or more people. Some intimates developed an interest in this kind of study and sketched events and conversations they thought relevant for me in my absence. Data collected by such persons obviously must be evaluated before use. Given the situations I have described, both the opportunity and inclination for personnel to distort are great. Here again, however, the possible returns outweigh the dangers and the labor of assessment.

About the effectiveness of Dalton's data-gathering methods there can be no doubt, but some of his techniques do raise ethical issues, which we reserve for discussion in Chapter 11.

MOTIVES FOR COLLABORATING WITH THE RESEARCHER

In our field work, researchers gain a great deal from collaborators. What do they gain from the relationship?

We have to consider not only what we researchers have to offer but also the limitations on what we can afford to offer. There are some benefits informants may want that we cannot give without jeopardizing our study or at least risking our future relationships.

To some extent, we simply offer sociability, friendship, and the exchange of favors characterizing any friendship. As I commented on my first field project:

> While I sought to avoid influencing individuals or groups, I tried to be helpful in the way a friend is expected to help in Cornerville. When one of the boys had to go downtown on an errand and wanted company, I went along with him. When somebody was trying to get a job and had to write a letter about himself, I helped him to compose it, and so on. This sort of behavior presented no problem, but, when it came to the matter of handling money, it was not at all clear just how I should behave. Of course, I sought to spend money on my friends just as they did on me. But what about lending money? It is expected in such a district that a man will help out his friends whenever he can, and often the help needed is financial. I lent money on several occasions, but I always felt uneasy about it. Naturally, a man appreciates it at the time you lend him the money, but how does he feel later when the time has come to pay, and he is not able to do so? Perhaps he is embarrassed and tries to avoid your company. On such occasions I tried to reassure the individual and tell him that I knew he did not have it just then and that I was not worried about it. Or I even told him to forget about the debt altogether. But that did not wipe it off the books; the uneasiness remained. I learned that it is possible to do a favor for a friend and cause a strain in the relationship in the process.
>
> I know no easy solution to this problem. I am sure there will be times when the researcher would be extremely ill advised to refuse to make a personal loan. On the other hand, I am convinced that, whatever his financial resources, he should not look for opportunities to lend money and should avoid doing so whenever he gracefully can [Whyte, 1981: 305-306].

Blau (1964: 30-31) discusses another dimension of the relationship:

> Interest in earning the observer's respect may be an informant's major motivating force for supplying information and explanations. Respondents make a contribution to the research in exchange for the respect they win by doing so, provided they care about being respected by the observer. The most competent officials can win respect by demonstrating their superior knowledge and skills, but the less competent ones cannot, and this leads them to seek to earn the observer's respect by acting as secondhand participant-observers and sharing their inside knowledge and insights with him.

This status enhancement clearly worked to my advantage on the street corner. The corner boys had a great respect for education and were impressed by my interest in associating with them, even though I was a college graduate with a fellowship at Harvard. This attitude manifested itself most clearly one evening when Chick, leader of a college men's club (to which I also belonged), stopped for a brief conversation on the street corner. At one point he said to me, "Bill, these fellows wouldn't understand, but you know what I mean." I felt impelled to tell Chick that he had underestimated the corner boys, that their lack of formal education did not mean that they were stupid. After Chick left, the corner boys expressed their antagonism toward him with a full load of profanity and then told me they appreciated the fact that, although I was more educated than Chick, I respected and understood them.

While it is advantageous up to a point, this status enhancement can lead to claims that the researcher has difficulty in fulfilling. I now believe that this was the underlying problem in my inability to establish a close relationship with one of the leading local racketeers, after a promising beginning. Shortly after we had met at a banquet honoring the police lieutenant's son, Tony Cataldo invited Kathleen and me to dinner. His wife told us later that she had been overwhelmed by the prospect, as he had described us to her as a Harvard professor and an artist. She thought she should have at least a week to prepare for such an event, and he'd only given her three to four days. After dinner, Tony drove us to the suburbs to meet some of his relatives. As we talked, it became clear that Tony considered himself and his family socially superior to others in the neighborhood. For example he would not allow his young son to associate with other boys on the street.

We reciprocated by inviting Tony and his wife to dinner. This kind of exchange went on for a while but then petered out. While a dramatic holdup of his horse room distracted Tony's attention, I don't believe this was sufficient to account for the cooling of our relationship. In the time we spent together, he had expressed a good deal of interest in Harvard and the people I knew there. Perhaps if I had invited Harvard people to dinner with the Cataldos it could have cemented the relationship. This might have been possible, but it did entail a risk, as I could not predict how my Harvard friends would behave in this setting. In any case, although the relationship with Tony Cataldo did not ripen to such an extent that I was able to penetrate the workings of the middle level of the rackets, I maintained some contact with him through membership in the

Cornerville Social and Athletic Club, although Tony only participated at times critical for his business.

There is another potential benefit to collaborators in field work that is seldom recognized. I became aware of this in my relationship with Angelo Ralph Orlandella (Sam Franco), who worked with me to figure out corner gang structures. Many years later, at my retirement ceremonies, Orlandella spoke about the "sociological insurance policy" that he had gained through working with me. He claimed that the methods we developed together for analyzing informal leadership and group structures had advanced his career in the military and later in civilian life (Whyte, 1981: 361-375).

Following a meeting in which I had interpreted to a management group what I had learned about organizational behavior in Peru, my collaborator, Robert Braun, told my wife:

> It is as if I had been living in the same house for years, so I knew where every chair and table was located. But I was in the dark. Then suddenly he turned on the light, and I could see everything clearly.

If the researcher can help collaborators to see the pattern of social life more clearly, that is an important reward. Furthermore, through working with us, a person who is a skilled and sensitive observer learns that these skills are of value, that they can be developed further, and that they can lead both to greater understanding and to more effective action. If we encourage people in the field to work with us in explaining human phenomena, they share with us the joys of discovery.

One final aspect of the researcher's relations in the field deserves special treatment later. So far I have been discussing simply the incentives that motivate individuals to collaborate with the researcher. When we are discussing action research and applied sociology, we will explore the potential benefits to communities and organizations when they participate in the research process.

5

Observational Methods

What should we observe in the field? Before answering that question, let us first deal with two common misconceptions. Since human beings are the only species with a language, the field worker is likely to assume that the verbal content of interpersonal interactions is all that matters. Speech is obviously important, and we will deal with verbal content later, but it is important to recognize that a great deal of what is important to observe is unspoken.

The beginner is inclined to assume that social observation takes a high level of skill and sensitivity. Indeed, there are some subtle behaviors that provide significant clues to what people are thinking and feeling. For example, a more active than usual movement of the Adam's apple may portray emotions that the informant is trying to suppress. Similarly, if the informant has been looking straight in the eyes of the researcher for most of the time but then looks away when discussing a particular topic, he or she may be dealing with a delicate subject. Such bodily clues are significant, but we should not assume that the major task of the observer is to discover emotional states that the subject is trying to conceal. Some of the most basic aspects of behavior are readily observable and recordable by anyone of normal intelligence.

FOCUS ON STRUCTURE AND LEADERSHIP

We assume that human behavior is not random but structured. Much of it is *socially* structured, and we need to discover the framework

Author's Note: Parts of this chapter are adapted from Whyte (1951b) and Whyte (1981). Material from W. F. Whyte, *Street Corner Society* (© 1981 University of Chicago Press), used by permission.

for such structuring. This is obvious enough when we are studying a formal organization, with titles, offices, and so on, but even there, behaviors may not closely conform to what we would expect from titles and office arrangements. We must go beyond the organization chart in order to discover the social uniformities of behavior.

Social anthropologist Eliot D. Chapple puts it most simply when he states that we need to answer the question, "Who does what with whom, when, and where?" Note that the question does not include *why*. Answers to the question why are based on inferences from research data. We cannot observe *why* anyone does anything. We can observe who the actors are, the time during which the interactions are taking place, and the location of those interactions. Such observations, over a period of time, provide essential evidence regarding social groupings, and the frequency and duration of interaction among those observed.

To go beyond groupings and interactional frequencies and durations so as to get at informal leadership and followership relations, we need to make the critical distinction suggested by Eliot D. Chapple and Conrad Arensberg (1940) between pair events and set events. A *pair event* is an interaction between two individuals. A *set event* involves interactions among three or more individuals.

If we observe only pair events, we often find it impossible to make valid judgments about who is influencing or dominating whom. At the extreme, if we observe several incidents in which A flatly tells B what to do and we subsequently observe B carrying out the action, A is clearly dominating B. But how are we to interpret an observation in which B suggests a course of action and A agrees, and they then jointly follow this course of action? Here B is initiating an activity for A, but A appears to have some freedom of action and could reject the suggestion.

In set events the structural relations become clear—and without our having to assume that the stimulus for the activity is an order, a direction, a suggestion, or an entreaty. We observe here the interaction, including conversation, through which there is an objective change in the pattern of group activity. These examples will serve as illustrations:

> Seven men are standing in the club room, in groups of two, two, and three. Individual X comes in and the three little groups immediately re-form into one larger group, with the seven men remaining silent while X talks and each man seeking to get the attention of X before he himself speaks.
>
> X says, "Let's take a walk." We then observe the group setting out for a walk. Or A says to X, "Let's go to the Orpheum." X says, "Naw, that

picture is no good." No change in group activity. Then B says to X, "Let's go to the State." X says, "O.K." The group is then off to the State.

Some of the fellows are sitting around a table in a cafeteria having their evening coffee-ands. A leaves the group to sit down for a few minutes with people at a nearby table. X remains at the original table, and the conversation continues much as it did when A was present. On another occasion, the same people are present in the same spatial arrangement in the cafeteria, but this time it is X who gets up and goes over to another table. The conversation at X's former table noticeably slows down and perhaps breaks up into twos and threes. The men talk about what X could be doing over at the other table, and their attention is frequently directed to that table. If X stays away for some time, we may observe his friends picking up their chairs and moving over to the other table with him.

Observations along these lines establish that X characteristically initiates action for this group, that he is the leader of the group.

CHARTING SPATIAL RELATIONS

When the observer is studying a small group, the record naturally notes the names of the individuals present and interacting during the period of observation. In studying a larger organization we cannot follow the interactions of all members in the same physical space and during the same time period, and therefore we must devise methods to help us sort out the subgroupings. I encountered this problem in a sudy of what I called the Cornerville S&A Club.

The club had fifty members. Fortunately, only about thirty of them were frequent attenders, so that I could concentrate on that smaller number, but even that presented a formidable problem.

I felt I would have to develop more formal and systematic procedures than I had used when I had been hanging on a street corner with a much smaller group of men. I began with positional mapmaking. Assuming that the men who associated together most closely socially would also be those who lined up together on the same side when decisions were to be made, I set about making a record of the groupings I observed each evening in the club. To some extent, I could do this from the front window of our apartment. I simply adjusted the venetian blind so that I was hidden from view and I could look down and into the store-front club. Unfortunately, however, our flat was two flights up, and the angle of vision was such that I could not see past the middle of the clubroom. To get the full picture, I had to go across the street and be with the men.

When evening activities were going full blast, I looked around the room to see which people were talking together, playing cards together, or otherwise interacting. I counted the number of men in the room, so as to know how many I would have to account for. Since I was familiar with the main physical objects of the clubroom, it was not difficult to get a mental picture of the men in relation to tables, chairs, couches, radio, and so on. When individuals moved about or when there was some interaction between these groupings, I sought to retain that in mind. In the course of an evening, there might be a general reshuffling of positions. I was not able to remember every movement, but I tried to observe with which members the movements began. And when another spatial arrangement developed, I went through the same mental process as I had with the first.

I managed to make a few notes on trips to the men's room, but most of the mapping was done from memory after I had gone home. At first, I went home once or twice for mapmaking during the evening, but, with practice, I got so that I could retain at least two positional arrangements in memory and could do all of my notes at the end of the evening.

I found this an extremely rewarding method, which well compensated me for the boring routines of endless mapping. As I piled up these maps, it became evident just what the major social groupings were and what people fluctuated between the two factions of the club. As issues arose within the club, I could predict who would stand where.

This observation of groupings did not, in itself, point out the influential people in the club. For that purpose, I tried to pay particular attention to events in which an individual originated activity for one or more others—where a proposal, suggestion, or request was followed by a positive response. Over a period of six months, in my notes I tabulated every observed incident where A had originated activity for B. The result of this for pair events (events involving only two people) was entirely negative. While I might have the impression that, in the relationship between A and B, B was definitely the subordinate individual, the tabulation might show that B originated for A approximately as much as A for B. However, when I tabulated the set events (those involving three or more people), the hierarchical structure of the organization clearly emerged.

In a study of a local union, George Strauss (1952) used similar methods. He attended every meeting of the union throughout a year. While there were hundreds of members in the local, attendance was generally limited to 35 to 50 more or less regulars, so it was not difficult for Strauss to learn the names of each person he was observing. The officers of the local conducted the meeting from a platform in the front of the hall. The members were seated on both sides of a central aisle. It did not take Strauss long to determine that the seating positions were structured rather than random. He observed the same individuals sitting together from meeting to meeting. He also observed that the seating pattern provided an unofficial separation of the members into two factions, those sitting on one side of the hall supporting the incumbent leaders and those sitting on the other side raising questions and arguments that clearly indicated their opposition. Beyond the formal positions as represented by those on the platform, Strauss observed an important difference in behavior among the rank and file members. Most of them were seated throughout the meeting, but there were a few individuals on both sides of the hall who would get up from time to time, move around, and seek out another member to whisper some message to him. Strauss learned that those who moved around were more influential members than those that sat still. In effect, the movers were initiating action for some of those sitting down, who were later observed to speak up in the meeting. Furthermore, as Strauss observed a shift in the number of members seated on the two sides of the aisle, he was able to predict correctly that the incumbent officers would lose in the next election.

As a footnote to methodological arguments, we should note that Strauss's paper was published in a journal then called *Sociometry*. The editor accepted the article with obvious reservations because he insisted that Strauss change the title of his article, making it "Direct Observation as a Source of Quasi-Sociometric Information." In effect, he was saying that what Strauss really should have done was circulate a questionnaire among the members attendng the meeting to ask them what other members they would like to sit next to, and so on. Unfortunately, he had not used the sociometric method, so the editor was willing to settle for the next best thing: observation of actual behavior.

These spatial relations and interaction patterns may remain stable for considerable periods of time, but they do change, and it is important to observe those changes. For example, when the members were planning the annual outing of the Cornerville S&A Club, a member who had previously shown no evidences of leadership spoke up with a glowing description of an amusement park in the suburbs of the city. The members responded favorably to his description, and the club president appointed him to the committee to plan the outing. At the meeting the following week, this suddenly prominent member was not even present. One of the members had discovered that the amusement park in question had burned down two years ago. Within eight days I had observed major gains and losses of influence in this case. Changes in groupings and in informal group structure can also be important in providing explanations for the behavior and the personal problems of individuals. In Chapter 2, I traced the onset and subsequent resolution of Long John's mental health problems in terms of a series of changes in patterns of interpersonal interaction. This demonstrates that these methods are useful, not only for charting group structures but also for understanding the emotional adjustment of individuals. Note also that these methods can provide systematic quantitative data. Although field observation provides much information that does not lend itself to quantification, it is a serious (but very common) error to assume that observation is simply a *qualitative* method.

CLASSIFYING AND QUANTIFYING VERBAL CONTENT

The study of interpersonal interactions, as illustrated above, can be carried out with minimal attention to the verbal content of the interactions. That is, if we observe a group of men in a street corner conversation and then walking together to the Orpheum Theater, it is important to note who proposed this walk and who endorsed the suggestion. To determine the structure of the group, we need to understand what is said only insofar as it enables us to observe who is initiating changes in activities for whom.

Important as these structural observations are, we will generally wish to go beyond counting to observing, recording, and interpreting the verbal content of conversations. In everyday life we are constantly interpreting such verbal content, but must this be entirely an intuitive operation, subject to no checks on its validity? There is also the question of reliability—the extent to which two observers of the same spoken words would interpret them in the same way. Without some standards of judgment regarding the classification of verbal content, it is impossible to advance beyond personal intuition.

R. Fried Bales (1950) developed a methodology he calls "interaction process analysis." The scheme involves classifying each utterance, gesture, or facial expression in terms of its assumed intent from the standpoint of the speaker. Bales uses six categories to represent expressions of agreement or disagreement, solidarity or tension, and six others centering around the task problems of asking or giving suggestion, opinion, or orientation. The Bales method also involves noting who speaks to whom, and in this way is related to methods concentrating strictly on the quantitative patterns, without verbal content.

Bales and his associates have used this methodology in observing and analyzing small group meetings in the Harvard social laboratory. They have been able to achieve a high enough degree of reliability among different observers and raters that they can claim a scientific foundation for the methodology. However, interaction process analysis is so complex that it takes considerable training for observers to reach a point at which reliability scores are high enough to warrant confidence. Furthermore, the methodology does not lend itself readily to use outside of the small groups laboratory.

In an unpublished study I made some years ago of a discussion group of 21 members in the National Training Laboratory for Group Development in Bethel, Maine, I devised a much simpler method that enabled me to focus particularly on questions of leadership and influence. I recorded who proposed a given action to the group and who supported it. I also noted who gave the proposal conditional support but modified it in some way. I noted who opposed a given proposal and then observed the outcome. In this situation the outcome was not limited to an either/or choice: acceptance or rejection of the proposal. I observed many proposals that seemed to die on the table, with no one speaking up in opposition and no one venturing to offer support.

As I recorded these observations in daily meetings over a two-week period, a clear pattern of leadership and followership and of factional cleavages emerged. Furthermore, my conclusions were supported by sociometric questionnaires in which members of the group put on paper their judgment of who were the most influential members. The combination of observation and the sociometric questionnaire also provided an interesting contrast in evaluations of popularity and influence. For example, I found that the most highly chosen person for leisure time activities did not figure at all among the sociometric ratings for influence. This fit my behavioral observations. I never observed this popular member making any proposal for action, nor did he play a prominent role in either supporting or opposing proposals made by others. While it may seem obvious that there is an important difference between popularity and leadership, in everyday life people all too often fail to recognize the difference.

Since I did not have other observers applying the same methodology on the group I observed, so that I have no evidence regarding the reliability of my simple methodology, I describe it here simply to indicate the possibility of field workers developing their own method of observation and classification, adapted to their own purposes.

The possibilities of using a simplified version of the Bales methodology in the field are illustrated by a study of changes in leadership behavior in a supermarket chain. Top management had committed itself to a program for decentralizing authority and responsibility. This required changes in the relationships between store managers and district managers, who oversaw the operations of a number of supermarkets. In order to determine whether the desired changes had actually taken place, it was necessary for Paul Lawrence and James Clark (1958) to make systematic and quantitative behavioral observations. They observed three district managers in their interactions with store managers.

Lawrence and Clark developed a twofold typology for the content of the verbal interactions. They classified topics as people, merchandise, records systems, physical plant, and small talk. They also categorized each statement as question, information, opinion, direction, or suggestion. They also measured the time that each member of the pair talked.

This scheme of analysis yielded a number of important distinctions. Researchers noted that when "people" were the topic discussed, this led to more talking time by the store manager, since most of the people discussed were working under him. The researchers discovered that, in conversations with their store managers, each district manager (DM) had his favorite topic. DM1 spent 48 percent of his talking time on people, DM2 spent 41 percent of his time talking on merchandise, DM3 spent 47 percent of his time on records systems. They also noted major differences in the amount of time devoted to small talk. DM3 devoted only .5 percent of his time to small talk, compared to 7 percent and 6 percent, respectively, for DM1 and DM2.

Two years later the researchers returned to check for any changes in the interactions between district managers and store managers. This time their observations were necessarily confined to two division managers since DM1 had been promoted. This in itself is of interest. Since the pattern of interaction of DM1 fit far better with the delegation objective of higher management, it is not surprising that he was the one promoted.

The researchers did find major changes in the interactions of DM2 and DM3 with their several subordinates. DM2 markedly reduced his expressions of opinions and suggestions or directions, while his store managers (SMs) showed approximately the same percentages. DM3 reduced his directions or suggestions by more than half, while his SMs remained constant. The researchers found no significant changes in DM3's proportions of opinions expressed or information offered but observed sharp increases in these categories by the SMs. Furthermore, while the DMs had used approximately three-quarters of the talking time in the first period, in the second period they were down to 55 percent and 62 percent.

A plant manager once described his experience under a former boss who thought he was delegating responsibility and authority:

> Of course he talked about delegation. I suppose he went home and told his wife, "We're doing things differently now in the plant. We're delegating."
>
> One day he called me into the office and he said, "Damn it, Ed, we've gotta delegate around here. Now you take this letter from the telephone company and handle it for me. They want to put six more lines in here. Hell, we can't afford it. You tell them that."
>
> I told him I would handle it, but I felt like asking him whether I should bring my letter back for him to sign [Whyte, 1961: 673].

Ridiculous as this case sounds, it illustrates a common management problem. I have never met an executive who didn't believe that he delegated. Most subordinates report that their bosses do not delegate enough. Why these opposing interpretations? The differences arise because the term "delegation" has no commonly accepted *behavioral* definition.

If management people are serious about delegation, they need to adopt behavioral indices reflecting degrees of delegation. The behavioral categories and observational methods of Lawrence and Clark demonstrate the possibility of producing quantitative measures reflecting behavior relevant to achieving any policy of increasing participative (or autocratic) leadership.

WORK FLOW, WORK STATIONS, AND STATUS

Here we are dealing with observations that are so simple to make that we may overlook them altogether. If so, we are likely to miss data basic to understanding group behavior at work. To a considerable extent the social relations at work, and the ability or inability of work groups to stick together and exert pressure on management, will be influenced not only by the nature of the jobs but also by the way work passes from one work station to another and by the physical location of the work stations (Sayles, 1958).

Jobs vary enormously in the amount of physical movement and social interaction allowed. The noise level is also important, since at some work stations people have to move close together and shout if they are to be understood. On the conventional automotive assembly line, workers have minimum freedom of movement and, while on the line, can only communicate—and that with difficulty—with those on immediately adjoining work stations. At the other extreme, in the control room of the Phillips Petroleum plant I studied, the workers had great freedom of movement since, except in emergencies, the required job activities consumed only a few minutes every hour. The engine operator responsible for monitoring and adjusting the process that furnished the motive power for the operations similarly devoted a minimum of his time to required work activities (again, except in emergencies), but his social situation was far different from that of the control room operators. The engine room was about a hundred yards from the control room, and the engine operator worked alone among his thundering engines.

It makes a difference in interactions whether those stationed close together are working on the same interrelated work operations, or whether each is doing an independent operation. Fully independent operations require no communication among the operators, whereas interrelated operations demand some communication, unless the work is completely machine-paced. On independent jobs it makes a difference whether the job involves direct production or machine tending. Donald Roy's job on the clicking machine required constant attention to the operations so that interaction was only possible during "banana time" and at other work breaks. On the other hand, some machine-tending jobs require work actions only to start and stop operations and, in between, to monitor operations only to be able to intervene when something goes wrong. When the machine is running smoothly, the operator may have considerable freedom of movement.

When people are working in groups, it makes a difference whether the group is hierarchically organized or whether all members have the same job classification and work responsibilities. In a labor gang, division of labor and leadership may arise, but these patterns develop informally. At the other extreme, the work teams in the Steuben Glass division of Corning Glass Works are stratified in formal titles and work responsibilities, with the production process being necessarily under the control of the gaffer, who holds the top position.

In offices, sociologists have long been familiar with the ways in which work location, size and style of desk, easy access to a telephone, and so on reflect the status of employees. The layout and furnishings of executive offices tell us something about the relative importance of the executives.

We tend to take such matters for granted, but we recognize their importance when we discover that organizations can differ from each other in the United States in the degree of emphasis on status distinctions. The importance of this point has been driven home by the recognition that the Japanese policy generally is to minimize the differentiation of status symbols. In the typical large Japanese plant, blue- and white-collar workers, and even many management people, wear the same basic uniform; the executive offices show minimal status distinctions; there is no separate management dining room; and so on. Some see this deemphasis of status distinctions as important in fostering the cohesiveness of the Japanese firm. In any case, status symbols are always important, and the observer can note the presence or absence of physical symbols that reflect status distinctions.

COMBINING INTERVIEWING WITH OBSERVATION

In directing the path-breaking Yankee City study in the 1930s, W. Lloyd Warner emphasized the importance of combining observation and interviewing. Whenever an event can be anticipated, it is important to interview the principal actors both beforehand and afterward. When an important meeting is scheduled, the researcher should talk in advance with those planning the meeting to get them to explain why it is being held, what they hope to accomplish, and what problems they may encounter. Where the researcher has identified prospective participants who are likely to oppose any proposal to be made by the organizers, they also should be interviewed. Following observation of the meeting, it is important to interview the same people again to get their interpretation of what happened and why.

Such interviewing can be exceedingly important as it is not always obvious from observation what is going on in the meeting. We are all familiar with the notion of the *hidden agenda*—objectives never explicitly stated, but that may nevertheless be more important to some of those participating than what people say the meeting is about.

Nor can the observer always readily judge how people feel about a particular issue by the way they speak and by the overt emotional accompaniment of the words. This is particularly likely to be the case in collective bargaining. For example, we may observe union negotiators pushing a particular demand very vigorously, with a great show of emotion, and then, after an extended and apparently fruitless interchange with management, setting aside that issue and going on to the next item, which they introduce without any emotional freight as if it were simply a minor matter. The expressions of emotion accompanying the two items would indicate that the first issue is of great importance to the union, whereas the second one is relatively minor. In fact, if the researcher has the opportunity to interview union negotiators before the meeting, he may learn that they raised the first issue with the full knowledge that it was going to be impossible to get management to concede on this point. Therefore, they pushed the issue with apparent vigor simply for the purpose of softening up the management people. Recognizing that bargaining involves both give and take, and having refused to give on the first item, managers might feel some subtle pressure to accommodate the union on the second item.

PLACING OBSERVATIONS IN CONTEXT

In stressing the importance of linking interviewing with observation, I have noted that observation alone does not reveal to us what people are trying to accomplish or why they act as they do. Furthermore, interviewing may not lead us to the underlying dynamics in some cases unless we are armed with advance knowledge of the rewards people are seeking or of the penalties they are trying to avoid.

Consider the way the media reported upon the national election in El Salvador in 1982 during the nation's civil war. Reporters provided the following information:

(1) Leaders of the guerrilla forces declined to offer themselves as candidates. They urged citizens to boycott the election and threatened to disrupt the voting.
(2) Nevertheless, the election was carried out with a minimum of disruption, and the voter turnout was over 80 percent—far higher than the average turnout in a national election in the United States.

Spokesmen for the Reagan administration hailed this turnout as reflecting the desire of the people for democracy and their rejection of the Marxist doctrines espoused by guerrilla leaders. Critics argued that the reported number of voters was exaggerated. Be that as it may, the argument misses the critical point: the following information that (so far as I have been able to discover) no U.S. reporter provided the U.S. public around the time of the 1982 election:

(1) As in many Latin American countries, voting in El Salvador was compulsory.
(2) To enforce this law, each adult was required to carry a *cedula,* a document to be stamped by election officials when the citizen voted.
(3) As a means of identification, citizens must have their cedulas with them at all times. Government and military officials had the right and the power to inspect these cedulas at any time.

What would have happened if a citizen failed to produce a stamped cedula upon official demand? Government officials had let it be known that they considered failure to vote an act of treason. The potential consequences of such a judgment would be evident to all citizens, who were aware that the right-wing death squads had murdered thousands of people on the basis of no more substantial evidence.

Armed with this information, we see that the turnout may only mean that people were more afraid of government-related violence if they did not vote than they were afraid of guerilla violence if they voted. Since there could be no voting in the still relatively small area controlled by the guerrillas, it would be only sensible to be more concerned, where voting did take place, with government reprisals against nonvoters.

Why did reporters miss information so crucial to the understanding of the election? Probably because they unconsciously projected what they were observing against their own cultural background and experience. Here were people turning out to vote in large numbers, in spite of a lack of previous democratic experience, and without any *observable* coercion to make them vote. (By the time of the 1984 election, the conditions I have described had been reported by some journalists.)

The case indicates that when we observe in another culture social processes that appear similar to those with which we are familiar, we should not jump to the conclusion that we know what is going on. Even in our own society, we should interpret what we observe with caution. Beyond contextual interviewing, we need to ask ourselves what would happen if those whom we are observing did not do what we see them doing. That "what if" question is unanswerable, but it may lead us to the discovery of potential positive and negative sanctions that are not obvious simply from observation.

CONCLUSION

I have argued that observation of behavior is important for research and that the operations involved can be specified, taught, and learned. Naturally, some individuals will be more skilled than others, but we should not think of observation as an activity requiring a rare type of skill. Much of what the observer does can be reduced to routines that are readily learned and practiced.

Field observation is often referred to in the sociological literature under the heading of "qualitative methods." While I do not argue that all important observations can be quantified, researchers have devised reasonably reliable methods to quantify much of the behavior we wish to record.

Finally, before proceeding to a discussion of interviewing, I stress the importance of linking interviewing and observation. Observation guides us to some of the important questions we want to ask the respondent, and interviewing helps us to interpret the significance of what we are observing. Whether through interviewing or other means of data gathering, we need to place the observed scene in context, searching for the potential positive or negative sanctions, which are not immediately observable but may be important in shaping behavior.

6

Interviewing Strategy and Tactics

Interviews may be of various types, ranging from the orally administered interview schedule of predetermined questions to the more freely structured interview common to studies in social anthropology.

In the present chapter I shall give only incidental attention to questionnaires and interview schedules, since they are systematically discussed in a number of books. I shall concentrate upon the method in which the interviewer does *not* follow a standard order and wording of questions.

NATURE OF THE INTERVIEW

The interview we use is often called "nondirective." This is a misnomer. The nondirective interview was a therapeutic development based on the theory that patients would make progress best if left free to express themselves on their problems as they wished, stimulated by an interested and sympathetic listener.

The good research interview is structured in terms of the research problem. The interview structure is not fixed by predetermined questions, as in the questionnaire, but is designed to provide the informant with freedom to introduce materials that were not anticipated by the interviewer.

Whatever its merits for therapy, a genuinely nondirective interviewing approach simply is not appropriate for research. Far from putting informants at their ease, it actually produces anxieties. Once, while

Author's Note: Some of the material in Chapters 6 and 7 is from Whyte (1960).

studying restaurants, I decided that I would be as nondirective as I could. I began each interview simply by asking informants to tell me whatever they cared to that was important to them about the job situation. The usual answers was: "What do you want to know?" Some informants were willing to respond to questions, but none poured out their feelings in response to my general invitation. Since the approach made my informants uneasy, I quickly shifted to providing more structure.

Sometimes, when an informant does need to get something off his or her chest, the researcher can appropriately play a nondirective role—at least for the first part of the interview. Even here, however, the informant will usually leave out aspects of the problem that are significant for the interviewer. These can be brought out only through questioning or otherwise encouraging talk along certain lines.

The rules we follow in interviewing are based on those for the nondirective interview. But there are important differences.

Like the therapist, the research interviewer listens more than he talks, and listens with a sympathetic and lively interest. We find it helpful occasionally to rephrase and reflect back to informants what they seem to be expressing and to summarize the remarks as a check on understanding.

The interviewer avoids giving advice and passing moral judgments. We accept statements that violate our own ethical, political, or other standards without showing disapproval in any way. Generally we do not argue with the informant, although there may be justification for stimulating an argument to determine how the informant will react. This, however, should be a part of a conscious plan and not simply because we disagree with the informant and cannot contain ourselves.

The therapist is told not to interrupt. For the researcher the advice should be: Don't interrupt *accidentally*. In normal social intercourse people interrupt because they are impatient and need to express themselves. This is no such justification in a research interview. However, some people will talk forever if not checked. Since they seldom pause for breath, anything that anyone says to them is an interruption. Such people circle the same topic with an infinite capacity for repeating themselves. The interviewer who waits patiently for new material will hear only variations on the same theme.

I have described an extreme type of informant, rarely encountered in pure form. However, experienced researchers recognize that for informants of this tendency one must learn to interrupt *gracefully*. This is not as difficult as it sounds; such people are quite accustomed to being interrupted in ordinary social intercourse, as this is the major way others communicate with them. The interviewer need not feel that an occasional interruption will antagonize the informant. Inserting a question may serve to move the informant to a new topic.

In nondirective therapy the interviewer designs questions to help patients express themselves more fully on matters of concern to them. In research we want the informant to talk about things of vital interest to them, but we also need their cooperation in covering matters of importance to us that are possibly of little interest to the informant.

I have thus far compared the nondirective with the research interview as if they were two different and distinct types, but it should be possible to measure the degree of directiveness that the interviewer uses. If so, we can vary the degree of directiveness not simply in terms of interviewer personality but in response to the interviewing situation and the problem under study. Research by Richardson, Dohrenwend, and Klein (1965) has shown the way here, and I shall present a modified and simplified version of their work.

The following scale should enable us to evaluate the degree of directiveness in any question or statement by the interviewer by examining it in the context of what immediately preceded it during the interview. The scale goes from low to high directiveness as we go from 1 to 6.

(1) *"Uh-huh,"* a nod of the head, or "That's interesting." Such responses simply encourage informants to continue and do not exert any overt influence on the direction of their conversation.

(2) *Reflection.* Let us say the informant concludes his or her statement with these words: "So I didn't feel to good about the job." the interviewer then says: "You didn't feel too good about the job?" — repeating the last phrase or sentence with a rising inflection. This adds a bit more direction than response 1, since it implies that the informant should continue discussing the thought that has just been reflected.

(3) *Probe the informant's last remark.* Here, as in response 2, attention is directed to the last idea expressed, but the informant's statement is not simply reflected back to him or her. The interviewer raises some question about this last remark or makes a statement about it.

(4) *Probe an idea* preceding the last remark by the informant, but still within the scope of a single informant statement. In one uninter-

rupted statement an informant may go over a half-dozen ideas. The interviewer probes on an idea expressed earlier in the informant's last statement.

(5) *Probe an idea* expressed by informant or interviewer in an earlier part of the interview (that is, not the block of talking that immediately preceded the interiewer's probe). By going further back in the interview to pick up a topic, the interviewer has a much broader choice and consequently exercises more control than is the case in limiting choice to immediately preceding remarks. It seems logical to distinguish between probes on ideas earlier expressed by the informant and those by the interviewer. However, I find in practice that this is a difficult discrimination to make because most probes of this type can be related back to remarks made both by the informant and the interviewer.

(6) *Introduction of a new topic.* Here the interviewer raises a question on a topic that has not been referred to before.

In using this scheme, I follow the convention of categorizing a remark with the lower number when it might be categorized by two or more different numbers. For example, a probe related to the last informant remark—3—may also refer to a remark made earlier in the interview—5. Following our convention, we would show it as 3.

If we were doing research on interviews of different degrees of directiveness, we would need to study the reliability of coding by several different coders and study interviews by a number of interviewers with a wide range of informants. I am simply suggesting here that this system of coding can be useful for training interviewers and for self-evaluations.

These coding schemes do not in themselves tell us whether interviewers are performing well or badly, but they do provide a reasonably objective basis whereby interviewers can evaluate themselves. For this purpose, we need to tape-record several interviews so that we will have an exact record. Memory is likely to be faulty in these matters.

The fact that an interviewer's statements average high on the directiveness scale does not necessarily mean that the interview was a poor one. However, a high-directiveness average, combined with the feeling that the interview was choppy and that the informant did not talk very freely, suggests that a less directive approach might be more effective with this particular informant. On the other hand, a very low average on the directiveness scale, combined with an apparent lack of progress from one idea to the next and a lack of materials relevant to the research, suggests the desirability of introducing more direction.

The authors also categorize interviewer behavior in terms of "restrictiveness": the extent to which the interviewer's remarks indicate the type of response called for or suggest the content of the answer. On type of response indicated, they distinguish between the open and the closed question. A closed question is one that can reasonably be answered yes or no, by a choice among alternatives, or by naming an individual or place.

Many informants will talk at length on a question that can be answered by a single word, but there are informants who answer in a word or two. Interviewers who begin with a number of closed questions may get answers before they can think up new questions—a most disturbing experience. With such informants, only as we use open questions calling for more extended statements in the early stages of the interview do we find that we can relax, listen, and develop useful questions out of the informant's responses.

In restrictiveness, the authors also distinguish among descriptive, evaluative, and nonspecific questions. A descriptive question is one in which the interviewer is asking what happened in a particular event of series of events. An evaluative question is one in which the interviewer asks how the informant *feels* (or felt at one time) about what happened or about the people or organizations involved in the events. A nonspecific question is one that can reasonably be answered with descriptive or evaluative statements or some combination of both.

The correct mix among descriptive, evaluative, and nonspecific questions depends upon the purpose of the interview and the nature of the responses. If the interviewer asks a high proportion of evaluative questions, responses are likely to provide too little information on events. With descriptive questions the case is not so clear because few people can report events without at the same time expressing feelings about them. However, the interviewer who asks few evaluative questions should consider whether the informant is providing sufficient evaluative material.

FOCUSING ON EVENTS

Some years ago I was studying a striking shift from conflict in cooperation in union-management relations (Whyte, 1951a). Early in this field work, in a conversation with the vice president for industrial relations of the parent company, I confessed that I was at a loss to explain this change. He commented, "Yes, that did puzzle me for a long time, but I have finally figured it out."

In eager anticipation, I asked for the answer. His reply: "They learned to trust each other."

For a moment I sat there speechless, waiting for something else, but that was all there was. I drew a deep breath and said, "Well, I guess you're right, but *how* did they learn to trust each other?"

The vice president laughed and said, "You're the sociologist. It is up to you to figure that out."

In that era even some social scientists were accepting the "answer" given me by the vice president. The National Planning Association was then publishing a series of studies on cases of union-management cooperation. In each case the writers emphasized "mutual trust" as a major part of the answer.

Such answers have neither practical nor scientific value. I have never heard of a case in which union and management shifted from conflict to cooperation because a consultant advised them that they should trust each other. In scientific terms, mutual trust may be a reasonable general characterization of the attitudes of the leaders of the two parties to each other at the time of the field work, but the conclusion is of little value unless we can discover the events that moved the parties from mistrust to trust.

If we wish to make a systematic and quantitative study of the attitudes of any body of people, the questionnaire or survey is the method of choice. If we want to determine how particular individuals arrived at the attitudes they hold, then we need to conduct semistructured interviewing.

When informants express strong attitudes toward other people or organizations or situations, they generally have in mind particular events. Therefore, if we are to understand *the shaping of* attitudes, we must probe for reports of experience.

My policy is first to get the informant to describe the events he or she has experienced that are relevant to my study. When the informant expresses an attitude apparently unconnected with any event already described, I say something like this: "That's interesting. Have you had some experience that has led you to feel this way?" Almost invariably the informant will respond with an account of one or more relevant experiences.

In focusing first on events, I do not mean to minimize the importance of the subjective side of life. I am simply arguing that we can get a better understanding of informant attitudes if we link them with the events experienced. Besides, once the linkage is established, if we still do not fully grasp the nature of the attitude expressed, it is easy to ask informants to elaborate on their feelings.

SPECIFYING PROCESS AND PEOPLE

We often find that an open-ended question is poorly answered the first time we put it. The problem is that most informants are vague in identifying people and in dealing with social process.

For example, the informant may say, "We faced a problem with them." He then goes on to state the nature of the problem and, in the next breath, the solution. No mention is made of who "we" or "they" are. Even when the identification of the individuals seems obvious, we would do well to check our understanding. I find that I have often gone wrong guessing on such identification. Furthermore, the informant has mentioned the nature of the problem and its solution but has said nothing about the social process of recognition, decision, choice of actions, and so on, all of which may be of more interest to the social researcher than the problem itself.

In one interview with a union leader, for example, my opening question elicited a response of about 500 words. No doubt the informant considered this a full response, as indeed it was, by ordinary conversational standards. However, I was dealing with a problem of some technical complexity, as well as one of specifying people and process. It took me eighteen questions or statements before I felt that I had it adequately covered. Even then, upon reviewing the transcription, I found important elements I had overlooked (Whyte, 1956).

A student was studying managerial succession in a large industrial plant. He reported that the previous plant manager had held weekly meetings in a conference room of all his operating department heads and heads of staff groups, the total attending numbering about 25. His successor eliminated these large weekly meetings. Instead, the student reported, the new manager just met "informally" with small groups, and his subordinates also took to meeting informally with small groups, with one or another subordinate taking the initiative to get a group together. These meetings took place in "various" management offices.

What is wrong with this report? Note that the information on the meeting pattern of the previous manager was reasonably precise and quantitative. With allowance for absences of the manager or of some of his subordinates and for vacation times, over 20 people were meeting up to 50 times a year, at weekly intervals. Regarding the new manager, the report gives us a feel of a different leadership style, but it gives us no information on which we can establish the resulting pattern of interpersonal relations. We don't know which people were meeting, with what frequency, where they were meeting, and which individuals were taking the initiative to bring which others together. To be sure, such information is more difficult to gather for the successor than for the former plant manager because the meetings varied in numbers of people involved. location, and source of the initiative. However, everything we know about human relations tells us that these people were not getting together on some random basis. No doubt management people told the field worker that they were now getting together informally in small groups and in various offices, and the student failed to establish the *patterns* of leadership and participation under the successor.

STAGES IN INTERVIEWING

The researcher should not hope to cover all relevant areas in the first interview. Often we are greeted with suspicion. Even though we promise that what people say will remain confidential, "most sensible people do not believe what a stranger tells them" (Wax, 1971: 365). Therefore, if we venture into the touchiest emotional areas at the outset, we find people responding in a guarded and superficial manner and observe unmistakable signs that they would be happier if we left them alone.

In any case, first interviews with informants during the early stages of an organizational study are likely to yield something like a normative picture: a statement that reflects how things *ought* to be done. After people get used to us and see us talking with others who may possibly give us ideas that may reflect negatively on them, they are much more likely to "tell it like it is." By this I do not mean that later statements are entirely accurate, but they are certainly more frank.

The first conern of the interviewer is to build rapport. The interviewer deliberately keeps the conversation away from evaluative topics and tries to get informants to make descriptive statements. We may begin asking informants just what their jobs entail, what they do at what time, and how their jobs fit into the whole production process. Then we may ask informants how they got their particular jobs, so as to learn something of their work history. On such topics the informants do not feel pushed to reveal their inner feelings about the company, the foreman, the union, or other possibly touchy topics. On the other hand, since these topics involve human relations, informants can easily refer to other people if they feel so inclined. In the first interview the researcher should follow up such references with caution. When they are not volunteered, the researcher must wait patiently for another occasion when increased familiarity may give informants more confidence and enable them to talk more easily.

Occasionally, in the first interview an informant will unburden him- or herself of a great deal of emotionally loaded material. The beginning interviewer may be delighted by such a reaction, but later the informant may become anxious and wonder if he or she has said too much. The interviewer may then find in the second interview that this particular informant is quite hesitant and reserved.[1]

In such a first interview we cannot refuse to listen, but we should recognize the hazards and not probe for further information. Also we should not terminate the interview just at the point at which the informant has discussed the most emotionally loaded materials but should conclude the interview with some casual small talk. Furthermore, to guard against the sudden cooling-off of such an informant, he or she should be contacted further for a casual discussion, if not another interview, soon after the first interview.

Every experienced field worker recognizes that informants are not of equal value to the research. No matter how skilled the interviewer, there are people who do not notice what is going on around them or have difficulty in expressing themselves. The best informants are those who have observed significant events and who are perceptive and reflective about them. Some such key individuals may be identified early in the study, if they hold important formal positions. Others, who hold key informal positions, are not so evident initially. To locate such people, the interviewer can make a practice of asking each informant to name several people who would be especially helpful to the study. The several lists are likely to converge on a few names.

As the study proceeds, the researcher should be thinking of getting some key individuals to become collaborators. It can be of inestimable value to have one or two individuals who know what the researcher is looking for and can give expert guidance and information.

PROJECTIVE AIDS TO INTERVIEWING

There are situations in which verbal stimuli are entirely inadequate to bring out the data the researcher is trying to elicit. In such cases the interviewer may wish to develop projective devices.

Projective techniques are commonly used in clinical psychology for personality studies. Our concern is with the individual's social world, and we therefore use devices much closer to the social environment we are studying than the Rorschach ink blot or even the Thematic Apperception Test pictures. Three examples will indicate the possibilities.

In the Sterling County study of mental health and social stress, John Collier (1957) photographed all the houses in a community and a number of work areas in a local factory. The project staff found the pictures a distinct aid in eliciting statements that went into full and rich detail. Talking about the pictures also added to the informant's enjoyment.

The pictures of factory interiors were particularly helpful in interviews in the home. Researchers have noted that the home is psychologically quite distant from the work place for most informants. The factory pictures helped the worker place himself in that scene and helped the interviewer place the informant in the technology and work space.

Leonard Sayles used photographs when studying the grievance procedure, where an individual or group of workers are represented by a union official who presents the worker's complaint to management. The union contract explicitly recognized the grievance procedure as an essential aspect of workplace democracy and implied that a worker should take pride in it. Nevertheless, Sayles suspected that workers were anxious about grievances.

To elicit such sentiments more readily and to probe more deeply, Sayles developed a set of seven photographs depicting significant social scenes at various stages in the process of grievance handling. He describes the selection of the scenes as follows:

> In general, people in the plant who thought about using the grievance procedure, envisioned themselves as participating in these group interactions or successive steps of the settlement process: (1) informal discussion with one's fellow workers on what to do about a complaint, (2) informal discussion with a union official, (3) informal meeting with the foreman and union official and worker involved, (4) formal meeting in personnel director's office with the union official and worker present, (5) a formal hearing for the union member before the union executive board, (6) formal discussion of the grievance with the union member present at the plant labor-management committee meeting, (7) an informal discussion in the work group concerning the outcome of the case [Sayles, 1954; quoted in Whyte, 1960: 169].

Sayles presented the pictures in sequence to each informant, accompanying each picture with a statement as to the situation it represented and as to who the characters were. The informant was then asked to give his impression of what was happening in the picture. In the following examples, Sayles compares projective and interview responses:

A. Response to the photograph:
   You can tell by their faces just what they're saying. They're telling him, "You can go ahead if you want to—*but*," and you can be sure it's a big *but* they're adding. The question is whether or not he has a legitimate grievance. You can see by how he looks that he's sure that he has a legitimate grievance, of course; that's always the way. He's probably still going through with it, in fact. But by the looks of them, it seems like he is making trouble for the group all the time. If those other fellows are a cross section of the plant, they'll probably be thinking the same as the grievance committee though, and he is going to lose his case. In fact, I'm sure he'll lose it. But at the end he will have made some trouble for them.

B. Interview response:
   Very few fellows in a department like to be in a position of having a grievance—it usually stops a lot of other people from getting something. Most of the grievances fellows have are against each other. You can tell though who it is who's going to have the grievances. It's just like in the Army—you know who's going to squawk.

   The average depth interview was two hours, and this did not include the researcher's previous efforts over a six-week period to develop rapport with his informants. On the other hand, the projective photographs were administered in approximately ten minutes to volunteer subjects that the reseacher had not met prior to the picture interview. To be successful, the depth interviews had to be undertaken at the informant's home; the picture interviews were done in the plant [quoted in Whyte, 1958: 171-173].

I found a projective method very helpful in a study of Steuben glass workers. We wondered whether the workers derived some aesthetic satisfaction from making these products, but we had difficulty in getting meaningful worker reactions to the mental and physical processes involved in the work.

Frustrated in our direct approach, we devised an indirect approach through asking the gaffer or the servitor to arrange a set of cards, each one representing a piece his team produced, in order of preference. We then asked each individual to explain why he ranked the cards the way he did. While we got no data of particular value out of the ranking itself, the explanations of the rankings revealed feelings about the work process that were not expressed in the ordinary interview.

Some of the gaffers were able to verbalize their pride in the creative process. One commented, "When you get done, you've got a nice piece of work there. . . . It really looks like something. . . . When I can say I made that piece, I really swell with pride." Another gaffer, after commenting on other aspects of a piece he disliked, said, "That little mug don't look like nothing when you're done." A third gaffer commented on his favorite piece, "When you're finished, you've got something." We also found them verbalizing feelings that could be categorized under their reactions to achievement, pressure and timing, amount of work, variety, and sense of contribution.

Finally, we found the card-ranking method exceedingly useful in some cases in bringing out data on personality, status, and human relations. For example, one ambitious young gaffer evaluated his pieces primarily in terms of the degree of difficulty each design offered. The more complex the production problem, the more prestige to him if he succeeded (Whyte, 1961).

RECIPROCITY OR CASH?

Should you pay informants for their time and information? I have never done so, and as a general rule this practice is to be avoided. Paying for information has some clear disadvantages. It can become expensive for us—and for those who follow us. In his action research at hacienda Vicos in the Peruvian highlands, Allan Holmberg did not pay Indian informants, but he was most generous in allowing other researchers access to this field site. One summer a group of well-financed psychologists and psychoanalysts moved in and paid informants willing to tell their life stories and describe their dreams. Having discovered that their information had a commercial value, naturally Vicosinos thereafter sought to charge researchers the going rate.

If we do not impose lengthy and repeated interviews on the same few individuals and confine our interviewing to leisure hours or to the job situation (but where the informant does not lose pay), then it seems preferable to avoid cash payments. There are, of course, cases where payment cannot and should not be avoided.

If the informant is not wealthy and has to make a financial sacrifice to talk with us, then clearly some material compensation is needed. If we want particular informants to submit to many hours of interviewing, then a cash payment may be necessary. Admittedly, it can be difficult to draw the line between a few hours and many hours.

If a key informant goes beyond that role to become an active collaborator, then the case for compensation is much stronger. In the North End study, I tried unsuccessfully to get Doc a job in private industry and then persuaded a settlement house director to hire him to run a storefront recreation center. I made loans to Doc, but he never asked money for his services. Looking back now on his crucial importance to my project, I think I should have sought a grant for him from Harvard's Society of Fellows. That possibility did not occur to me until toward the end of my study, when I was working with Angelo Ralph Orlandella in figuring out the structures of corner gangs known to him. Ralph enjoyed the work and did not expect any money for it, but I believed he could not concentrate on our work without some relief from financial worries. Besides, I was getting so much from him that I felt guilty in not being able to pay him. I therefore secured a $100 grant from Harvard. In other cases, I have sought to compensate an informant/collaborator with joint authorship of research publications (Garfield and Whyte, 1950-1951; Whyte and Braun, 1966, 1968).

With these exceptions and qualifications, I believe it is desirable to secure information on a volunteered basis. Besides the expense of paying informants, the introduction of cash tends to distort what we would like to be a friendly relationship based on mutual interests. However, this mutuality of interests need not be limited to interpersonal reciprocity—what the informant does for us and what we do for him or her. We need also to think of the informant's interest in benefiting his group, organization, or community through participating in our project. (see Chapter 10).

STUDIES FROM A DISTANCE

In studying a community, we would like to interview a variety of people representative of different social classes, ethnic groups, and organizational memberships. Similarly, in studying a work organization, we would like to interview a range of people holding different jobs and different positions in the hierarchy. In either case, we would seek opportunities to observe some of our informants in their natural settings. Beyond this, we would want to gather documentary materials providing presumably factual information about the community or organization.

For many years, such research designs could not be carried out by U.S. students of the People's Republic of China. Even today restrictions severely limit field work by behavioral scientists inside China. Our social research knowledge regarding the People's Republic has depended primarily upon interviewing people coming and settling in or passing through Hong Kong. The drawbacks of Hong Kong-based studies may seem obvious, but sinologists argue that much valuable data can be secured, even operating from such a distance. Martin K. Whyte (1983) gives this general description of research procedures:

> Interviews typically require several sessions, often of about three hours each. A variety of procedures are followed to try to get full and accurate information from informants: assurances of privacy and anonymity, assurances of mundane research purposes, questions designed not to be leading or threatening, a focus on concrete personal experiences and observations, and steering clear of directly inquiring about political attitudes or conveying one's own attitudes. The general practice has been to pay informants for their time and trouble (for a number of years the "going rate" was HK $15 per hour), although if one interviews fewer informants for longer periods of time it may be possible to establish a more personal relationship and not use the potentially embarrassing hourly payments.

The researcher must deal with the question of political bias:

> "If these people decided to leave China, surely they must have an anti-communist bias and will give a distorted view of Chinese society." We feel this is a less severe problem than is often assumed. First, most refugees are not committed anti-communists. They come to Hong Kong for a variety of reasons, most having to do with their search for greater personal opportunities, and many retain strong patriotic sentiments toward China and admire many aspects of the society they have left. For instance, in comparing the quality of interpersonal relationships in China and Hong Kong, informants we have interviewed almost universally see China as far superior. Second, by avoiding sensitive issues and questions of political attitudes, and by

focusing on organizational specifics and personal experiences, the interviewer can confine the interviews to areas where personal biases are less likely to have much influence. Third, there is a substantial variety in the backgrounds and orientations of refugees, and if a sufficient number of diverse people are interviewed, the researcher can qualitatively or even statistically check whether those expected to be more anti-communist yield different accounts, and correct for this factor [M. K. Whyte, 1983; see also Parish and Whyte, 1978: methodological appendix].

Whyte adds that on some points accuracy can be checked against the accounts of other informants or items in the Chinese press or through consulting other researchers who have interviewed the same informant.

Is there a problem with "professional informants" who tailor their stories so as to make a living being interviewed? This is not a big problem. At any time, there is a large pool of potential informants and only a few Hong Kong researchers, and the researchers generally have such different interests as to rule out the all-purpose subject bent on maximizing his employment opportunities.

There are more serious problems of bias due to geographical origins and social class backgrounds of informants.

A disproportionate share of these illegal refugees come from Guandong Province, adjacent to Hong Kong, and they tend to be younger, better educated, more male, and of worse class background than the general population in that province [M. K. Whyte, 1983].

(In this case "worse class background" means that the parents of the informants did not have the politically appropriate industrial worker or lower peasant status.)

Then there are legal refugees, people given exit visas by Chinese authorities.

They are almost all people who had returned to China from abroad and then wanted to leave again, or people born in China who have overseas relatives. Unlike the illegals, they come from all over China, but they also tend to be relatively well-educated and predominantly urban, and their overseas connections generally give them higher incomes and a separate status from the rest of the population within China.

How does the researcher minimize the effects of biased selection?

Generally speaking, it is easiest to interview about common areas of social life that many people are likely to have knowledge about—schooling, neighborhood organization, village life, and so forth.

Another technique, according to M. K. Whyte,

is to ask informants to supply information not so much about themselves and their families, but about close neighbors and co-workers, people still in China who are not likely to be as atypical as the informants themselves.

On the potential for such interviewing, M. K. Whyte (1983) makes this evaluation:

Through Hong Kong interviewing whole new worlds of Chinese social life open up to us. We can learn rich details about daily life experiences and inquire about areas rarely discussed in the press. How does rationing work? What determines which middle school urban children attend? How do people now celebrate traditional festivals? Who gets the bonuses and pay raises in a unit and why? How is the garbage collected? . . . We can learn how certain policies were actually carried out in various settings, as opposed to the way they were supposed to be carried out. We can discover the many other features of social life that influence people's lives in addition to current government policies.

The researcher cannot expect to encounter enough informants from a particular village or factory to make it possible to study such an individual unit. Nor can the researcher expect to generalize regarding current political attitudes within China based on Hong Kong interviews. However, it is not yet possible to study political attitudes through interviewing inside China, and it has been exceedingly difficult for foreigners to gain access to a particular factory or community for research purposes. Therefore, if China is worth studying, we must make the most of our opportunities for research from a distance, while awaiting openings for on-site research.

NOTE

1. I am indebted to Stephen A. Richardson for this point.

7

Recording, Indexing, and Evaluating Interview Data

I nterviewing yields of voluminous data that must be recorded in some form, indexed so that they will be readily available, and subjected to some process of evaluation long before we reach the point of analyzing and writing research reports.

RECORDING THE INTERVIEW

How are the data to be recorded? That depends upon the nature of the study, the stage of learning of the researcher, and the stage of development of the study. Whatever the purpose of an interview, a student should learn early in training to record answers as nearly verbatim as possible. Among other things, this helps the student stretch powers of observation and memory. It is easy enough later to cut down on the volume of recording; it is very difficult to build up an adequate record later on the basis of brief skeleton reports.

When beginning a study it is wise to strive for a fuller recording than will be needed later on. By recording only items that are apparently significant at the time, the researcher loses data that later could open up promising new avenues of exploration.

For the mechanics of recording the interview, the researcher has three choices: (1) tape-recording the interview, (2) taking notes on the interview as it progresses and writing a fuller report later, and (3) making notes on the interview after it has terminated and then writing or dictating a report later.

While a tape recorder on the spot provides the fullest recording, it is expensive and formal. The expense of the machine is the smallest part of the problem. Transcription of an interview is an exceedingly time-consuming task, even for an experienced stenographer. If expense is no problem, the interviewer still has to cope with the additional formality provided by the recording equipment. Informants are likely to talk more for the record with the machine than without, even when they have been told that the interviewer is going to write up the interview later. Where the interviewer has strong rapport, informants may accept the machine with little hesitation, but in the early stages of the study its introduction may damage rapport.

The use of concealed recording machines raises both ethical and practical questions. The practical question involves the chances of detection. After a number of months in the same community or organization, the chances are that the researcher will give away the secret through carelessness or that an informant will somehow stumble upon it. Once out, the secret will spread through the organization or community in no time at all. At this point no explanation will satisfy the people in the study. Even on strictly practical grounds, the risk is not worth taking.

Should the interviewer take notes in the course of the interview? While this provides a fuller and more accurate record than can possibly be recaptured by memory, this choice must be balanced against possible disadvantages.

Note-taking adds to formality and may inhibit the informant— especially in the early stages of the study. This is not always and uniformly the case. There are some informants who express anxiety when the interviewer is *not* taking notes, or who feel that this means that what they are saying is not worth remembering.

Even if the assets and liabilities of note-taking balance each other out from the standpoint of their effect upon the informant, they have an effect on the interviewer. An interviewer who takes notes cannot give full attention to the informant. Physical movements, gestures, and facial expressions give clues not to be found in the words themselves, and some of these fleeting nonverbal cues will be missed while the interviewer is writing.

Furthermore, a good interviewer cannot be passive. At all times we must reflect upon what is being said, ask ourselves what each statement means and how best to encourage the informant to clarify a point or give detail on an item only hinted at. We must be ready at the conclusion of each informant statement to raise a question or make a comment to further develop the items most pertinent at this stage. The interviewer who is busy taking notes cannot be as alert for productive leads as one who is paying full attention to the informant.

Note-taking is likely to interfere with the flow of the interview in another way. The writer is always a little behind the informant. Let us say that the informant has just concluded a statement, rich in data, that should be followed up at once. Instead, we need time to finish writing. Then, after rushing the note-taking to a conclusion, we need a few seconds to formulate a good comment to stimulate further discussion. Such delays embarrass interviewers and make us hurry our own statements, with a consequent deterioration in quality.

The beginning student who makes notes later and tries to reconstruct the interview completely from memory will be depressed by how little he or she can bring back. Even a small amount of practice enormously increases one's ability to reconstruct what has been said. However, even the most skillful interviewer will not come very close to a verbatim recording in this method. At best, we present an interview that is accurate in its main outlines but that condenses and organizes the data. This is probably an inevitable feature of such a recording process. Our memory needs pegs to hang things on, and we tend to think in terms of topics. The informant may have talked on a certain topic on three or four occasions during the interview, but we tend to group comments on the same topic together and record them together.

Condensation and reorganization in themselves rarely lead to serious errors, but distortion may occur in the process. There are no sure ways of detecting distortions, but one method for checking is to arrange for practice interviews with a tape recorder. Following the interview, the student writes it up from memory, and then checks it against the tape recorder for ommissions and, particularly, for distortions.

Often the interviewer is unable to write up the interview immediately after it has been concluded. We may have no dictating machine or typewriter handy and no time for a full pencil-and-paper report. If we have an opportunity to make a second interview immediately after the first, as a general rule, it is not wise to forgo potentially productive interviews simply to record others. When pressed for time the interviewer should try to jot down brief notes referring to points in the interview and a few key phrases or sentences that suggest particularly telling points that we will want to write in detail later. Such brief notes are of inestimable value when the interviewer is not able to handle the full recording until some hours later.

INDEXING

The researcher who uses questionnaires has little difficulty with problems of indexing. A well-designed questionnaire provides its own organization of data.

The type of interview we describe does not automatically order the data. Furthermore, it provides a voluminous body of data. At first the researcher may remember where to find any particular point, but as interviews pile up, this becomes impossible. We may spend endless hours rereading our notes unless we have devised some effective manner of indexing them.

In *Street Corner Society,* I described how I approached the indexing problem:

As I gathered my early research data, I had to decide how I was to organize the written notes. In the very early stage of exploration, I simply put all the notes, in chronological order, in a single folder. As I was to go on to study a number of different groups and problems, it was obvious that this was no solution at all.

I had to subdivide the notes. There seemed to be two main possibilities. I could organize the notes topically, with folders for politics, rackets, the church, the family, and so on. Or I could organize the notes in terms of the groups on which they were based, which would mean having folders on the Nortons, the Italian Community Club and so on. Without really thinking the problem through, I began filing material on the group basis, reasoning that I could redivide it on a topical basis when I had a better knowledge of what the relevant topics should be.

As the material in the folders piled up, I came to realize that the organization of notes by social groups fitted in with the way in which my study was developing. For example, we have a college-boy member of the Italian Community Club saying: "These racketeers give our district a bad name. They should really be cleaned out of here." And we have a member of the Nortons saying: "These racketeers are really all right. When you need help, they'll give it to you. The legitimate businessman—he won't give you the time of day." Should those quotes be filed under "Racketeers, attitudes toward"? If so, they would only show that there are conflicting attitudes toward racketeers in Cornerville. Only a questionnaire (which is hardly feasible for such a topic) would show the distribution of attitudes in the district. Furthermore, how important would it be to know how many people felt one way or another on this topic? It seemed to me of much greater scientific interest to be able to relate the attitude to the *group* in which the individual participated. This shows why two individuals could be expected to have quite different attitudes on a given topic.

As time went on, even the notes in one folder grew beyond the point where my memory would allow me to locate any given item rapidly. Then I devised a rudimentary indexing system: a page in three columns containing, for each interview or observation report, the date, the person or people interviewed or observed, and a brief summary of the interview or observation record. Such an index would cover from three to eight pages. When I came to review the notes or to write from them, a five-to-ten minute perusal of the index was enough to give me a reasonably full picture of what I had and of where any given item could be located [Whyte, 1981: 307-308].

As I moved on into industrial studies, I made the index somewhat more elaborate. In one column, together with names of people interviewed, I added, in parentheses, the names of people referred to in the interview. Thus I was able to note at a glance not only whom I interviewed but what people were referred to or discussed in the interview. In another column I recorded not only topics but also relationships. For example, a discussion of a problem of incentives might be indexed with the following headings: piece rates, foremen—time-study man, foreman—worker, worker—steward, steward—foreman. This would indicate that a certain section of the interview, in which the informant is describing a piece-rate problem, contains statements referring to events or sentiments between people in the categories separated by the dashes. I have not found it profitable to separate sentiments from interactions in my index because informants almost invariably run them together in their *own* statements.

I do not consider it advisable for the researcher to determine his or her indexing categories before he or she starts the field study. While most significant relationships can be set forth on the basis of the formal structure of the organization, exactly what topics will be most significant to the study cannot be predetermined completely. After eight or ten interviews, the researcher should have the feel of the situation sufficiently to develop a reasonably adequate indexing system. At this point, we might reread the first interviews and pencil the appropriate indexing categories on the margins of each page. If we then continue this practice as we go along, we will find that it takes just a few minutes of typing to transfer marginal notes from the interviews to index pages.

In writing a report we can work directly from the index to the outline of the paper. A few minutes spent in rereading the whole index gives a systematic idea of the material to be drawn on. Then, for each topic covered in the report, we can write into the outline the numbers of the interviews and the page numbers of relevant material. For example, in writing a section on relations between hostesses and waitresses, we write in the outline some general heading referring to the supervision of waitresses. Then we note in the outline all interviews where we find in the index "waitresses—hostess"—plus the page numbers of those particular interview sections. This may refer us to a dozen or more interviews. Perusal of the index will refresh our memory on these interviews, and we will recall that some of them merely duplicate each other. We pull out of the file perhaps a half dozen interviews, turn to the sections where "waitress—hostess" is marked on the margin, reread these sections, and finally use materials from three or four.

Since we cannot know in advance what many items important for later analysis will be, we need a method that will provide some general guidance, yet be flexible enough for adjustment to what we are learning in the course of field work. Any organizing scheme is at least implicitly based on theory—consciously or unconsciously we apply certain standards of judgment to sort out the important from the unimportant.

Glaser and Strauss (1967) discuss two types or levels of theory: substantive theory designed to arrive at hypotheses derived from and applicable to a particular situation and formal theory in which those hypotheses are restated in more abstract terms that may be applied to other situations. For organizing data, I add another type, *orienting theory,* which precedes both substantive and formal theory.

Orienting theory simply tells us in the most general terms what data we are likely to need at the point of analysis. I prefer to call the ordering process *indexing* rather than *coding,* as that term used by Glaser and Strauss implies going farther into theory building than I want to go while I am still orienting myself to the data.

For any field study my orienting theory tells me to index in these two categories:

(1) *Actors and their relationships:* Identification of informant and those mentioned in the interview. Identification of formal positions and titles of informant and people mentioned (in cases where formal positions and titles apply—beyond the informal group).

(2) *Events:* Informant's references to what happened in situations described. Also salient topics: references to problems of importance to informant and/or others mentioned by informant.

Initially the focus of attention is on behavior rather than upon attitudes or sentiments. For category 1, we want to be able to locate quickly all references to particular individuals or to particular relationships. For example, to discuss worker relations with their immediate supervisors, we want to locate all notations of "worker-foreman." Within category 1, we do not note whether a particular relationship is friendly or hostile. Such discriminations emerge as we review what we have indexed under "worker-foreman."

Notations under category 1 emerge almost automatically as the study proceeds. As new people are interviewed or mentioned, we simply record their names. When new relationships are mentioned, we simply add them to the index.

Notations under category 2 refer us to particular events, for example: 1946 strike, air hose case, discharge (of worker), and so on. Salient topics refer to more general problem areas, for example: absenteeism, turnover, rate setting, grievances, and the like.

With some initial background information, we may anticipate some of the items to note in category 2, but many of them will only emerge as the study proceeds. In the later stages of a study, the same events and topics will be referred to frequently, so we do not constantly need to add new index items.

This scheme tells us simply that we should index each interview so as to be able to answer the question of *who did what with whom, when, and where.* Further interviews provide information on the frequency of interactions and upon activities. Though this indexing method is not organized in terms of attitudes, sentiments, and values, such data emerge as we review the record on interactions and activities. In mentioning another person, the informant will often give us a clue as to how he or she feels about that person. Events and salient topics tend to be described in ways that reveal how the informant feels about them. Of course, the same item will generally be indexed in both categories 1 and 2: actors and their relationships; events and salient topics.

EVALUATING INTERVIEW DATA

Evaluation of our interviews should precede the analysis process. This enables us to take advantage of the flexibility possible with anthropological methods. With a survey, the data are all gathered in a short time span and then, if we discover some problems with the survey instrument or with the way it was applied, those problems can be handled only by fielding a new and improved survey. In anthropological field work, we are in the field for longer periods of time and have opportunities to reinterview informants and to cross-check our data through interviewing several informants about the same events. The nature of the method enables us to evaluate our data as we go along so that we can correct errors and deepen our understanding.

We use interviews to find out (A) what has been going on in the experience of the informant and (B) how the informant feels about those events, about other people and organizations important in these events, and about him- or herself. It is important to relate A with B, events with sentiments or attitudes. If we do not, we are left with a picture of sentiments floating in the air with no connection to personal experience.

This means that one of our primary objectives is to determine as best we can *what actually happened* in the events discussed by the informant. Because each informant colors his or her description with personal biases, and because different informants will give different accounts of the same events, we can never guarantee the absolute accuracy of what we piece together from several informants. There is no substitute for being there and observing the events, but the reconstruction process can provide us with reasonably accurate data if we are able to evaluate the credibility of the informant and check the account with what other people tell us about the same events.

Even when two informants give us what initially seem highly contradictory accounts of events and relationships, by concentrating on the pattern of interactions in those events, we are able to resolve most of the apparent contradictions. For example, in the Stouffer's Restaurant study, I was examing a conflict between Mr. Stanton, the recently appointed manager, and Miss Ellis, who had been directress of service until she quit the job. In interviews both informants acknowledged that there had been a conflict, but each gave a markedly different account of how the conflict arose and of the motivations of the other. However, I learned from Miss Ellis and from a number of other interviews that there was a marked contrast in the interaction patterns of Mr. Potter, the former manager, and Mr. Stanton. Potter had spent about half his working day circulating about the restaurant, observing and chatting informally with the employees. He was easily accessible, and supervisors or rank and file employees did not hesitate to approach him and initiate a conversation. In contrast, Stanton was rarely seen out on the floor. He spent most of his time in his office. Miss Ellis reported that she found Stanton unapproachable and rarely took the initiative to go into his office. Stanton told me that he had been unaware of Miss Ellis's unhappiness about her job. He added, "If she felt that way, why didn't she come in to see me?"

Of course, the interviews did not determine the "real" motivations of Miss Ellis or Stanton, but they provided clear and consistent data on the changes in interactions between the manager and directress of services, following the substitution of Stanton for Potter. This indicates how it is possible to get confirmatory evidence on social relations even from informants who are quite hostile to each other.

I am not suggesting that an informant's distorted account of events is of no value. If we recognize the nature of the distortion, this can aid us in understanding the way informants look at themselves and the world around them. However, we will usually also want to determine, as best we can, what actually happened. For this purpose, we need to evaluate both the informants' reports of *evaluative* data and their reports of *descriptive* data.

The Informant's Report of Evaluative Data

The problem here is how to assess the informant's feelings about some subject under investigation. At the outset we must recognize that there are different kinds of evaluative data: (a) the informant's *current emotional state,* such as anger, fear, anxiety, or depression; (b) the *values* of the informant, that is, the feelings that may be presumed to underlie opinions, attitudes, and behavior; (c) the informant's *attitudes* or *sentiments,* emotional reactions to the subjects under discussion; and (d) the informant's *opinions* or cognitive formulation of ideas on a subject.

There is no reason to expect that the data gathered in these four categories will fit together consistently. Nor, in case of a conflict, do we try to determine which data represent the informant's "real" feelings. Discovery of the conflict may indeed be the most important information we obtain.

This approach puts a different light on the problem of using behavior as a way of validating attitudes. For example, a young housewife reported herself so much in favor of careful budgeting that she and her husband made out envelopes in which they put the money allocated for various purposes. When shopping with a close friend with whom she felt a good deal of social competition, however, she bought a dress which was out of line with the budget. It is not very meaningful to say that her behavior in buying the dress "invalidates" her opinions in favor of budgeting or to ask what her "real" attitudes are. Even if this young housewife had been asked what she would do if she ran across an unusually attractive dress which was not within her budgetary planning, she might have said that she would refuse to buy it and would work out some way to purchase such a dress in the future. The sophisticated interviewer expects neither consistent well-thought-out attitudes and values on the subjects discussed nor rational and consistent pictures of informant's sentiments and behavior.

The difficulties in interpreting subjective data are increased when the informant is recollecting past feelings or attitudes. Recollections of past feelings are generally selected to fit more comfortably into one's current point of view.

But perhaps the major consideration that complicates the assessment of evaluative reports is that they are so *highly situational.* If, for example, a Democrat is among Republican friends whose opinions he values highly, he will hesitate to express sentiments that might antagonize or disconcert these friends. With other friends, who think pretty much as he does, however, he will not hesitate to express a Democratic point of view, and if he is at a Democratic party meeting he may be swept up in this enthusiasm and express such sentiments even more strongly. The interview situation must be seen as just *one* of many situations in which an informant may reveal subjective data in different ways.

The key question is this: What factors may influence an informant's reporting in the interview situation? The following factors are likely to be important:

(1) *Ulterior motives.* On one occasion a foreman of a South American company expressed great interest in being interviewed. He went on to express enthusiasm about every aspect of the company. When the interview closed, he said, "I hope you will give me a good recommendation to the management."

(2) The informant may *desire to please* the interviewer so that his opinions will be well received. An interviewer identified with better race relations might well find informants expressing opinions more favorable to minority groups than they would express among their own friends.

(3) *Idiosyncratic factors* may cause the informant to express only one facet of his reactions to a subject. For example, in a follow-up interview an informant was told that she had changed her attitude toward Jews. She then recalled that just before the initial interview she had

felt that a Jewish dealer had tried to cheat her. She recalled that she was still angry about this incident and had reacted in terms of it to the questions about Jews in the interview. A few days earlier or a few days later she would probably have expressed herself quite differently. On the other hand, her earlier statement revealed an underlying anti-Semitism she was apparently trying to submerge under more socially acceptable sentiments.

While we never assume a one-to-one relationship between sentiments and overt behavior, we should try to relate the sentiments expressed to the behavior observed—or to what we would expect to observe in the situation under discussion.

In one case, the informant was a supervisor in a large restaurant. The restaurant owner was a graduate dietician who placed a great deal of stress upon maintaining high professional standards. In the course of the interview the supervisor casually remarked that she herself was the only supervisor in the restaurant who was not a college graduate. She did not elaborate, nor did I probe the point at this time. A few minutes later I returned to the topic: "I was interested in something you said earlier: that you are the only supervisor here who is not a college graduate." Before another word was uttered, the supervisor burst into tears. Clearly the affect attached to the earlier statement was repressed and became evident only in subsequent behavior, when she cried.

In some cases the informant may be trying to convince himself, as well as the interviewer, that he does not have a certain sentiment. In the case of Joe Sloan, a highly ambitious gasoline-plant operator, the interview took place shortly after Sloan had been demoted. He reported calmly that in a subsequent talk with the plant manager and the personnel manager they had not been able to encourage him about his future with the company. Given that Sloan had earlier expressed strong sentiments against management—with apparent relish—I expected him to be even more explosive with this new provocation. I was puzzled when he said, "I'm nonchalant now. Those things don't bother me any more." Neither his gestures nor his facial expression revealed any emotion.

A week later, Sloan suddenly walked off the job in response to a minor condition that had recurred often in the past. Reflecting on the incident later, I could see that Sloan's "nonchalant" statement was a danger signal. Recent events had intensified his negative sentiments toward management, and he was making an effort to repress these sentiments. Probably, being unable or unwilling to "blow his top" as before, he no longer had a safety valve and might have been expected to take some rash and erratic action (Whyte, 1956).

These cases suggest the importance of seeing discrepancies between sentiments and observed (or expected) behavior as an open invitation to focus interviewing and observation in this problem area.

The Informant's Report of Descriptive Data

An informant who reports that people are plotting against him may reveal merely his own paranoid tendencies. But even though plots of this kind are rare, it may just happen that people actually *are* trying to undermine the informant. The researcher must know in what respects an informant's statement reflects his personality and perception and in what respects it is a reasonably accurate record of actual events.

The objectivity of an informant's report depends on how much distortion has been introduced and how this can be corrected. The major sources of distortion in firsthand reports of informants are these:

(1) The respondent did not observe what happened, or cannot recollect what he did observe, and reports instead what he supposes happened.

(2) The respondent reports as accurately as he can, but, because his mental set has selectively perceived the situation, the data reported give a distorted impression of what occurred. Awareness of the "true" facts might be so uncomfortable that the informant wants to protect himself against his awareness.

(3) The informant quite consciously modifies the facts as he perceives them in order to convey a distorted impression of what occured.

Trained field workers are alert to detect distortion wherever it occurs. How can we do this? First of all, there is an important negative check—*implausibility*. If an account just does not seem at all plausible, we are justified in suspecting distortion. For example, an informant living near the campus of a coeducational college reported that a college girl had been raped in a classroom during hours of instruction by some of the male students. She was quite vague as to the precise circumstances, for example, as to what the professor was doing at the time. (Did he, perhaps, rap the blackboard and say, "May I have your attention, please?") While this account lacked plausibility, it did throw light on the informant's personal world. Through other reports we learned that a college girl had indeed been raped, but the offense had taken place at night, the girl was not on the college campus, and the men were not college students. The woman who told the original story was a devout member of a fundamentalist sect that was highly suspicious of the "Godless university." In this context, the story makes sense as a distortion unconsciously introduced to make the story conform to her perception of the university. The test of implausibility must be used with caution, of course, because sometimes the implausible *does* happen.

A second aid in detecting distortion is any knowledge of the *unreliability of the informant* as an accurate reporter. In the courtroom the story of a witness is undermined by any evidence that he has been inaccurate in reporting some important point. First interviews provide little evidence on an informant's reliability unless he is reporting on a situation about which we have prior knowledge. After what the informant has told us has been checked or corroborated by other reports, we can form some idea of how much we can rely on his account. Even though we learn to distinguish reliable from unreliable informants, we must never assume that an informant who has proved reliable in the past will never require further checking.

A third aid is *knowledge of an informant's mental set* and how it may influence his perception and interpretation of events. Thus we would be on guard for distortion in a labor-union leader's report of how management welched upon a promise it made in a closed meeting.

Perhaps the major way to detect and correct distortion is by *comparing an informant's account with accounts given by other informants.* And here the situation resembles the courtroom setting, since we must weigh and balance testimony of different witnesses, evaluate the validity of eyewitness data, compare the reliability of witnesses, take circumstantial evidence into account, appraise the motives of key persons, and consider the admissibility of hearsay information. We may have little opportunity in field research for anything that resembles cross-examination, but we can *cross-check* accounts of different informants for discrepancies and try to clear these up by asking for further clarification.

Since we assure informants that what they say is confidential, we are not free to tell one informant what another has told us. Even if the informant says he does not care, it is wise to treat the interview as confidential, since repeating what informants say stirs up anxiety and suspicion. Of course the researcher may be able to tell what he has heard without revealing the source; this may be appropriate where a story has wide currency, so that an informant cannot infer the source of the information. But if an event is not widely known, the mere mention of it may reveal what a specific informant has said about the situation. How can data be cross-checked in these circumstances?

In a field study in a glass works, gaffer Jack Carter described a serious argument on another work team that had arisen between gaffer Al Lucido and his servitor. Lucido and his servitor had been known as close friends. Since the effect of intrateam relations on morale and productivity were central to the study, it was important (1) to check this situation for distortion and (2) to develop the details.

Carter's account of the situation seemed plausible, and my experience indicated that he was a reliable informant. I had no reason to believe that he was so emotionally involved or biased toward this other work team as to give him an especially jaundiced view of the situation. Furthermore, some of the events he described he had actually witnessed, and others he had heard about directly from the men on the particular work team. Nevertheless, wishing an account from one of the men directly involved, I scheduled an appointment with Lucido one day after work. To avoid disturbing Lucido and the others by asking directly about the argument, I sought to reach this point without revealing my purpose. I encouraged Lucido to talk about the nature of his work and about the problems that arose on his job, with the focus gradually moving toward problems of cooperation within the work team. After Lucido had discussed at length the importance of maintaining harmonious relationships within the work team, I said, "Yes, that certainly is important. You know I've been impressed with the harmonious relationships you have on your team. Since you and the servitor have to work closely together, I guess it's important that you and Sammy are such close friends. Still, I suppose that even the closest of friends can have disagreements. Has there ever been a time when there was any friction between you and Sammy?" Lucido remarked that indeed this had happened just recently. When I expressed interest, he went on to give a detailed account of how the friction arose and how the problem between the two men had finally worked out. It was then possible to use Lucido's account to amplify the data on a number of points that Carter had not covered. The informant in this case probably never realized that I had any prior knowledge of the argument. This suggests how the use of information already in hand can guide the researcher toward data that will cross-check the initial account and give a more complete understanding of what actually happened.

Secondhand reports compound the problems of distortion, since they combine the original distortion by the witness with subsequent distortions by the informant. Of course, a shrewd informant may be able to take into account distortions or bias in the reports he receives, and it may even be that his lines of communication are more direct and intimate than any the research worker can establish. If so, the picture the informant gives may have greater objectivity than the reports of eyewitnesses.

This is illustrated in the case of Doc in *Street Corner Society.* Doc was an extraordinarily valuable informant. Whenever checked, his accounts seemed highly reliable. He was also well-informed about what was happening in his own and other groups and organizations in his district. This was due to the position he occupied in the community social structure. Other leaders discussed with him what they were doing and what they should do. Hence we knew developments in the "foreign relations" of the group before his followers, and usually in more direct and accurate form.

Because of the wide variation in quality of informants, the researcher is always on the lookout for informants such as Doc, who can give a reasonably accurate and perceptive account of events. These special informants are frequently found at key positions in the communication structure, often as formal or informal leaders in the organization. They can weigh and balance the evidence themselves and correct for the distortions incorporated by their sources of information. Of course, they may withhold or distort information too, so wherever the researcher has to rely on secondhand reports he or she must be particularly cautious in his or her interpretation.

We should be aware of the dangers of relying too heavily upon any single informant. Gerald Berreman (1961), reporting on a field study in rural India, used a local man as interpreter-informant. Halfway through the field period, he had to work with a different interpreter-informant. He then found that he was getting quite a different picture of the community than he had received in working with his previous assistant. The two individuals occupied quite different positions in the social structure of the community. As Berreman explained, the social positions of the two assistants led each of them, consciously or unconsciously to guide the researcher toward his own views of the community.

This case indicates that it is not enough to assess the reliability of an informant simply in terms of the personality and character of the individual. We need also to recognize how the individual's position in the social structure is likely to shape his or her perceptions, recollections, and descriptions.

8

Integrating Methods
in Team Research

At the 1970 meeting of the American Sociological Association, I participated in a panel discussion on observational and interviewing methods in field research. At the end, a graduate student came up, shook my hand and said, "I want you to know that your talk has been an inspiration to me." When I asked what had been so inspiring, he replied, "Your talk will be most helpful to me in a campaign I am organizing to eliminate the required course in statistics from our sociology curriculum."

I was dumbfounded. I asked myself what I could have said that might be interpreted as a condemnation of statistics. My only reference to the survey or questionnaire was a statement that it is not an all-purpose method. Apparently, since I had been advocating interviewing and observation, it must have followed that I was against surveys and statistics.

The student's remark was an extreme reflection of a commonly accepted dichotomy. Sociological sessions on methods are still commonly divided into two categories: quantitative and qualitative. In past sociological practice, "quantitative" was a code word for surveys. This meant that the less structured interviewing and observational methods were implicitly defined as qualitative—even when they yielded concrete numbers.

Author's Note: Some material in this chapter is adapted from Whyte and Alberti (1976).

RECOGNIZING THE NEED FOR INTEGRATION

My first studies (1936-1948) were based entirely on interviewing and observation. I took a dim view of surveys and thus reinforced the fruitless argument of surveys versus anthropological methods.

Working with students and colleagues at Cornell, I came to recognize that surveys could provide useful data, so that I must develop some competence in that method. First I learned from students designing and carrying out their own surveys, and, during my first sabbatical year (Venezuela, 1954-1955) I assumed primary responsibility for designing and supervising a survey. My next sabbatical (Peru, 1961-1962) was to focus on an anthropological study of "human problems of industrial development," but this led me into a cross-cultural organizational survey (Whyte and Williams, 1963) and also a broad study of Peruvian culture as reflected in surveys of attitudes and beliefs of high school students (Whyte, 1963b).

I no longer questioned the potential value of surveys, but I felt that their value could be enhanced if they were integrated with other field methods. It seemed to me that most attempts to use surveys with anthropological methods did not fully exploit the possibilities of either approach. Survey research was then dominant in sociology, and the surveyors cast anthropological methods in a preliminary and subsidiary role, using anthropological field work only to provide "insights" leading to the formulation of hypotheses—the implication being that solid scientific work was confined to survey research.

I believed we could advance our knowledge more rapidly if we planned for the systematic integration of anthropological methods with surveys, interviewing and observing before the surveys, during the survey process, and in follow-up studies to help us make sense of the survey findings.

Carrying out studies through several research methods in a number of different organizations or communities is not a one-person job. My work in Peru from 1961 to 1976 therefore led me into some major problems of managing team research in comparative multimethod studies.

THE IEP-CORNELL PROGRAM

When I began research in Peru in 1961, I did not plan any rural studies. A Cornell graduate student of anthropology, John Hickman, was doing a thesis on several Indian villages in the highlands around

Lake Titicaca. He became interested in our high school values questionnaire and asked permission to use a number of our items. With translations into the indigenous languages of Quechua and Aymara, he got these surveys carried out in six villages. His results led me to consider the possibilities of combining surveys with anthropological methods in village studies.

The hotly contested Peruvian presidential election took place in June 1962 and was shortly nullified by a military coup. The following year there was a rerun with the same major candidates, and Fernando Belaunde Terry became president. I was interested in the Belaunde candidacy because of his strong campaign commitments to land reform and community development in poor rural areas. When he took office in July 1963 I felt that it could be important to plan field research to monitor these changes.

This would require establishing a baseline in a number of communities just as soon as we could get surveys in the field, beginning in early 1964. Three to five years later, we would resurvey some of the same communities to measure changes in attitudes, perceptions, and the like. With the initial surveys, and during the period between the surveys, we would continue with anthropological studies to explain the course of change in the various communities. In spite of formidable political and financial problems, we were able in general to carry out the original plans, and to add some additional elements.

At Cornell I teamed up with Lawrence K. Williams. Co-Director for Peru was José Matos Mar, a distinguished anthropologist who had just established the Instituto de Estudios Peruanos. J. Oscar Alers, and then Giorgio Alberti, served as field coordinators for Cornell with the IEP, and Williams spent a sabbatical year in Peru. Julio Cotler joined Matos as coordinator for IEP. Our Peruvian associates were full partners in all phases of the program. Peruvian students and professors did most of the field work, and were also fully involved in planning, analyzing the data, and publishing research reports. In 1964 we carried out surveys in 26 communities in 5 regions. In 1969 we resurveyed 12 communities where we had the most solid anthropological data.

INTEGRATING METHODS IN COMPARATIVE CASE STUDIES

To illustrate the value of combining surveys with anthropological methods, I shall use several examples from our studies of Huayopampa and Pacaraos, two villages on the western slope of the Andes in the Chancay Valley, north of Lima. They were in the same culture area and shared the institutional forms characteristic of that area, yet we found marked differences between them.

Consider the responses to the item referring to their community government, the *junta comunal:* "How much power does the junta comunal have to solve the problems of this village?" In Pacaraos, 23 percent responded, "all the power necessary," and 40 percent responded, "the power to do certain things but not others." Do these figures suggest that the people of Pacaraos had much or little confidence in the power of their junta comunal? It might be argued that when 63 percent of the villagers feel that the junta has either all the power necessary or the power to do some things but not others, this is a substantial vote of confidence in this local government institution. But when we look at the figures for Huayopampa and find that 90 percent say that their junta has "all the power necessary," we get a more valuable perspective on our figures. We still cannot say whether the Pacareños are expressing much or little confidence in the power of their junta, but we can say that the Huayopampans have much greater confidence in the power of theirs. In other words, the responses to a survey item are not very useful until we compare one village with another, and such comparison requirs some degree of standardization, which a survey provides.

Both communities had a system of *faenas,* or community work bees. The community assembly and the junta comunal would decide upon a project, calling upon each family to provide an adult male for the period of required work. Fines were imposed upon those families that failed to comply.

Faena attendance was higher in Huayopampa than in Pacaraos (70 percent compared to 59 percent), but the major difference was in rule enforcement. In Huayopampa, 100 percent of the fines levied were collected. The accounts on fines due were closed annually at the time of the community cattle roundup. If delinquents did not pay up, officials sold one or more of their animals to collect the fines. These levies, together with annual rental of some of the farmlands and the fees per head of cattle for grazing on community lands, gave Huayopampa an income substantially above that of Pacaraos.

In Pacaraos, the collection rate for fines ranged from 13 percent to 32 percent. Furthermore, when our field workers divided Pacaraos into socioeconomic strata, they found the bottom stratum paying 32 percent of fines, whereas the top stratum got away with only 13 percent.

When fines failed to secure compliance, the Pacaraos junta comunal had little success with other means. When the junta cut off electricity from the home of one recalcitrant citizen, he appealed to the national authorities. The national government had built and owned the electric power system, and the authorities ruled that the electric service must be restored. In a comparable case in Huayopampa, the recalcitrant citizen had no recourse when his electricity had been cut off—Huayopampa had built its own power system. Data such as these not only confirm the survey finding on the perception of the power of local government in the two villages, they show us how local officials sought to exercise power and the different degrees to which they were able to implement the decisions of their juntas.

We relied on intensive anthropological field work for our data on socioeconomic stratification. For example, interviews and observations over many months enabled our Huayopampa team to divide that community into five strata in terms of quantifiable or otherwise objective indices. Table 1 summarizes the findings. (The family income figures in dollars are for 1966, when the rate of exchange was 26.80 soles per dollar.)

Having converted from traditional crops to growing fruit for coastal markets, Huayopampa was the most affluent of all the villages we studied. Families in the top two strata included ten school teachers, but otherwise the bulk of family income in all strata came from farming.

Pacaraos contrasted sharply with Huayopampa in wealth and income distribution. The ratio from top to bottom strata in Huayopampa for monthly income was only about 4 to 1, whereas in much poorer Pacaraos the ratio was about 18 to 1—$209 for the top 12 percent of the families, $11.60 for the bottom 35 percent of the families. Also, while the largest stratum in Huayopampa fell in the middle of the scale, 60 percent of the Pacaraos families in the bottom two strata had average monthly incomes below $22.40. Finally, in Pacaraos we found an inverse relationship between family income and dependence upon farming. The top stratum families gained 69 percent of their incomes from commerce, 24 percent from cattle, and only 7 percent from raising crops. The number of families whose income came primarily from agricultural crops rose steadily with each step down the strata, reaching 83 percent for families at the bottom.

These figures emphasize a point that should be obvious but that is all too often unrecognized: Anthropological methods can yield highly quantitative and objective data. I do not claim that the figures are exact, yet for Huayopampa they are based on intensive field work over five

TABLE 1

Huayopampa Socioeconomic Stratification

Strata	Number of Families	Hectares Irrigated Land	Labor Use	Machines	Average Monthly Income (in dollars)
1	5	1.64	hired labor	owned machines	474
2	9	1.15	hired labor	rented machines	332
3	57	1.00	reciprocal: relatives and friends	little use	261
4	28	.76	perform part-time labor for others	little use	175
5	52	.54	family labor only on own farm	little use	119

SOURCE: Adapted from Whyte and Alberti (1976: 175). For further detail on Huayopampa, see Fuenzalida et al. (1982).

months by six field workers living in the community. The Pacaraos figures are based upon the work of two researchers who each spent several months in that community; the figures may be somewhat less exact, but the data comparing strata in income and sources of income yield such sharp contrasts that minor errors would be of little consequence. It was on the basis of figures such as these (combined with the survey data and the historical record) that we built up comparative studies of these two villages (Whyte and Alberti, 1976: 164-182).

The survey data for 1964 supported in every respect the contrast observed by the field workers between a poor, stagnating community with sharp internal divisions (Pacaraos) and an affluent, cohesive, and dynamic community (Huayopampa). For the five items measuring interpersonal trust, Huayopampans showed more faith in people than any of the other communities studied, whereas Pacareños trailed most of the others.

On perceptions of cooperation and conflict within the community, we also found a marked contrast. To the question, "When it comes to cooperating on some project for the community, how well do the people cooperate?" in 1964, 97 percent of males and 86 percent of females in Huayopampa chose the top response: "much cooperation." In

Pacaraos, the corresponding figures were 68 percent and 55 percent, respectively. Responding to the question, "Is there much conflict or division between the people of this village?" in Huayopampa no males and only 9 percent of the females perceived "much conflict," whereas 59 percent of both sexes perceived no conflict. In Pacaraos, 24 percent of the males and 18 percent of the females perceived "much conflict" and 30 percent of the males and 45 percent of the females saw "no conflict."

In response to a question regarding respect for old people, we encountered a finding that would have seemed inexplicable if we had depended entirely upon survey data. One might have expected that a stagnant community would show more respect for age than would a dynamic community, yet Huayopampa respondents showed markedly more respect for older citizens. This led us to hypothesize that the dynamism of Huayopampa was not a recent phenomenon, and that people old at the time of our study had played leading roles toward progressive change. Our interviews confirmed this interpretation.

FOCUSING ANTHROPOLOGICAL RESEARCH ON BEHAVIOR AND SOCIAL PROCESSES

Our objective led us away from the approaches that were then becoming most popular in social anthropology. Frank Cancian (1955: 2-3) expressed the options then commonly practiced in this way:

> The use of extensive samples of individual behavior may be contrasted with two other approaches to the study of social structure: (1) the approach that generalizes about social structure on the basis of intensive analysis of a few "crucial" cases, and therefore carries little information about the actual proportion of the population that follows any particular pattern; and (2) the approach that generalizes about social structure on the basis of information about norms, and therefore carries virtually no information about what people actually do. Many anthropologists are able to argue convincingly that the proper goal of a field study is the production of a report showing how the native system makes coherent sense as a way of looking at the world and a way of living. I cannot object to this goal, but I think that the usual way of attaining it leaves too much to the imagination of the anthropologist. The more powerful his intellect and imagination, the more likely the anthropologist is to use this power to create coherence, whatever the actual situation. Careful attention to extensive samples of behavior may help avoid these dangers.

We rejected the first of Cancian's "other approaches" because we assumed (correctly) that we would find considerable variability within a given community in both attitudes and behavior. Therefore we could not base any interpretation on a few "crucial" cases.

We rejected the second option because we wanted to focus primarily on behavior rather than on norms and beliefs. We were interested in norms but we did *not* assume that the villagers uniformly adhered to the norms they articulated to us. We studied behavior to determine what happened when individuals did not do what they were supposed to do. We recognized the growing interest in the symbolic interpretations designed to reveal the ethos of a given culture, in the style of the eminent French anthropologist, Claude Lévi-Strauss (1967), but we suspected that this approach would lead us to assume a spurious uniformity in any area we studied. We were more interested in the differences among different communities in the same culture area than in any overarching cultural interpretation. For this purpose, we had to gather "extensive samples of individual behavior."

I now find that our research strategy provides means to tackle one of the most controversial issues in the history of social anthropology: the conflicting interpretations of the same village or culture published by highly respected researchers. Robert Redfield (1930) found the Mexican village of Tepoztlan to be characterized by high levels of social cohesion and cooperation. Oscar Lewis (1951) described the same village as fraught with conflict and mutual suspicion. Since the Lewis study was done more than 20 years after the Redfield study, it might be argued that they were not studying the same community. However, Redfield did not make that claim, so the conflict in interpretations remained unresolved.

Some years later, George Foster built on the Lewis interpretation to generalize about the nature of peasant communities. In his influential article, "Peasant Society and the Image of the Limited Good," Foster (1966) argued that peasants tend to regard all good things in life, from land to health, as existing in short supply, so that one family's gain is another family's loss. With this world view goes a high degree of envy and interpersonal mistrust.

Some of the villages we studied conformed to the limited good model, but others did not. Huayopampa manifested high degrees of interpersonal trust and perceived cooperation and low perceptions of conflict in our 1964 survey, and several other villages were not far behind. But then we found in our 1969 survey that Huayopampa had experienced a marked drop in its scores for trust and cooperation and a marked rise in perceptions of conflict. Such findings lead us to these general conclusions:

(1) There is substantial variation among peasant communities in some of the characteristics of most interest to sociologists or anthropologists. The limited good model therefore is useful only insofar as it suggests certain conditions that lead to psychological orientations emphasizing envy, mistrust, and conflict. As we examine communities that do not fit the limited good model, the contrast should enable us to advance knowledge of the relations among socioeconomic structure, social processes, and psychological orientations.

(2) In the course of a few years, a village can change markedly in structure, social processes, and psychological orientations. It is therefore important to factor the time dimension into our analysis.

We can extend this analysis to the recent controversy precipitated by Derek Freeman's (1983) attack on Margaret Mead's (1973) classic study, *Coming of Age in Samoa*. Mead had died before the attack, but many anthropologists rallied to her support.

Mead set out to discover whether the stressful period of adolescence in Western societies was universal and therefore rooted primarily in biology, or whether the nature of coming of age was shaped primarily by culture. Concentrating upon interviewing primarily girls and young women, she reported that adolescence in Samoa was generally a peaceful and happy period. Beyond this age-sex group, she found Samoan life characterized by relatively harmonious and cooperative relationships.

On the contrary, Freeman reported Samoan life as being fraught with the tensions of sexual repression, conflict, and violence. One would think that the two anthropologists had studied different cultures, but Freeman rejected that interpretation. He insisted that he was right and that Mead had gone wrong in trying to support a belief in cultural determinism allegedly held by her mentor, Franz Boas.

To make sense out of this conflict, we do not need to read the two books or weigh the lengthy critiques (for example, 39 pages in *American Anthropologist* [Weiner, 1983] and 8 pages in *Human Organization* [Schleper-Hughes, 1983]). A few facts regarding time, geography, and demography should suffice.

Freeman began his research in Samoa about 15 years after Mead had completed her field work, and continued for many years thereafter. Regarding geography and demography,

> Freeman argues that Samoans all have the same culture, regardless of whether they live in American or Western Samoa. Therefore, he feels free to use his findings from the island of Upolu, Western Samoa, where he did his fieldwork, to criticize Mead's work on Ta'u, an island located at the extreme eastern end of the Samoan archipelago approximately 256 km from the island of Upolu. Upolu, which is 1,040 km² in size, has the highest population (106,000 in the census of 1971) of all the Samoan islands. Ta'u, part of American Samoa, is about 44 km² in size, and in 1925 Mead reported the population at about 1,150. Historically, Ta'u . . . underwent a very different period of colonization compared to the rest of Samoa [Weiner, 1983: 913].

These facts alone should discredit Freeman's attack on Mead. On the other hand, they do not prove that Mead's interpretation of Samoa was correct and that Freeman's interpretation was wrong. They simply indicate the absurdity of Freeman's claim that both anthropologists were studying the same phenomena.

Let me again refer to the comparison between Huayopampa and Pacaraos. Anthropologists consider those two villages, along with 25 other officially recognized indigenous communities in the upper part of the Chancay Valley, to share the same culture. Indeed, these villagers all spoke the same language (Spanish) and had the same political structures, cultural practices, and norms regarding community obligations. These were all small, predominantly farming communities. (In 1967 we estimated that Huayopampa had a population of 471, compared to 829 for Pacaraos.) They all had the same basic political structure: *personero* (elected representative to the national government), *junta comunal* (local government), monthly community meetings, and so on. Each community had at least one patron saint and a fiesta system combining Catholic and folk elements. Each community had a system of communal labor known as the *faena*.

In spite of these important common elements, we found striking differences between Huayopampa and Pacaraos, even during the same time period. Freeman considers the fifteen-year lapse between the two Samoan projects of no consequence, yet we found a marked deterioration in perceived cooperation and a sharp rise in perceived conflict in Huayopampa within a five-year period.

Freeman also refuses to recognize the importance of differences in geography and history, which helped us to explain the contrast between Huayopampa and Pacaraos. The two villages were not far apart by road, but they were located in different ecological and climatic zones. At an altitude of about 6,000 feet, Huayopampa had been able to shift from the traditional crops of corn and potatoes into much more profitable tropical fruits for the coastal market. The climate at Pacaraos at 10,000 feet would not support such a shift.

ON RESTUDIES AND TEAM RESEARCH

In some cases, a study of a given community was done by a single student, but in the Chancay Valley, with Huayopampa and Pacaraos, we had teams of two to six people in the community at the same time. The results showed the value of team efforts. A team can provide for a division of labor, with one individual examining the records of the communal government, observing *junta* meetings, and interviewing about local government activities, and another concentrating on the organization of economic activities and the measurement of income. A team also provides protection against the biases of a single individual. In the course of the field period, the team members learn from each other as they spend hours discussing and comparing their findings and arguing about interpretations.

We had originally hoped that during 1964 we would complete not only the surveys but also the anthropological studies in each of our villages. Between 1964 and 1969 we had planned only brief field expeditions to check anything that might have changed since the previous studies. Instead of simply bringing each village up to date, we carried out full-scale restudies, to check the original findings, fill in gaps, and reexamine interpretations made on the basis of the original study.

In some cases, restudies revealed serious errors in the previous work. Our first study of one community described an unusual type of committee functioning under the local government. The restudy provided no information on this committee. When we checked with the research team of the restudy, we found that the committee in question did not exist and had never existed. How could such a mistake be made? The student who did the first study described the committee on the basis of information given him by a single informant. This informant had a record for urging changes that frequently were not carried out. The minutes of the meetings of local government record the establishment of the committee, but the idea was never implemented.

In another community, after making a much more careful and systematic examination of the economic aspects of community life, our restudy team developed figures indicating that the first study's family income estimate was twice as large as it should have been.

It might be argued that such errors can be avoided by a good anthropologist using good methods. I agree that a well-trained and experienced anthropologist will bring in more adequate field data than will beginning students, but the history of social anthropology should raise doubts about the wisdom of relying entirely upon the field reports of a single anthropologist, no matter how well trained or how large his or her professional reputation.

The checking and rechecking process also stimulated our students to raise their standards of performance. They explained to us, "The information you had was simply wrong because the man who made the study got it from a single informant and did not check it with anybody else." Or, "Those original income estimates were just based on sloppy methods. We have talked with X, and he has admitted that this part of his study was not good." The students were thinking not only of the professors who would read their reports, but also of future students who would follow them and check on their work.

The quality of our studies has been improved by the writing of comparative descriptions and analyses about pairs or sets of communities. When a research director reads reports on communities A and B, deficiencies may escape his attention until he is required to write a comparison of the two. He then finds that he has excellent information on one aspect of life in community A, but the information from community B does not refer to some points considered important by the writers of the A report. For example, impressed by the Pacaraos report on the low frequency of collection of fines, we looked for comparable data in the Huayopampa monograph—and did not find any. Since Huayopampans paid 100 percent of their fines, collection did not seem a problem and was not reported. When we compared the two villages, Huayopampa's success in collecting fines was clearly as important as Pacaraos's failure.

ON MANAGING THE INTEGRATION
OF FIELD METHODS

Surveys and anthropological field work call for different styles of supervision. Traditionally, for the student about to study a primitive tribe, supervision by a senior anthropologist consisted of planning discussions before the student set forth and discussions when he or she returned, supplemented perhaps by an exchange of letters while the student was in the field. While this type of supervision hardly seems optimal to me, anthropological field work allows great flexibility and necessarily leaves the initiative very much in the hands of the field worker. The student does not embark upon field work with a tight research design, and can make major changes in the direction of the study as new problems and opportunities present themselves.

The planning and implementation of surveys requires a rigid research design and tight supervision throughout the process. To secure representative data, the sampling design must be systematically worked out and adhered to in the field. The questionnaire must be pretested to assure comprehension by the respondents. To make it practical to analyze the data, the questionnaire should consist mainly of closed-ended questions. (An anthropologist told me of an earlier survey in Peru that had contained 84 open-ended questions. After struggling for some months to code and analyze the responses, the researchers gave up.) The wording of the items should be standardized, and, so far as possible, the survey should be administered in the same form to all respondents.

Tight supervision is also necessary for quality control of the field interviewing process. For a student without previous survey experience, the first few questionnaires applied through personal interviewing may provide interesting experiences, but the process is repetitive and becomes dull work. There is a natural temptation to fill out the questionnaire without taking the time to get the cooperation of the respondent and go through the proper procedures. Even for survey researchers with far more experience than I, this can be a serious problem (Roth, 1975). To secure adequate quality control, the interviewers should turn in their questionnaires to the field supervisor at the end of each day. The supervisor can then check to make sure that all of the items have been covered and can discuss any problems with those carrying out the field work. It may also be advisable for the supervisor to make spot checks in the field, going back to certain respondents to make sure they have actually been interviewed.

All of this I knew in advance, but I did not adequately understand the problems this posed for my own direction of the field work. My natural style of supervision fits much better with anthropological studies than with surveys. I tend to trust people to do what they promise to do, and I find it difficult to provide the tight supervision good surveys require. Since I did not direct every step of the survey process in every area myself, this problem would have been minimized to the extent that I secured Peruvian field directors who would provide the close supervision required. However, while I was able to secure field directors who were generally highly regarded by their colleagues, none of them had previous survey experience. Beyond their learning problems, at least one of them did not take seriously the exacting requirements I sought to place upon the supervisory process. Furthermore, it was difficult for me to provide close supervision to the field supervisors.

I also faced serious problems in the time I had available for the field work and in the scope of the surveying operations. We proposed to survey villages in five areas. In order to secure a professor to direct the operation and students to do the field work, we worked through San Marcos National University in Lima and four provincial universities. Since the plan called for establishing a baseline and resurveys three to five years later, we aimed to cover what turned out to be 26 villages in 1964. Finally, since I had regular teaching obligations, I could be in Peru only between semesters in January and during summer vacation. Cornell's co-director, Lawrence K. Williams, who is far better qualified in skill and experience for the direction of surveys, was unable to go to Peru until his sabbatical year, 1967-1968.

In the summer of 1963, when I discussed the general plans with José Matos Mar, then chairman of the Department of Anthropology at San Marcos National University, he told me that he had support for a group of students to do field work in the Chancay Valley, about 50 miles north of Lima, during the January through March university vacation period. The students were to carry out anthropological studies in several coastal villages and also in one village in the highlands. He invited me to join them to fit the surveys into the other studies.

In the fall of 1963, Williams and I worked with a student seminar to write a first draft of a questionnaire, which we had translated into Spanish. For most of January 1964 I worked wih Matos and students in the field. I went with them as we pretested the questionnaire and then tried to utilize our experiences and ideas from the pretest in devising a final survey instrument. Regarding sampling, I called for advice from a Peruvian professional highly regarded in this field. We agreed that the basic plan would be to sample every fifth household in each village, increasing the percentage for very small villages, and decreasing the percentage somewhat for much larger villages. He also gave us advice that turned out to be based more on sex bias than professional expertise. He told us that we would be wasting our time surveying the women because they would just give the same answers as their husbands. When we disregarded this advice, we found that there were marked sex differences.

Matos worked closely with the students, and deputized two of the most advanced and mature students, Heraclio Bonilla and Cesar Fonseca, to provide close supervision of the survey process. I had to return to Cornell when the actual survey was just getting under way, but some months later I was delighted to find that we had Chancay Valley data that appeared to be of high quality and systematically gathered.

In the summer of 1964, I returned to Peru to organize surveys in the departments of Cuzco and Arequipa, the Mantaro Valley in the central highlands, and in a couple of villages on the north coast. These operations went as well as I could have hoped, but when we came to the surveys planned for one area, we encountered an unmitigated disaster.

THE SWISS CHEESE PHENOMENON

For reasons that will shortly become obvious, I will give our field director for this area the pseudonym of Juan Fulano. He had done previous research in the Mantaro Valley and was assuming a professorship at the university in our next study area. I worked with him in organizing and starting the Mantaro Valley project, with the expectation that, following this experience, he would repeat it in the next project.

That summer, toward the end of my stay in Peru, Fulano returned to Lima. As I went through his questionnaires, I was appalled at the number of problems I found. As I learned later, after I left town Fulano had just handed students the questionnaire forms, dispatched them to the field, and, upon their return, gathered the forms without giving them any attention. Meanwhile, he had been doing his own thing—whatever that was—around the Mantaro Valley. There was one redeeming feature in this set of questionnaires. While I had serious doubts that any sampling plan had been followed, the students had interviewed so many people in each village that the large numbers might offset the lack of systematic sample. In any case, I decided that some of the damage could be repaired, and was able to send a conscientious student, Hernan Castillo (who had worked with me in the 1961-1962 industrial studies) to the Mantaro Valley to fill in some of the gaps.

At this point, I should have told Fulano that, since his work in the Mantaro Valley had been unsatisfactory, I could not proceed with the next study. However, I had already made a commitment to the university authorities. Beyond that, I faced a problem that I have since come to recognize was characteristic of me. I find it very difficult to admit defeat, even when the rational decision would be to cut my losses by abandoning an operation.

Professor Fulano promised to do better, so, after a long talk, I agreed to proceed. For some of the villages in the Cuzco area, Oscar Núñez del Prado had prepared a Quechua version of our questionnaire. Since I knew that the new study was in an area where a somewhat different Quechua dialect was spoken, I asked Fulano if we should prepare a new translation. He assured me that this would not be necessary. In all the villages to be studied "everybody speaks Spanish." I suggested that he conduct a pretest, even though our Spanish-language questionnaire had been adequate for other areas, except for the indigenous communities in Cuzco—but I did not demand that such a pretest be done and the results reported to me before the final operation.

The surveys were to be done in the fall of 1964. I had planned to visit their university the following January to review the field experience with the students and Fulano. During the fall, Fulano reported that there had been delays beyond his control, but he still promised that the surveys would be done before my visit. As I later learned, the mimeographing of 200 questionnaires had been completed only shortly before the Christmas vacation. At that time, Fulano had hired eight students for surveys in four villages. He simply divided them up into teams of two and handed each team fifty questionnaires. Then he left for a long Christmas vacation.

In my feedback discussion in January, I asked the students to tell me frankly of any problems they had encountered in applying the surveys. One student spoke up: "In the villages where I worked, some of the people did not understand Spanish." I looked at Fulano, who laughed and said, "That surprised us all."

The next question was obvious, but it took me a while before I could face it. Finally, I went back to the student and asked, "In the villages where you worked, what percentage of the respondents would you say could not understand Spanish."

He thought that over and then replied, "I would say about 95 percent."

What did the students do with such respondents? Most of the students were bilingual, so they claimed that they just translated the questions as they went along, giving each Quechua-speaking respondent an individualized translation.

Back at Cornell, out of curiosity we decided to put the responses on the data cards we then used. It was at this point that we discovered what we called the "swiss cheese phenomenon." One day Williams had a deck of these cards and happened to hold them before the window. He discovered that he could see completely through the deck at a number of points. We thus encountered a phenomenon that may never have been experienced in survey research before: In some of these villages, every single respondent expressed the same opinion on several items. The students had not even taken the pains to fake the questionnaires with any skill. Needless to say, we abandoned that survey.

No doubt there were less catastrophic problems that we did not recognize in other area studies. If our research data had been limited to the surveys, we would have had some doubts about their validity. As it was, comparison between the survey responses and the anthropological data seemed to justify our confidence in the surveys. To be sure, we could not make sense out of the responses to some items. For example, the Mantaro Valley responses were relatively high on items designed to measure degrees of fatalism, yet we knew from our own anthropological studies and from ample previous research that this was one of the most dynamic areas of rural Peru. Faced with this apparent conflict between psychological orientation and behavior, we speculated that the villagers were simply voicing conventional beliefs that had little influence on behavior, and we made no further analyses of these survey items. Fortunately, on most of the items of importance to us, survey responses fitted well with the independently gathered anthropological data, strengthening our confidence in both bodies of data.

PARTICIPATION VERSUS STANDARDIZATION: THE 1969 RESURVEY

By the time we were planning the 1969 resurvey, we were far better prepared than we had been in 1964. Not only did we have the 1964 experience behind us, but now we had working with us in Peru two men with substantial survey experience. An Italian sociologist who had worked with us while doing his thesis in Peru, Giorgio Alberti, now became Cornell's full-time local representative. His Peruvian counterpart, Julio Cotler, had had experience working with an MIT group on surveys in Venezuela. We realized that our 1964 program involving surveys in 26 villages had been too ambitious. Beyond problems encountered in the survey, we had included more villages than could be covered adequately with anthropological field studies. Then political problems within the University of Arequipa forced us to drop villages in that area from the resurvey. So we came down to 12 villages in 4 areas of Peru. Now, in addition to using students from the provincial universities, the Instituto de Estudios Peruanos sent out for each area a person experienced in surveys to provide field direction.

We have the impression that the quality of the 1969 surveys was superior to that of the 1964 program, but we did encounter one unanticipated problem. For the resurvey, we planned to maintain what appeared to be useful items from the 1964 instrument for comparison, but to drop unproductive ones and substitute new items based on what we had learned. With that plan, we would be able to compare 1964 and 1969 on many items and gather further items of interest, even if we could not compare them with 1964. We expected that this revision would be carried out while I was in Lima during January 1969. Unfortunately, the IEP people were not ready until shortly before I had to return to Ithaca. Therefore, I left it up to Giorgio Alberti to conduct the discussions with the field workers and arrive at the final version. I had no problems with the competence or conscientiousness of Alberti, who knew more about surveys than I, but I overlooked one problem. In any survey, the final design of the instrument must be centralized, and I had failed to work out arrangements making it clear that Alberti would have the ultimate authority. He got along well with the students and had their respect, but he had worked closely with them and was much younger than I. As the students got involved in a highly participative discussion, they naturally developed some ego involvement in getting their particular ideas into the questionnaire. Where certain 1964 items had not proven useful, we had no hesitation in eliminating them, and this left space for new items. Some additions did prove useful, but we had a problem with the "improvements" students wanted to make on items we had planned to retain. Alberti held the line as far as he could but had to concede some points in the face of group pressures. In some cases, the reworded questions may have been superior to the 1964 versions, but, of course, we could not use these items for 1964-1969 comparisons. Fortunately, our losses through this process were not serious, but the experience did drive home the lesson that participation in decision making on a questionnaire must be limited by the need to adhere to a systematic research design.

GAINING ACCEPTANCE FOR
INTEGRATION OF METHODS

When reviewing the first reports submitted by the team of anthropology students after their intensive study of Huayopampa in 1966, I was impressed by two aspects of their work: (1) the anthropological data confirmed the survey findings in all important respects, and yet (2) the students made no references to the survey data.

When I discussed this with the team, one of the field workers replied:

> Yes, we did know about the survey, and we looked at it before we started our field work. But we couldn't believe that answers to a questionnaire in a peasant village would have any real meaning, so we just decided to forget about the questionnaire when we did our anthropological study.

I pointed out that it was not too late to reexamine the survey so that their final report could draw upon both types of data. However, neither the case study of Huayopampa nor a later edition enriched by a follow-up study made any reference to the Huayopampa surveys, though the bibliographies of these two volumes cited many works far less relevant (Fuenzalida et al., 1982). The explanation for this glaring omission in books otherwise noteworthy for their comprehensive and systematic scholarship is probably to be found in a combination of personal experience and personality.

The first Huayopampa book (published in 1968; see Fuenzalida et al., 1982) was based on anthropological field work in 1966 by six students who had not taken part in the 1964 survey program. One of them was invited to participate in the 1969 surveys but withdrew after a very brief time in the field. He got the impression that the respondents did not understand what was going on and were uncertain whether their answers would make clear what they *really* believed or felt. Therefore the whole project must be a waste of time.

Experienced survey interviewers do not react so drastically to their first few respondents. When respondents answer a series of questions posed by a stranger, we do not assume that they express what they *really and deeply feel*. In fact, sometimes we advise respondents just to give us the first response that comes to mind, since we know that if they took time to consider some items at length, none of the responses offered would seem exactly right, or they would rather answer questions we have not asked. Each individual questionnaire gives us only a rough and superficial reflection of the respondent's psychological orientation, but we believe that there is some safety in numbers—providing the questionnaire is reasonably well designed and, is administered to a systematic sample, and the survey interviews have been carried out conscientiously. Under those conditions, when we find patterns in the responses we think we have meaningful results. Furthermore, when these patterns are confirmed by our anthropological data, we are on more solid ground than if we were relying exclusively on either set of data.

On the positive side, we found several students who, having less resistance to questionnaires and having gained experience in field surveys and in survey data analysis, were able to write and publish reports based both on surveys and anthropological research. This has encouraged us to believe that the integration of research methods may yet have a future in Peru.

Are U.S. anthropologists receptive to the integration of surveys with anthropological studies? The review of our book in the *American Anthropologist* provides no support for that hope. Among other criticisms, Paul L. Doughty (1978) wrote:

> For anthropologists, the book sharpens methodological differences with sociologists: a dominant dependence on questionnaire data which provide insight on synchronic attitudes of peasants, but cannot really address matters of process.

Our "dominant dependence on questionnaire data" struck me as an interesting misperception. In only 5 of our 22 chapters do we report any survey data—but that is apparently 5 too many for the traditionally minded anthropologist.

Are U.S. sociologists more receptive than anthropologists to the integration of research methods? I see some encouraging signs. Without abandoning survey methods, some sociologists are coming to recognize that even the most advanced computerized statistical or mathematical analysis cannot overcome the inherent limitations of survey data.

The recent surge of interest in applied sociology is stimulating this broadening of methodological interests. Leaders of client organizations often are not content with survey reports on attitudes and perceptions, thus raising questions that cannot be answered exclusively with survey data.

When we were working on *Applied Sociology* (Freeman et al., 1983), Peter Rossi suggested that he and I co-author the introductory chapter, "The Applied Side of Sociology." Although Rossi is known for his survey research and highly quantitative data analysis, we had no trouble agreeing that the applied sociologist should develop some competence in a broad range of methods, including those commonly associated with the field work of social anthropologists.

CONCLUSIONS

Reliance upon a single research method is bound to impede the progress of science. If we use the survey alone, we may gather highly quantitative data measuring the subjective states of respondents, in relation to certain demographic characteristics. Surveys may also yield self-reports on behavior; for example, we asked respondents if they had ever lived outside of their villages—and if so, for how long—and how often during a year they visited a city. Some apparently objective questions may yield answers of doubtful validity, as we found in asking U.S. factory workers how often they attended union meetings (see the Dean-Strauss study reported in Chapter 11). In any case, the survey yields a snapshot of responses at a particular time. We can fill in this dimension partially with a resurvey, but this by itself only provides evidence of the direction and magnitude of changes. Without the use of other methods, we can only speculate on the dynamics of change.

In the past, anthropological studies of individual communities have had limited value for comparative and theoretical purposes because of the wide variation in purposes and procedures of social anthropologists. We can seldom find comparable data gathered in two or more communities at the same time or in the same community at different times. For example, in the Freeman-Mead controversy, in addition to the differences in historical background, geography, and demography between the two Samoan projects, we should note the differences in the selection of people interviewed and observed. Appropriately, in terms of her interest, Mead concentrated on adolescent girls and young women. Freeman did not similarly concentrate. Even if he had decided to do so, it is unlikely that an older man could have elicited such full and apparently frank interviews as did 23-year-old Margaret Mead.

If, in addition to her anthropological studies, Mead had used a survey including items on perceived conflict and cooperation, sexual norms and practices, and so on, and if Freeman had applied those same items in his study, the resulting data would have clarified one aspect of the controversy. Then the compatibility or incompatibility of the survey findings with the anthropological interpretation of each researcher would have influenced our confidence in the validity of that interpretation. Conceivably this combination of methods might have confirmed Mead's interpretation of Ta'u and Freeman's interpretation of Upolu, leading us back to the obvious fact that the two researchers had studied two different communities in two very different times and places. Or the combination of methods might have indicated that both researchers had oversimplified their interpretations.

I am not claiming there is one best way to do anthropological research. Currently the strategy I favor is distinctly a minority view, overshadowed in prestige and popularity by the ingenious and sophisticated interpretations of whole cultures as practiced by Claude Lévi-Strauss (1967) and Clifford Geertz (1973) and their many followers. While one may admire the intellectual brilliance of this work, I do not see how these efforts to discover the essence of a given culture can provide useful information and ideas on the actual behavior of the people who supposedly share this culture. If one wishes to study behavior and also provide data that can be integrated with historical research and surveys, then there are other anthropological models to follow (for example, see Greenwood, 1976; Cancian, 1955).

I did not invent the idea of integrating surveys with anthropological methods. A growing number of others have recognized the potential value in such triangulation of methods (see, for example, Burawoy, 1979; Cole, 1981; Thomas, 1984; Jick, 1983; Denzin, 1970). Since few researchers have made such an ambitious attempt at integration, I thought it worthwhile to report on our Peruvian experience.

Our experience also suggests some future developments in the integration of methods. Our program was so large in cost and number of researchers and so long in duration that it is not likely to be duplicated often. Since the surveys were applied in each village in a week to ten days, anthropological methods offer the only area for development of shortcuts that could make our strategy more accessible to others. In the first place, it must be recognized that, able as many of them were, this was the first extensive field experience for most of our anthropological researchers. Therefore, the time and money invested must be counted toward teaching and learning as well as toward data gathering. From this experience I now see possibilities of gathering comprehensive data on socioeconomic stratification without studying each family. Field workers might seek the assistance of key informants, who could give us a general picture of the social and economic levels in the community and identify one or two families at each level. We could then undertake intensive studies of these representative families. We could go back to our key informants to ask them to evaluate the socioeconomic status of all other families in the village in relation to those we had studied. We could not be as confident of our results as if we had studied each family, but the quality of the data might be good enough to let us cover more cases in less time.

I am not advocating such a shortcut. I simply suggest that, if one wishes to achieve a more efficient integration of methodologies, there is much further work to be done in methodological testing and development.

9

Using History in Social Research

When we began our Peruvian research program, I viewed history as having little value for understanding the current scene. I thought I was only being sympathetic to the interests of our Peruvian researchers in suggesting that they gather historical data on each village for the last 50 years.

Fortunately, the Peruvians refused to accept the 50-year limit and in some cases probed up to 500 years in the history of villages or areas. Much of these data on rural communities would be of interest only to historians. However, understanding the paradox of the Mantaro Valley required us to go back to the conquest of Peru, and, in the Chancay Valley, we traced the beginnings of the differentiation of Huayopampa from Pacaraos back more than a century.

THE MANTARO VALLEY

In the culture and social structure of the highlands of Peru, the Mantaro Valley departs sharply from the general pattern of mestizos, owning the large haciendas, controlling political power, and dominating and exploiting the indigenous population. The mestizo-Indian cleavage is less marked than elsewhere, and, at least in the villages along the Mantaro River, nearly everyone is fluent in Spanish. In contrast to the rigid structures of political and economic control elsewhere in the highlands, the Mantaro Valley villages are characterized by a high degree of grass-roots participatory democracy.

Author's Note: Parts of this chapter are adapted from Whyte and Alberti (1976).

A major economic base for the more democratic society and culture of the Mantaro Valley is readily apparent: This is an area of small family holdings, largely unaffected by the large haciendas or estates that dominate most of the highlands. But how this differentiation came about is not apparent to the current observer.

The Huancas, who occupied the Mantaro Valley, had been defeated and incorporated into the Inca empire only about 1460 and at the time of the conquest still regarded the Incas as enemies. When Pizarro and his men reached this valley in 1532, they were greeted by a large crowd. Five days of feasting, drinking, and dancing led to the signing of a treaty whereby, in return for their military support, the Huancas were guaranteed continued possession of their lands and local autonomy.

After Pizarro's death, the treaty was disregarded. Huanca delegations complained in vain to the government at Lima. In 1560, two Huanca leaders somehow made their way to Spain and secured an audience with King Philip II. The King upheld the treaty, signed by Pizarro, with a decree that the haciendas already established in the valley should be eliminated and that, in the future, no Spaniards should be permitted to own large estates in that area (Espinosa, 1973).

Later influences strengthened the independence of the small farmers and tradesmen of the valley and contributed to the growth of Huancayo, which became the area's dynamic urban center. In 1854, in his struggle against a rival general, who had the support of large landowners, Ramón Castilla, who became one of Peru's great presidents, established his headquarters in Huancayo. In return for Indian support, he abrogated discriminatory taxes.

Early in the twentieth century, copper mining became important around La Oroya, in the mountains between the Mantaro Valley and the coast. Many sons of Mantaro Valley farmers worked in the mines and returned not only with money but also with experience and ideas gained through membership in a militant union. In 1908 the Central Railroad from Lima to La Oroya was extended to Huancayo, and in the early 1930s the central highway from Lima to Huancayo was completed. These major transportation links stimulated the movement of merchandise, people, and ideas through the central highlands and to the coast, where Peru's industrial development was concentrated.

Our three villages in the Mantaro Valley presented a contrast that made no sense until we put our data in the context of history and geography. Pucará and San Antonio de Cajas were the dynamic self-propelled communities that we had been led to expect, but Mito appeared to be a stagnating and decaying community. We found our explanations in the rivalry of the cities of Huancayo and Jauja, located at opposite ends of the Mantaro Valley. Cajas and Pucará are close to Huancayo, a force for democratization since Castilla's victorious campaign in 1854. Mito is in the Mantaro Valley but adjoins Jauja, where the Mantaro and Yanamarca Valley meet. The conquerors and early settlers had subjugated the Indians and acquired large haciendas in the Yanamarca Valley, beyond the liberating edict of King Philip II. The large landowners in the Yanamacra Valley generally lived in Jauja, and they dominated the economy and the politics of that city and its surrounding area.

Early in the twentieth centry, Mito was a large municipality, with the mestizo elite controlling and exploiting the Indians who lived in its outlying districts, then called *anexos*. The alliance of the Mito elite with its counterpart in Jauja is illustrated by the fact that Jauja levied tolls on all roads and bridges leading from Jauja to Mito and granted Mito half of this income.

The mobilization of people in the anexos brought about their separation from Mito and recognition as independent villages in three stages (1917, 1929, and 1941). In this process, Mito lost about two-thirds of its former territory. Then, beginning in the 1950s, peasant movements in the Yanamarca Valley were gradually overcoming the large landholders and transforming that valley in the image of the Mantaro Valley. The elite in both Jauja and Mito were losing both wealth and political power.

As they lost control of lands and cheap labor, the Mito elite faced a dilemma. Many of them could still have made a living farming, but only by working the land themselves. The alternative was to migrate to a city, selling or renting the land, or working out a sharecropping arrangement. Increasing numbers of Mito's mestizos chose to leave town, and Mito experienced a marked decline in population.

At the time of our first field study in 1964, Mito still showed signs of its elite background. It remained markedly above both Cajas and Pucará in average educational level. Only 20 percent of the Miteños claimed to be able to speak Quechua, compared to 60 percent for Cajas and 95 percent for Pucará. In ethnic self-identification, over two-thirds of the Miteños claimed to be mestizos, compared to less than 50 percent for the comparison communities. Miteños could still claim social superiority, but they had given up the struggle to improve their community. Mito was living in its past.

THE CHANCAY VALLEY

We also drew upon the historical record to explain the differences between Huayopampa and Pacaraos. As already noted, they were similar in culture, but Huayopampa enjoyed a marked climate advantage. At an altitude of over 10,000 feet, Pacaraos was limited to the traditional crops of potatoes and corn. At 6000 feet, Huayopampa had converted to tropical fruits for coastal markets. However, climate cannot account for all of the important differences between the two.

The records of both communities since the mid-nineteenth century reveal frequent statements on the importance of education to put the villagers in touch with modern urban life, but Huayopampa built its educational base much earlier and deeper than Pacaraos. A Catholic missionary school was established in Huayopampa around 1850. Although it was short lived, it raised the literacy level substantially above that of other villages in the area. When petitions to the government from area villages brought no action, in 1886 Huayopampa built its own school and hired a teacher. It was 1922 before any other community in the area got its own school.

In 1902 both Huayopampa and Pacaraos were running short of unoccupied arable land for new families. Pacaraos distributed its remaining plots, but Huayopampa retained community ownership and rented the land for three-year periods. This rental income contributed importantly to the resources of the communal government and helped to make Huayopampa's junta comunal more effective than that of Pacaraos, as reflected in our surveys more than half a century later.

In 1904, Huayopampa built a new school and attracted as teachers a remarkable couple, the Ceferino Villars. Since their two sons succeeded them, Huayopampa remained under the influence of the Villars family until 1925. They are still remembered today, the main street bearing the name of Ceferino Villar and one of the school buildings being named after his wife.

The Villars family was also influential in persuading the Archbishop of Lima to establish the *Seminario Menor* in Huayopampa, extending education for several grades beyond the level of other communities in the area. Although that school burned to the ground in 1927, its impact was lasting. Most of the leaders in the development of Huayopampa in the 1940s and 1950s had been students there.

The pattern of education established by the Villars and followed by their successors differed markedly from the traditional Peruvian emphasis upon rote learning and the glorification of national heroes. The Huayopampa children studied the flora and fauna, the archaeology and history of the area, and teachers led the pupils to understand and appreciate their local community and culture. In contrast to the individualistic orientation of education elsewhere, the Villars stressed the collective arrangements of their indigenous past. They organized the children into work groups, with elected leaders, for maintenance work in and around the school. They emphasized the value and dignity of manual labor, establishing school garden plots and a reforestation project, where the pupils integrated what they had learned from their farm families with the information and ideas the teachers introduced from government agricultural research and extension.

In 1964 only two out of the ten Pacaraos teachers were natives of the village, and only one of these took part in community activities. In Huayopampa all ten teachers were natives, and the pattern of young people returning from higher education to teach in Huayopampa had prevailed for many years. Furthermore, since the days of the Ceferino Villars, school teachers had always been among the most active and influential citizens of Huayopampa.

Lampián, a community not far from Huayopampa, also provides a comparison that requires historical explanations. Lampián and Huayopampa had populations of almost identical size, and both had shifted from traditional crops into tropical fruits after building roads giving them access to coastal markets in the late 1940s. Both were relatively affluent in the 1960s, but the wealth and land holdings were much more equally distributed in Huayopampa. Since Lampián was not included among the villages we surveyed, we cannot compare the two on survey items reflecting conflict, cooperation, and respect for old people, but the anthropological data indicate that, compared to Huayopampa in 1964, Lampián manifested markedly more conflict, less cooperation, and less respect for old people. One old-timer commented,

> There are coming to be more and more people who do not respect the traditional customs of the community. Often neither the old agreements nor the new decisions of the community are respected. There is a lack of consideration for the ideas of the old people. Because of that we (old timers) no longer go to community meetings. Neither do the authorities have the power to lead the community as before. They are just interested in their own private benefits [Whyte and Alberti, 1976: 193].

In the 1920s the local government of Lampián was a gerontocracy, with the higher positions being reached only through increasing age. This traditional system began to break down under the stress of population pressure. Population rose by 25 percent between 1926 and 1936. By 1938, 30 of the 120 adult males had no land and so had to postpone marriage. During the 1930s they were working on their fathers' farms, assuming their fathers' duties in faenas and attending the monthly communal assemblies—where they had neither voice nor vote.

The discontents of the young men were fueled by a talented and enterprising school teacher who served in the community from 1927 to 1937. As some of them later learned, he taught them well enough so that they could more than hold their own with pupils in coastal cities. His influence extended beyond the classroom. An ardent follower of Haya de la Torre, he organized the young men into cells supporting APRA, which was then a radical reform party.

The generational conflict came to a head in 1938 with the parcelization of a 10 hectare plot. The authorities allocated the best land to themselves and relatives and friends of their generation, handing out miniscule plots in the worst terrain to the landless young men. This provoked an open revolt. Now the young men spoke up in a community meeting, accusing the authorities of "betraying the necessities of youth." The elders attacked the young men for their disloyalty to traditional values and voted to expel all 30 of them from the community. Thus began seven years of exile for the young men of Lampián.

The young men went down to the coast to find jobs in Lima or on coastal haciendas. Some of them continued their education as they struggled to support themselves. Throughout this period, they kept in touch with each other and took pride in the fact that they were doing better economically than the old people they had left behind.

Meanwhile, those remaining in Lampián were encountering increasing difficulties. They had problems managing the heavy work that had been done by the young men, and they could not afford to hire competent help. They also encountered increasingly severe problems in coping with the national government, which was imposing new laws and regulations on indigenous communities, and with neighboring villages in endless boundary disputes.

At last the local authorities recognized they could not do without the strength, knowledge, political contacts, and social skills of the exiles.

Responding to the invitation of the village authorities, all 30 young men returned to Lampián in 1945. Having learned how to grow tropical fruits on the coastal haciendas, the young men organized the road building project to give Lampián access to urban markets, and they led the movement to transform local agriculture.

By the early 1950s the former exiles had taken over local government. By the mid-1960s, their economic and political success had divided the social structure into two distinct segments. At the top were 40 families, the original migrants plus friends and relatives. In 1967, these families, 36 percent of the population, controlled 80 percent of the land, with average holdings of 4 hectares per family—almost 2.5 the average holding in Huayopampa's top stratum. The remaining 64 percent of the families held an average of about .9 hectare. Land use was also strikingly different. Whereas the 40 families devoted 45 percent of their cultivated land to fruit, the others used less than 6 percent of their land this way. In animal husbandry, we found the same cleavage. The 40 families owned 73 percent of the cattle, averaging 23.7 head per family, while the others averaged slightly under 5 head.

In following the history of these three villages into the late 1960s, we found that education—both inside and outside of the community—was a major factor in explaining the differences. The boys of Pacaraos had received just a minimal elementary education. When young people emigrated from Pacaraos, they entered the labor markets of the coast or of the highland mines as unskilled workers. Some returned to settle in Pacaraos with their savings but without additional education. What they had learned in the mines or in tropical agriculture had little application to life in Pacaraos.

Besides learning to grow tropical fruit and developing the social skills to cope with urban life, many of the exiled youth of Lampián continued their education through high school. The combination of superior education with increased technical and social skills enabled them to return and dominate the economic and political life of their village.

Paradoxically, education had led Huayopampa to a broadly shared prosperity, as teachers of the Villars family established a program of high intellectual quality built on values of social solidarity, yet by 1969 we found that education was increasing stresses within the community. The young people of Huayopampa were not expelled from their village, but their families sent them to Lima for further education—and beyond high school. By 1966 Huayopampa had produced 95 males and 52 females who were established professionals or were university students. As evidence of the profound influence of the village school teachers, we found that 52.6 percent of these men and 82.7 percent of these women had become or were becoming school teachers. And the Huayopampa schools had only ten teaching positions and no current vacancies. When we met with a group of Huayopampa university students in Lima, we found them very proud of the progress of their home town and committed to frequent visits there, but not a single one was considering settling down in Huayopampa.

Traditionally in these villages, as well as helping their parents with farm work, young people had shouldered some of the heavier communal work responsibilities and then passed them on to the age cohort following them. Higher education for young Huayopampans has undermining this age-graded division of labor, and the older people were experiencing growing difficulties in managing their own work and the communal labor obligations. Increasingly they were turning to hired labor, thus substituting the problems of labor relations for the customary understandings of shared communal work. In just the short period from 1964 to 1969, survey responses showed marked increases in perceived conflict and marked decreases in perceived cooperation and interpersonal trust.

CONCLUSIONS

The cases described here, along with many others, transformed my conceptions of the value of history in social research. I began my Peruvian experience thinking of history as just providing a general context for solid social research. Indeed, at the national level, that is how we used history. Writing in English for people not familiar with Peru (Whyte and Alberti, 1976), we had to provide some of the essential facts of history, geography, economics, and politics. This brief background simply provided a context for what was to follow.

As we advanced in area and community studies, it became obvious that history could no longer be treated simply as background. To understand the Convención Valley and the Yanamarca Valley in the mid-1960s, we had to study the peasant movements that had begun to transform those valleys in the 1950s. Our students took us back to the Conquest of Peru to explain how the Mantaro Valley had come to differ so markedly from other highland valleys. We had to study the different lines of development of the neighboring Mantaro and Yanamarca Valleys and the rivalry between the cities of Huancayo and Jauja to understand how Mito had come to differ so markedly from Pucará and

Agustín de Cajas. Documents in village offices showed us that events occurring more than a century earlier had begun the marked differentiation of Huayopampa from the other villages in the highlands above the Chancay Valley. Whereas climate accounted in part for the differences between Pacaraos and Huayopampa, it did not differentiate Huayopampa from Lampián; only history could account for the contrast between those two villages.

I now believe that any study of an organization or a community must be built on a firm historical base. Historical data should be integrated into our analysis of current structural and social process data.

Without historical data, our theories of development and change are bound to be faulty. Furthermore, for any practitioner of community development, gaining some historical perspective should be a sobering and enlightening experience. Such experience should turn us away from "quick fix" strategies based solely upon an interpretation of current conditions. History does not tell us that inducing change is impossible; even within a few years we observed major changes in some of these Peruvian villages. From our experience, I draw this practical lesson: successful introduction of change into village or organization requires devising a strategy that can be linked with structures and social processes that have deep roots in history.

From the beginning of my field studies on the street corner, I had recognized the importance of following social processes through time. In the Phillips Petroleum project, I needed to extend the time line back a quarter century to the early days of the company. We had planned in the Peruvian program to study changes through a five year period. Important changes did take place even in that short period, yet we came to recognize that understanding the dynamics of current social processes required us to extend the time line back many decades or even centuries.

10

Types of Applied Social Research

In spite of the growing interest of students in putting what they learn about the social sciences to some practical use in academia, one still finds the traditional view that the "pure" or basic researcher is more of a scientist than those doing studies designed to benefit particular client organizations. While recognizing the prestige implications of this view, I argue that good or bad science can be practiced in either the pure or applied forms and that there is no reason to believe that purer is better. Since this point has been argued elsewhere by many of us (see, for example, Rossi and Whyte, 1983), I decline to elaborate upon it here. In the final chapter, I consider the general question of the scientific legitimacy of various types of social research.

I believe there are possibilities for learning through applied research that are not available to those who stick to basic research, but those possibilities become apparent only as we recognize that *there are distinctively different types of applied social research.* I categorize these types in terms of the nature of the involvement of the research subjects in the research process.

In basic research, those studied do not participate in the design or implementation of the study or in the interpretation of the results. In terms of the influence the researcher exerts on the subjects, basic research comes in two forms. At one extreme, the researcher seeks to maintain sufficient detachment so as to minimize his or her influence upon the behavior studied. At the other extreme, the researcher seeks to maximize control over the subjects so as to measure the effects of the social experiment imposed on them. At neither extreme do the subjects have any say about what is going on—beyond allowing themselves to be studied.

Applied social research can be done in either of those two forms, but it can also be done in forms in which subjects participate in the research process. The main purpose of this chapter is to explore the potential of participatory forms of applied social research. I find it useful to think in terms ranging from no subject participation (ASR-1) to increasing degrees of subject participation (ASR-2 and ASR-3).

ASR-1: THE RESEARCHER
AS PROFESSIONAL EXPERT

This type differs from basic research mainly in terms of who chooses the problem for study and to what publics the results are to be offered. The basic researcher selects the problem for study and reports the results primarily to professional colleagues. In applied research, decision makers in the client organization invite the researcher to study a problem they select, or the researcher selects the problem and then seeks to persuade the decision makers that they should finance the study. Even when members of the client organization make the selection, it is often necessary for the researcher to reformulate the problem to make it researchable, in which case the client must be persuaded that the reformulation meets the needs of the organization. Although researchers often go on to publish their findings in academic journals, as far as clients are concerned, the project is completed when the researcher has presented conclusions, with an emphasis upon implications for action. How members of the client organization use those conclusions—if they use them at all—is up to them.

ASR-1 is inherently elitist in two respects: (1) The researcher is the expert, telling people what they should do; (2) the researcher is responsible solely to the heads of the client organization, who pay the bill. To be sure, ethical considerations often lead ASR-1 researchers to be concerned about the effects of their work, and committees in the various social science disciplines have standards of professional ethics to guide and limit social researchers, in an effort to safeguard the interests of less powerful people in the client organization. However, these safeguards involve the relation of the researcher's work to his or her conscience and the relations of researchers to colleagues in the discipline. They are not inherent in the relationship between the researcher and the client organization, under ASR-1.

ASR-1 is still probably the most common model for applied social research, and I would not want to rule it out on either scientific or ethical grounds. Clients often want objective answers to questions to help them decide on a policy or action. The researcher may decide against accepting a particular project because of concerns about the ways in which the findings are likely to be used, but that is an ethical rather than a scientific judgment. And, because client organizations draw on financial, engineering, and other technical data in making their decisions, one would hardly argue that it is morally wrong to provide them with the best behavioral science data and ideas we can supply. Clearly it is important for us to do research designed to help answer policy questions.

The action problem arises when the project calls for the researcher to go beyond policy questions in order to help the organization to improve its functioning, over a period of time. When that is the assignment, ASR-1 rarely yields any constructive results. The organization's needs cannot be satisfied with clear-cut factual answers. To contribute to the improved functioning of an organization, the researcher needs not only an understanding of its structure and social processes but also the ability to work effectively with organization members throughout the change process. For that purpose, we must look to other models.

ASR-2: RESEARCH IN AN ORGANIZATION DEVELOPMENT FRAMEWORK

In recent years organization development (OD) has become a popular label for management training. Here the researcher or consultant is generally an outsider, brought in by management, but some large companies have their own OD specialists. The aim is to help management people resolve their problems of communication and interpersonal frictions and sensitize them to the thoughts and feelings of others. Generally OD specialists encourage management to stimulate participation by workers and first line supervisors in order to share some power with lower levels of the organization. In effect, th OD specialist is seeking to teach higher level people how to deal with workers, but without workers being directly involved in the teaching and learning process. Full participation is further limited by two factors: (1) The OD specialist is in charge of the process, and (2) he or she is officially responsible to the organization heads, although the trainer may feel an obligation to serve the interests of workers as well.

I have had enough experience with this model to appreciate its potentials and also to recognize some of the dilemmas it poses. As noted earlier, local union leaders often complain to the researcher that they are unable to get management to understand problems workers face, or appreciate how workers could help solve production problems. Using the researcher as an alternative communication channel, they hope to overcome the blockage in regular channels.

At first I enjoyed the intellectual and social challenges involved in providing that alternative channel. I found it stimulating to devise strategies to interpret my findings to management in ways that would help management, workers, and union leaders solve problems to their mutual satisfaction. I had only modest success along these lines, but, even so, I came to recognize the basic dilemma in my role. The more successful I was, the more the parties became dependent upon me. My successes could deprive them of opportunities to learn how to solve problems themselves.

This is a dilemma commonly faced by organizational consultants. We give lip service to the maxim that the aim of the consultant should be to work himself out of a job—to help the parties to improve their problem solving to the point where the outsider is no longer necessary. On the other hand, success in such an assignment ends the consultant's role in the organization. This tempts the consultant to look for other problems so as to keep working with the organization. This is likely to lead to the definition of problems in terms of the needs of the consultant instead of the needs of the client organization.

I found this an important intellectual and professional challenge. I wanted to find ways in which an outsider could influence an organization, and at the same time increase the abilities of members to define and resolve their problems, with minimal reliance on the outsider.

Early in my research career (1945-1946), I took my first tentative steps in that direction. Upon hearing my talk, "Human Elements in Supervision," Byron Calhoun, vice president and general manager of the Radisson Hotel in Minneapolis, asked me to help recruit a new personnel manager. When I learned that three people had been in and out of that position within the past year, I realized that there was something basically wrong with the position that could not be solved simply by hiring a good personnel man. I proposed an applied research project. I would recommend a personnel man who had been trained within our Committee on Human Relations in Industry at the University of Chicago, if the hotel would also support a full-time human relations researcher. A veteran of the restaurant study, Edith Lentz (later Edith

Lentz Hamilton) became the field worker and kept notes and reports that were seen only by me and by personnel manager Meredith Wiley. I visited the Radisson monthly, and Lentz, or sometimes Wiley, came monthly to Chicago, so the three of us worked closely together (Whyte and Hamilton, 1965).

It was my role as project director and consultant to provide early interpretations of our research to Calhoun and at the same time try to keep the hard-driving executive from pressuring Wiley into activities that would get him bogged down in the conventional functions of a personnel office. As our project became established, Wiley was able to take over much of the consultation with Calhoun. Together, Lentz, Wiley, and I advanced beyond giving advice and began a program of regular discussion meetings between workers and supervisors in the various departments. Starting in the food service departments, when Lentz had done enough interviewing and observing to give us a sense of the state of relations, Wiley would approach a supervisor to suggest the value of group meetings and help the supervisor overcome anxieties by discussing what might be accomplished and how such meetings might best be conducted. Edith Lentz would attend meetings as a nonparticipating observer. Following each meeting, she would seek out a number of the workers to get their reactions and evaluations. This provided Wiley with information and ideas that enabled him to compliment the supervisors on constructive outcomes and also to suggest ways to conduct the meetings more skillfully. We used the same general procedures in dealing with interdepartmental problems. For example, Wiley overcame the chef's initial resistance and got him to attend a meeting with the Coffee Shop waitresses and their supervisors, thus leading to the relief of some persistent friction.

In order to establish some credibility at the top, we began by providing Byron Calhoun with information on practical problems on the work floor, but, beginning with the group meetings, we steadily opened up channels through which workers were getting action on their problems and improving the efficiency of hotel operations. In this way, we were moving beyond ASR-2 and toward ASR-3, but the project did not last long enough to consolidate this changed pattern of organizational behavior. The contract provided a year of support. Calhoun was prepared to finance a second year, but only if Edith Lentz remained with the project; however, she decided to return to her studies at the University of Chicago.

ASR-3: PARTICIPATORY ACTION RESEARCH

In this still new but now rapidly developing field of activity, there may be considerable variation from project to project. Nevertheless, all ASR-3 projects share these features: (1) The professional researcher is responsible not simply to organizational heads, but structures relations so as to be accountable also to lower-level officials and the rank and file. In industry, this may be done particularly by working with and through a union. (2) Organization members at various levels participate in the project design and research process including reporting findings. In what follows, I present case examples of ASR-3.

The Norwegian Industrial Democracy Program

The intellectual stimulus to the Norwegian Industrial Democracy Program came from England through Eric Trist, a social psychologist who has had an extraordinary impact on applied social research throughout the world (Trist, 1981). In his early work with the Tavistock Institute of Human Relations in London, Trist developed the sociotechnical systems framework, which has guided much of the work in subsequent years. The basic idea is that organizational changes can be most effectively brought about through an integrated strategy, in which changes in technology and in human relations are worked out at the same time by the same groups of people. While this notion may now seem obvious, in earlier years social researchers tended to concentrate almost exclusively on human relations. We gave lip service to the importance of technology but tended to treat it as a constant instead of as a variable, which could be changed along with changes in human relations.

The sociotechnical systems framework requires that social researchers and technology specialists work together in any planned change and that workers, who operate the machines and do the work, participate actively in the diagnosis of problems and in the implementation of changes.

Although the first work on sociotechnical systems changes was done in England, Trist stimulated the interest of Scandinavian social researchers, and shortly Norway and Sweden had overtaken England in this rapidly expanding field.

Following Max Elden, I find it useful to recognize "Three Generations of Work-Democracy Experiments in Norway" (Elden, 1979a). In the first generation (1964-1967), the researcher served in the role of expert. Working under a labor-management committee, the researcher analyzed problems, recommended changes, managed the change process, and evaluated the results. In the second generation (1968-early 1970s), the researcher served as a consultant. He was more involved with workers, who participated in working out recommendations and also assumed some responsibility for implementing and evaluating. In the third generation (early 1970s onward), Elden describes the researcher as a "colearner." Employee redesign teams work actively with the researcher to analyze their own organization, to develop recommendations, to implement changes, and to evaluate results.

I had established my own categories before Elden's came to my attention, but I am encouraged to discover the close correspondence bewteen ASR-1, ASR-2, and ASR-3 and his typology of three generations. Here we concentrate on Norwegian third-generation cases.

The ship-redesign program was carried out under the leadership of Einar Thorsrud (1977). The program arose in response to increasing foreign competition, and also because of increasing dissatisfaction among seamen with the conditions of life and work in Norwegian shipping. The Norwegian merchant marine had long been one of the most efficient and largest fleets of any nation, but by the early 1960s the Norwegian competitive position was being undermined by the much lower wages paid on ships from developing nations and those flying "flags of convenience." The distinctive feature of the Norwegian program was its participatory nature. The union was a joint partner with management, and seamen as well as ships' officers were actively involved.

Workers and union leaders were interested in protecting jobs against foreign competition, and, with management, were also concerned about serious human problems. There was a high turnover among seamen, so that it was difficult to maintain adequate crews. Furthermore, although seamen's pay compared favorably with that of shore jobs, the ready availability of employment on shore, combined with the hardships involved in spending weeks and months at sea away from their families, had created a situation in which few seamen remained really committed to a lifelong career. Management and union leaders realized that the problem of turnover was not simply one of making shipboard employment more attractive so as to keep seamen for longer periods. If most of them would inevitably seek employment on shore long before retirement age, planners had to examine shipboard jobs in terms of the extent to which they provided skills and knowledge that might eventually be valuable for shore employment. They recognized that the traditional shipboard social and technical division between the engine room crew and the deck crew had a major impact upon later job opportunities on shore.

Engine room personnel had distinct advantages, since their work in machine operation and maintenance built skills and knowledge that could be applied to manufacturing jobs, whereas the skills of deckhands had no ready application on shore. This led the decision makers to recognize the advantage of breaking down the physical and social barriers separating the engine room from the deck, so that deckhands could learn some of the engine room skills.

There was also interest in changing the traditional organizational hierarchy among officers and that separating officers from seamen, which supported a traditional authoritarian style of leadership.

Thorsrud and his associates recognized that changing the distribution of labor and making the work more interesting and conditions more appealing required basic structural changes in the design of ships. They would have to integrate changes in the physical structure with changes in the distribution of labor, the job descriptions, and styles of managerial leadership.

Thorsrud and his behavioral science associates served as facilitators and resource persons. They designed and guided the social processes involved in problem diagnosis, study of alternatives, evaluation, and decision making. While the researchers participated in various discussions, members of labor and management, including seamen, carried the bulk of the activity in studying current problems, visualizing improved models for the sociotechnical system of the ship, and working out their model in detail. This process went on simultaneously among the crews of several ships. The researchers also promoted ship-to-ship conferences, in which members of the study teams on each ship presented their analyses and preliminary plans to other teams, actively interchanging information and ideas.

The ship-redesign program resulted in major physical and social changes. The structure was changed to provide more comfortable and attractive accommodations for seamen, and to break down the social barriers between deck and engine room and between officers and men. A major change involved substituting a common dining room for all personnel for the eating quarters that had separated officers from men.

In the job descriptions and the assignment of positions, the new model provided for a reduction of personnel, but also for a reduction in the previous rigidities of job descriptions to promote the development of multiskilled workers.

The other projects briefly described here have been reported by Max Elden, an American political scientist who went to Norway to study participatory organizational change. Elden became so well integrated into Norwegian society that he became head of the Institute for Social Research in Industry in Trondheim, a sister institution to the Institute for Work Research in Oslo, directed by Einar Thorsrud.

The bank project arose when leaders of labor and management recognized that technological changes had been having major effects upon bank organization and functioning (Elden, 1983). Elden first met with representatives from labor and management to devise an interview form for the diagnosis of problems. He then interviewed employees, supervisors, and managers and to summarize the identification and perception of problems at all levels. Although the interviewing was done entirely by the researcher, Elden (personal correspondence) writes that "representatives from management and the employees determined both the research design and most significantly the interpretation of the data that resulted from the interview round."

The analysis of the responses yielded an important theoretical and practical outcome: the establishment of what Elden calls "local theory." In the past, social researchers have generally been concerned with theory only insofar as they have tried to develop an adequate social theory to account for the phenomena studied. We have tended to overlook the fact that people working in an organization necessarily have their own theories about what is going on and how the organization functions, although they do not use the word "theory." Elden argues that unless social researchers understand the local theories that guide the behavior of the actors in the organization, they will be seriously handicapped in helping to devise a change strategy to resolve the problems perceived by organization members.

It is important to recognize that in this case—and probably in any complex organization—there is not simply a single "local theory." Elden found that top management had its own local theory, whereas employees had another. There were some points of overlap, but, for the employees and management people to get together on a mutually acceptable plan of action, they had to recognize the existence of two local theories. This recognition required discussions in which employees and management people worked toward a local theory that would encompass the problems perceived by both parties.

Elden interprets the local theories in the bank:

> If one tries to map the employees' theory onto the managers' theory, one finds that at the center of each theory is the same complex of problems. Its implications however are much more developed in the employees' theory: theirs is richer, more complex and more extensive. The important result concerning action potential is that the employees' theory included the two action possibilities suggested by management, plus numerous additional possibilities. By the way, this does not indicate that managers were simple-minded or stupid concerning workplace problems. It is more likely that they are too remote from the worker's situation to have a refined and complex theory about it. I would guess that if the workers are asked to describe the managers' work situation, then the workers' theory would be equally .simplistic compared to the managers' theory of managerial work. The main point is that with only minimal external support people can develop a quite adequate theory of their own situation. Usually their theory is more comprehensive and action-oriented than the theory of outsiders regardless of how much expertise these outsiders have [personal correspondence].

When Elden helped employees and managers to recognize and integrate the two local theories and then agree on remedial actions, the parties devised their own solutions to the technical and human problems of the bank. The project resulted in a number of major changes, including delegation of responsibilities from officers to employees, a new plan covering absences, appointment of an assistant manager of customer services, a physical shift in the location of the office manager's office, and some degree of "flexitime" in work scheduling.

Elden (1979: 249) explains:

> Perhaps more important than any of the single concrete changes is the way the change process itself operated. Initiative clearly rested with the employees themselves. They developed their own strategy, designed changes, and saw to it that these were tested out in consultation with those affected. If we compare this kind of employee-managed change with the unilateral way that managers decided about the changes implied by the new computer technology less than a year previously, we see what might be called a democratization of the change process itself.

The aluminum industry technological change study was a project carried out by Elden and his associates at the request of the union, with the active participation of union leaders and members and without the participation of management (Elden, 1983). The study documented three major technological changes that had taken place during the preceding 25 years. Up to this point, the union leaders and workers had simply reacted to changes planned and introduced by management. The union leaders had become increasingly concerned about the impact of these technological changes on job security and the quality of working life. In order to play a more active role in the planning and introduction of future changes, the union leaders thought it essential to gain systematic knowledge of the course of technological change in the three preceding decades and its impact on workers and their jobs. Elden and Morton Levin worked with a committee of local union leaders and workers to design the study. Much could be learned about the nature of the various technologies through examination of publications and other reports. A major part of the process involved social researchers helping workers design a systematic study of changes in the nature of work as reflected in official job descriptions written by the company over 25 years. To supplement these data, workers interviewed high seniority coworkers about the nature of jobs and job-related problems under the earlier technologies.

It is important to note that the workers developed their own categories of needed information regarding jobs under each technology. In other words, instead of using the research literature to establish the categories of relevant information, the workers, with help from social scientists, built the categories on the basis of those characteristics that made sense to them—that is, that were derived from their own local theory. This was an extension of the local theory idea from the bank project.

This project not only supplied union leaders and members with systematic information on technological changes and their social impacts and enabled them to deal more effectively with management on future technological changes. In the process, workers developed competence in systematic analysis of the nature of jobs from the standpoint of worker interests. Workers reached two important conclusions: (1) Most of the benefits of previous technological changes had accrued to the company in the form of increased productivity, and (2) the workers' physical working environment improved, but the changes had an adverse impact upon their social psychological environment (social contacts, learning opportunities, challenging work, and so on). As a direct result, the union was able to stop the acquisition of a new technology until a full-fledged quality of working life assessment was made—with participation by workers and union leaders.

The Sky River Project

The Sky River project (Kennedy, 1982) did not begin as research but its creator, Timothy Kennedy, is using it for his doctoral thesis. He began work in Alaska as a VISTA volunteer and then extended his stay with the Eskimos eleven years to work on organization and community development projects. Kennedy's experience as an organizer led him to identify three types of change agent roles that can be played by outsiders: power broker, liberal advocate, and facilitator.[1]

Although Eskimos do not consider themselves Indians, in some parts of Eskimo territory the Bureau of Indian Affairs is an important and powerful organization. The local representative of the BIA may act the role of power broker, seeing himself as an intermediary between the Eskimos and the bureaucracy. That is, he takes it upon himself to interpret the needs and interests of the Eskimos to his organizational superiors and interpret the policies of the bureaucracy to the Eskimos. The head of the local school, always in the past a non-Eskimo, can also play this power broker role.

The liberal advocate seeks to deal with the political and economic establishment on a confrontational basis. He tries to organize the Eskimos (or workers or peasants) so that he can lead them in making demands for change.

From the outset of his experience in Alaska, Kennedy was hostile to power brokers, seeing them as maintaining the dependency relationship that had kept the Eskimos powerless and divided. He began his work as a liberal advocate but lost faith in this role. He came to realize that, if he was successful in organizing Eskimos to exert pressure on the bureaucracy, this served to reinforce the Eskimos' dependency relationship—but they would be depending upon the liberal advocate rather than the power broker. Observing other liberal advocates, he became convinced that their confrontational strategy tended to build up resistance among bureaucrats and politicians, some of whom sincerely wanted to understand the Eskimos and respond to their needs and interests. He also noted the burnout phenomenon, which is probably common among liberal advocates. They see themselves as self-sacrificing individuals, serving the common people. This self-conception may support them for a while, particularly if their organizing efforts produce some movement from the establishment, but sooner or later the inherent weaknesses of the role manifest themselves. The "common people" are quite content to follow the liberal advocate when he or she is successful, but take no initiative themselves. If the next project proposed by the liberal advocate fails, support for him or her crumble. This leads the liberal advocate to become disillusioned and cynical, feeling something like, "After all I have done for them, is this all the reward I get?" The liberal advocate then abandons the struggle and settles for some more conventional role.

Kennedy came to see the basic problem as the dependency of the Eskimos and the misguided paternalism of government. It was in this context that he worked out the role of facilitator.

Kennedy arrived at this diagnosis of Eskimo culture, social organization, and communication problems:

(1) Eskimos tend to live in small villages, isolated from each other, with little intervillage recognition of shared problems.
(2) Eskimo culture is group oriented and highly egalitarian. The individual who stands out from the group is rejected and cannot exercise any real leadership.
(3) Communication between Eskimos and bureaucrats or politicians is hampered and distorted by physical and social distances.

Bureaucrats and politicians do make an effort to get around the country and talk with Eskimos face to face, but, given the great distances, the outside official cannot afford to spend much time in any one place. He or she therefore resorts to calling public hearings and meetings so as to meet with a number of Eskimos in a short period of time, flying into a village, spending two or three hours talking to the inhabitants, and then flying to the next village.

Kennedy provides a picture of the typical public hearing or meeting between the government official or politician and the Eskimo villagers. If the outside official had someone precede him into the community to organize the public hearing, that individual would look for Eskimos who would speak up. Inevitably he would pick the more aggressive Eskimos who were already partly alienated from their own culture and could in no sense be considered representatives of their fellows. If no advance preparations were made and the official made an introductory statement and then asked Eskimos about their concerns, invariably it would be one of these more aggressive individuals who would speak up. In some cases, that individual might be an official of the village, which would lead outsiders to assume that he was a leader—but Kennedy discovered that the Eskimo word for such individuals meant "playboss." They played the role of leader to the outsiders but had no influence with their fellow Eskimos.

Kennedy (1982: 36) describes how he came to turn against the liberal advocate role and seek to develop a more participatory role:

> Advocates frequently act as a buffer between community members and decision-makers. In so doing they unwittingly protect officials from being directly accountable to constituents, thus making it easier for them to ignore the consequences of their actions. This negative aspect of advocacy became apparent to me when I confronted a BIA official on the culturally irrelevant readers used by the BIA day schools. It seemed obvious that these readers, showing a very white Dick and Jane living in a comfortable middle-class neighborhood, could only serve as a hindrance to learning, and would reinforce the Eskimo children's already low image of themselves and their culture. The BIA official listened very politely to my comments, thanked me for my input, and then summarily dismissed what I said. He then proceeded to inform me that in his eighteen years of serving Native Alaskans he had never heard even one complaint from an Eskimo or Indian parent about the readers. He was not about to let a young "cheechako" influence his opinions, and his response was in some ways perfectly understandable. After all, his constituency was Native Alaskans, not VISTA Volunteers.
>
> While I had my doubts about how this particular official would have responded to direct complaints, the encounter certainly raised some interesting questions. For instance: how could officials be made more accountable for their actions? Was I really representing the interests of the villagers, or was I setting my own agenda, meeting my own needs? Weren't advocates such as myself actually preventing the citizen participation we espoused? How could responsible bureaucrats, those who are genuinely interested in being responsive to community needs, be brought together with villagers so that direct interaction could occur? Why was it that community members could articulate very coherent ideas about local problems and solutions to me during informal conversations, and then remain mute during official meetings on the same issues?

By the time Kennedy was ready to try to stimulate effective communication between Eskimos and bureaucrats and politicians, he had helped the Eskimos organize a fish processing cooperative on the Yukon

River. The cooperative was so successful that it drove out of business a private firm headquartered in Seattle. By now, Kennedy enjoyed the friendship and trust of increasing numbers of Eskimos, but he resolved not to use these sentiments to build his own power. Instead, he set about developing a way to build community organization and strengthen Eskimo communication to government.

With support from the Office of Economic Opportunity, Kennedy went about putting modern technology at the service of the people. His organizational model went through thirteen steps.

(1) Presenting to the community the idea for the project. Kennedy arranged to meet with villagers to explain his plan to help them use videotape and film technology to strengthen their communication with the authorities and help them to understand and organize themselves better. They agreed to work with him, presumably, more because they trusted Kennedy than because they had a very clear idea of what was going to happen.

(2) Demystifying the technology. Kennedy believed that this approach would only be successful if the Eskimos came to regard the technology as something they could handle themselves, rather than a specialized instrument from another culture. Therefore, after demonstrating briefly the battery-operated videotape recording equipment, Kennedy invited several of the adults to use it to film their children at play or anything else they wished. He also suggested that they focus not only upon their problems but also upon the aspects of Eskimo life that they took pride in.

(3) Community group discussions to select one high priority problem. Recognizing that the villagers could not operate effectively on all of their problems at once, he encouraged them to choose one particular problem that was most urgent.

(4) Videotaping of group discussion of the selected problem and the proposed solution. Here the villagers expressed their problems in their own way but did not stop there; going beyond complaining, they proposed concrete actions.

(5) Group viewing of videotape. The villagers viewed the tape and decided whether it adequately and accurately represented their views. Kennedy granted them full power to edit the tape or to reject it and start over. It was essential that they accept ownership of the videotape rather

than let it appear to outsiders as a documentary prepared by a film expert.

(6) Group selection of spokesperson. The group selected the person they believed could most faithfully represent their views.

(7) Interview of the spokesperson on the designated problem. In the early stages of the project, Kennedy did the interviewing, and his Eskimo apprentice learning the process so that later he could carry on independently. So as to give the spokesperson full control over the process, Kennedy invited him to select the time and the physical setting in which he felt most comfortable. For example, in the film on the high school problem, William Trader chose to be interviewed in the backyard of his home while he was repairing his fishing net.

(8) Viewing of film or videotape by the spokesperson and the group. Again the Eskimos had full power to edit the tape or require that the filming be done over. Before the tape or film was shown beyond the group, the spokesperson had to be satisfied that the tape fully and adequately represented his views. Similarly, members of the group had to agree that the tape fairly and accurately represented the views of their community. Kennedy formalized these agreements by asking the spokesperson and members of the group to sign a document affirming that the tape represented their common views. This document was important, not only because it gave the Eskimos a tangible sense of ownership of the tape, but also because it represented evidence that the film was an authentic communication of Eskimo views.

(9) Group decision of where and how the tape will be shown. The Eskimos needed to know which individuals and which government agency had the responsibility and power to act on their complaints and proposals. Here Kennedy served as a resource person, providing essential background information about the structure of the State Government and the responsibilities of key officials. However, he refrained from urging them to take any particular course of action.

(10) Showing of tape to designated government officials. In the early stages of the project, Kennedy and his Eskimo apprentice went, unaccompanied by other Eskimos, to show the tape to the officials. As the program became better known and stirred up wide interest both among Eskimos and officials, the tapes were shown at regional meetings bringing together larger numbers of Eskimos and officials of agencies concerned with the problem.

(11) Videotaping the answers to the Eskimos from the key official responsible for the problem area. Here Kennedy not only offered the official the right to reply in his own way, he also granted the official the same rights to view the tape, to edit it, or to have it redone in case he was not fully satisfied. Kennedy explained to the officials that he was not there to put them on the spot—as is characteristic of investigative reporting—but to facilitate authentic communication between the Eskimos and the officials.

(12) Community viewing of the government response. The tape of the response from the official now returned to the community that had produced the original tape. After viewing the response, the Eskimos had an opportunity to discuss what they had accomplished, what more needed to be done, and what the next step should be.

(13) Showing of the videotapes in neighboring villages. Here the tape embodying the community articulation of a key problem was shown, along with the tape of the government response, in several neighboring communities. This was followed by discussions with representatives of the initiating community present to provide further background.

The Sky River project produced an extraordinary series of changes in relations between the Eskimos and the government and among the Eskimos themselves. For example, the videotape on the high school problem was only 15 minutes long, but in it William Trader not only discussed the problem but had selected a final scene of Eskimo parents bidding goodbye to their children, who were boarding the plane to be flown out to schools in Oregon or Oklahoma. No viewer could fail to grasp the traumatic experience imposed upon Eskimo families by the current educational policies. Before this time, educational authorities had considered the possibility of building rural high schools for Eskimos but had rejected the project as too costly. Since they had heard no complaints from Eskimos, they had no reason to think that the Eskimos were dissatisfied. The initial showing of the tape to education officials reopened the question and led directly to a $149 million high school building program.

In another case, the Eskimos were concerned about the frequent breakdowns of electrical power in some of their communities. The electricity was supplied through a loan from the Rural Electrification Administration to the Alaskan Village Electrification Cooperative (AVEC). The work was done at a time when REA officials in Washington were very conscious of environmental concerns and had therefore decreed that power lines be laid underground. When the engineers began work in rural Alaska, some Eskimos advised against the plan, pointing out that the ground heaving under permafrost conditions would rupture the cables. The construction people had their orders and proceeded to lay the cables underground. To demonstrate to the REA the folly of this decision, the Eskimos filmed a small group talking about the problem, standing on both sides of a rift in the snow and earth.

By this time REA in Washington had received complaints over ruptured cables from 35 villages, but all had been referred to the REA officials who had made the original feasibility study so the complaints had been buried along with the cables. The manager of AVEC had recognized the validity of the complaints but had been unable to move Washington. Delighted with the film, he secured permission to take it to Washington. Shortly after the showings, REA abandoned the cable program and accepted the Eskimo suggestion to authorize AVEC to string overhead wires connecting village homes to local oil-fired generators.

The Eskimos had complained about the houses constructed for them by the government, but the head of the housing authority had responded with an engineering study that claimed the walls were insulated adequately and that no floor sagged more than a quarter of an inch. The Eskimos countered with a videotape showing ice forming on the interior walls of several homes. To demonstrate the sagging floor problem, an Eskimo placed a child's kaleidoscope against one wall and released it, whereupon it rolled down to the middle of the room and up almost to the opposite wall. The camera followed it as it rolled back and forth.

When this tape was shown to the board of directors responsible for the Eskimo housing program, it precipitated a long and heated meeting. When the executive still refused to acknowledge any serious deficiencies, the board voted to discharge him and to change the program to meet the Eskimo complaints.

The showing of films and tapes from village to village had dramatic effects upon intervillage relations. Previously, these villages had been separated by physical distance and rivalries. The villagers had not recognized that they had common problems. Now as these tapes were shown, villagers pitched into the subsequent discussion to testify that the problems depicted by the people of Emanok were their problems also. This led some of them to make their own videotapes elaborating on the work previously done. This kind of interchange forged links that enabled Eskimos from large numbers of villages to establish regional organizations to consult on common problems and exercise collective pressure on the government.

Today we find frequent reports in the media that the Eskimos are no longer passive, they are organizing to do things for themselves and to press the government to be more responsive to their needs and interests. No one can claim that the Sky River Project alone is responsible for this major advance, but it seems clear that the Project did stimulate Eskimo organization.

Cornell's New Systems of Work and Participation Program

Since 1975 I have been working with Cornell colleagues and students in what we called the New Systems of Work and Participation Program.

We got involved in a major study of the Mondragón cooperative complex in the Basque country of Spain. Ana Gutiérrez-Johnson (a graduate student from Peru) and I were the first to publish research in English on Mondragón (Johnson and Wayne, 1977; Whyte, 1982). The Mondragón complex has grown from one worker cooperative founded in 1956 by five men with eighteen coworkers, to a system of industrial, construction, service, and agricultural cooperatives that at the end of 1982 numbered almost 100, with close to 16,000 worker-members, associated with a cooperative bank, housing cooperatives, a cooperative educational program, and a research and development coop.

Since the conventional wisdom among social scientists had long held that worker cooperatives were not a viable form of organization (Blumberg, 1968: 3-4), we thought it important to understand the operating principles and social processes that had made possible Mondragón extraordinary success. Perhaps the lessons we could draw from this case might help activists develop successful worker cooperatives in the United States and elsewhere. This is indeed happening as increasing numbers of people seek to learn and apply the lessons of Mondragón. But that is a story to be told elsewhere. Here I shall focus on the researchers' direct involvement in action programs in private industry and in employee owned firms.

With Christopher Meek, a graduate assistant and then research associate (now at Brigham Young University), for five years I was involved with the Jamestown Area Labor-Management Committee. This is a communitywide program established by a very creative mayor, Stanley Lundine (now congressman), who brought labor and management leaders together to arrest the steady decline of what seemed to be a dying industrial city through saving plants that were going out of business and through developing labor-management cooperation to improve productivity and quality of working life (Whyte et al., 1983).

We studied a number of other cases of saving jobs through a shift to employee ownership: Byers Transport, Ltd., Vermont Asbestos Group, Saratoga Knitting Mill and the Mohawk Valley Community Corporation, the latter two in New York State. In this period we were also gathering whatever we could from the media and from colleagues' reports on this emerging trend of employee buyouts, which began in some numbers only in the 1970s.

As we were studying cases of job saving through employee buyouts, some of us were also trying to help workers and union leaders take action in other shutdown situations. In two cases where we were involved, we were unsuccessful, yet the experience yielded valuable information and ideas. Through comparing successful and unsuccessful employee buyout attempts (Stern and Hammer, 1978), we were learning about the combination of resources and activities necessary for success.

We began to move more deeply into applied work when we learned about Rath Packing Company, headquartered in Waterloo, Iowa, which had been a major meat producer. Rath had been going down hill with increasing speed in the 1970s, but the company still had about 3,000 employees, mainly in Waterloo, and was 499 on the Fortune 500 list. It wasn't its size that attracted us; rather, it was the contrast between what was happening at Rath and the characteristics of other cases familiar to us.

Up to this time the cases we studied or heard about all had this in common: the leaders of the drive to save the plant through an employee buyout had been members of local management, sometimes with the close collaboration of community leaders. Workers had gone along. Local union leaders cooperated with management and made no demands for participation or control. International union officials wrung their hands, not knowing what to do.

Although the workers at first made no demands for participation or control, if they were in fact excluded from any participation after they became owners, eventually the contradiction between sharing in ownership and not sharing in management in any form began to get to them. Some dramatic conflicts arose out of this contradiction. At Vermont Asbestos Group there was a shift in management with the hero of the job-saving campaign, John Lupien, being fired. We believe that Lupien was ousted because his leadership of VAG made no allowance for worker participation. Whenever anybody asked Lupien if he had thought about worker participation, he had a stock answer: "If you own stock in General Motors, that doesn't give you the right to run General Motors." True enough, but we figured that anybody who could see a close analogy between General Motors and a company of 170 employees who owned 80 percent of the stock was heading for trouble. Later other well-publicized conflicts were to occur: a strike of South Bend Lathe and at one plant of the Okonite Corporation (Whyte et al., 1983).

We first heard about Rath from Randy Barber, then with the Citizens Business Commission in Washington, D.C. He had been part of our academic/activist network on employee ownership, and had been involved in our abortive efforts to make employee ownership happen. Barber called to tell me: "I've just been out to Waterloo where something exciting is going on. I talked to Lyle Taylor, President of Local 46 of the United Food and Commercial Workers Union, and Chuck Mueller, Chief Steward. They are trying to buy the Rath Packing Company to keep it from going down the tube. They are interested in control as well as ownership, and they need all the help they can get. Could you do something?" I immediately sent Lyle Taylor (April 16, 1979) a letter, congratulating him on what he was trying to do and offering our assistance. We also sent him some of our research reports. I learned later that Chief Steward Mueller read the materials with interest.

In May of 1979 Professors Tove Hammer and Robert Stern went to Waterloo to explore the possibilities of including Rath in a new research project. At the time, they were not thinking of applied research. They were beginning a study of the role of workers on company boards of directors or employee stock ownership trusts. Since few such cases yet existed in the United States and the union leaders at Rath proposed to place workers on the board of their company, Rath promised to be important to their research design.

On the evening of their first day in Waterloo, Hammer and Stern had dinner with the Charles Muellers. The chief steward asked for their help "We're at a critical point—the negotiating committee is trying to decide what form of ownership and control we will accept when we get 60 percent of the stock." Through payroll deductions of $20 per week, workers would own newly issued stock which would constitute 60 percent of the total, 40 percent remaining in private hands. He continued, "The company lawyer and our own lawyer have advised us that the only practical way to go is with the usual stock ownership arrangement: one share of stock, one vote, no trust, no way of consolidating worker voting power. The negotiating committee stands nine to one for going this way, and I'm the one that's holding out. Can you come in and talk the negotiating committee out of this?" My colleagues said, as I would have myself, "We don't think we should intervene in internal union politics, but if you'd like us to sit down with the negotiating committee and review what we've learned about ownership and control in past cases of employee ownership, that we'd be happy to do." And that was arranged. They went into an extraordinarily productive seminar. They did not exhort the union leaders to do anything, but simply laid out what happens when you follow the conventional route. Sooner or later individual employee stock owners let it slip away from them. They soon lose any chance for control. If it survives, the company reverts to private ownership.

After my colleagues left town, the negotiating committee reconvened and voted ten to nothing to insist upon a stock ownership trust, which would be structured in a novel way. The trustees would vote the 60 percent of the stock owned by the employees, and the trustees would be elected by the workers on a one-worker, one-vote basis. In other words, they plugged the principle of a worker cooperative into this employee stock ownership plan.

They had already agreed on the board of directors. The six people representing private management would become a minority. Ten people would be chosen by the union. Tove Hammer, to her surprise, was nominated by the union. After some hesitation over whether her action role would contaminate the design of the worker-directors study, she accepted. (She agreed that Stern would conduct the interviews at Rath.) Since June of 1980 she has been a participant observer in a very critical position in this landmark case. While many boards of directors are rubber stamps for management, this board has had to change the orientation and mode of operation of the whole company. So, while Hammer has been doing her best to help them, she has been a participant observer, busily writing notes throughout the meetings and compiling a unique record.

We also became involved at lower levels. Chris Meek joined Warner Woodworth from Brigham Young to propose a labor-management cooperative problem solving program, based on the Jamestown model.

I joined them at one point (November 1979) to help management to accept the idea of cooperation even before the shift in power.

Meek and/or Woodworth were in Waterloo every month for two to three days, helping the parties to set up the top level joint steering committee for the cooperation program, the joint long-range planning committee, and the action research teams in the various departments. In this case the word "research" is not a misnomer because the workers were not just giving offhand comments. Workers, union stewards, and supervisors met together (generally on their own time) to analyze problems and devise solutions. Following the appointment of former union leader Lyle Taylor as president and chief executive officer of Rath in March 1983, Meek spent two summer months at Waterloo to work on an intensive management training program and on the research documentation of the case.

We cannot call Rath successful from a financial standpoint. In November 1983, Rath was forced to seek protection from its creditors under Chapter 11 of the Bankruptcy Act and, at this writing, workers and management are struggling to find ways to avoid the final shutdown. However, to put this in context, we should note that employee ownership at Rath was established under extraordinarily adverse conditions. The meat packing industry was in financial difficulties even before the onset of the most severe post-World War II recession, beginning in 1981. In the late 1970s, widespread plant closings and company bankruptcies were reported.

Meek has documented productivity improvements of approximately 20 percent in manufacturing operations, but at Rath production costs constitute only about 15 percent of total company costs. In such a situation, productivity improvements in the factory can be overwhelmed by rising material costs (the price of hogs, principally), high interest payments, and inefficiencies in marketing and business administration.

At most, we can say that the shift to employee ownership and the cooperative program enabled Rath to maintain jobs for a majority of those employed in 1980 for more than three years, whereas without those changes all those jobs would have been lost.

The Xerox-Amalgamated Job Preservation Program

Since the early 1940s human relations researchers have been speaking and writing about the potential benefits of worker participation for both management and workers, but for years we could get few management people to take these ideas seriously (Whyte, 1983). The feats of production of our "great arsenal of democracy" during World War II gave U.S. managers enormous prestige all around the world, and productivity teams from many countries came seeking the secrets of U.S. know-how. Since U.S. managers already had the answers, why should they listen to workers or professors?

That situation has dramatically changed within the last ten years. Foreign competition, and particularly the Japanese challenge, have turned complacency into insecurity. Having discovered that Japan's success depends in part upon a much fuller utilization of the total human resources of the firm—including the brains of workers—thousands of U.S. companies have sought to catch up by instituting their own participation programs. Manifestations of this surge of interest are currently found under various titles: quality circles, quaity of working life programs, employee involvement, and so on. Whatever the title, such programs aim to encourage worker participation in decisions on shop floor problems.

In most of these programs, the scope of worker participation is severely limited, as matters covered by the labor contract and by managerial prerogatives are excluded from the discussion process. Furthermore, for fear that workers and union leaders will see this as just a new approach to getting workers to work harder, management has concentrated primarily on improved quality, reduced absenteeism and turnover, increased job satisfaction, and fewer grievances, thus avoiding a focus on the tough but touchy problems of productivity and costs.

It is widely believed that these efforts have yielded benefits to both labor and management, but hard evidence is scarce (Katz et al., 1983). Our Cornell research suggests that, when participation is confined within the customary limits, the changes achieved will be relatively minor, and many such programs will prove to be passing fads, abandoned when managers and workers lose interest.

This analysis indicates why we consider the Xerox-Amalgamated Job Preservation Program of special importance. Here the Xerox management and the Amalgamated Clothing and Textile Workers Union broke through the customary barriers to carry out joint programs to reduce costs and save jobs (Lazes and Costanza, 1983).

A consulting psychologist in organizational development, Peter Lazes, has served as trainer and facilitator for the Xerox program, through a contract with Cornell University. A Quality of Working Life program was introduced into several Xerox plants, and, by the time our story begins, QWL had gained some modest successes and, more important, the confidence of workers and union leaders and managers.

In assessing its competitive position, Xerox management found that the company could buy from vendors components produced in one department for $3.2 million less than the current annual production costs in that department, a saving of slightly over 25 percent. Management therefore informed the union of its intention to buy these components and lay off 180 workers in the department affected. Encouraged by Lazes, the union leaders responded by proposing a joint study to determine the possibilities of cutting production costs enough to save the jobs. Management people saw little chance of effecting such a marked improvement through a cooperative project but agreed to give it a try.

The QWL program was structured in three tiers, with joint representation at each level: Labor/Management Policy and Planning Committee, Labor/Management Departmental Steering Committees, and Labor/Management Problem Solving Teams. Until the Policy and Planning Committee agreed upon the job-saving project, members of Problem Solving Teams (composed of the foreman and workers) had been meeting for two hours a week to diagnose, analyze, and solve problems in their particular work areas. They were limited not only by time but also by policies that placed matters affecting company policy or the labor agreement out of bounds.

So as to provide the time and scope necessary for working on such a major problem, labor and management agreed to set up an 8-person team to devote full time for six months to the study—and without any policy or contractual restrictions. The team consisted of 6 workers, 1 manager, and 1 engineer. When the project was announced, 160 of the 180 workers volunteered. Examining records of work experience and interviewing 20 of the volunteers, the union leaders selected 6 as representative of the various skills and jobs involved. Before the final decision, leaders of labor and management exchanged lists of nominees so as to check for any possible personality conflicts within the proposed team.

The team had complete access to all company records and all company people. Beyond the company, team members visited three plants capable of producing the components manufactured in the Xerox department. In addition to consulting with workers and supervisors individually in the department, team members held regular reporting meetings with all workers and supervisors. These meetings also allowed people not on the team to make valuable suggestions and criticisms.

At the end of the six-month study period, the team presented to labor and management a plan producing over $3.5 million in annual savings. Major savings were made in the redeployment of workers and the consolidation of jobs. The team proposed a number of improvements in equipment, in the use of space, heat, and lighting, and in the reduction of scrap. The reduction in production control and company overhead costs of over half a million dollars is especially significant in indicating the scope of the project. Here the team had to negotiate with higher management to eliminate unnecessary services and absorb within the department functions that had been performed by staff people reporting to higher levels of management. In other words, the project not only reached its cost-cutting goal, but also opened up a reexamination of relations and functions within the management organization far above the departmental level. Furthermore, the savings were achieved without cutting worker pay or fringe benefits.

This was not a study submitted to management by an outside expert. Workers and management members of the team, in full consultation with their fellow workers and managers, analyzed the problem, evaluated a wide range of options, presented a written report, and then persuaded management to take the actions necessary to save 180 jobs. The outsider, Peter Lazes, did not devise the technical solutions. Instead, he played the vital facilitator role essential to participatory action research. He conducted training sessions on worker-management cooperation and group problem-solving methods with members of the team. He sat with them in many discussion meetings, not telling them what to do, but intervening occasionally when they hit road blocks, to help them to develop a social process that would enable them to overcome both technical and interpersonal problems. He also consulted with leaders of labor and management and with team members so as to help them to structure a social process that would yield solutions that were both technically and financially adequate and that were socially acceptable.

The significance of this project can be appreciated best in the context of concession bargaining that became a common management program in the early 1980s. In this period, management negotiators would argue that the company could not survive or could not retain current levels of employment unless the union agreed to major cuts in pay and benefits. This appealed to many management people because it enabled them to take the offensive in bargaining and also because of its conceptual simplicity. To open its offensive, management simply had to figure the number of dollars of savings needed, divide this figure by the number of workers involved, and then calculate the percentage of cuts in each pay package. This also reflected a generally popular strategy of "blaming the victim." That is, the deteriorating competitive position of the company was blamed entirely on the workers, who were therefore called upon to make the entire sacrifice.

Instead, the parties recognized that productivity and costs in this department were *mutual responsibilities* of both labor and management and therefore established a cooperative project, which enabled them to solve their problems without cutting the pay of workers.

Success in this project has institutionalized this strategy of problem solving at Xerox. The union was able to persuade management to accept a new contract provision on job security. In any future case in which the company can purchase components below the costs of manufacturing them, before contracting out the work, management will collaborate with the union in setting up a joint study team. Thus, Xerox jobs will be lost only if the study team fails to work out a practical plan for reducing costs to competitive levels. At this writing, such joint study teams are well advanced in projects to reduce costs in three other departments. With the guidance of Lazes, Xerox management and union have gone far beyond shop level improvements in the quality of working life, effecting fundamental transformations in styles of managerial leadership and in the nature of labor relations.

This Xerox experience, along with our work on employee ownership, had led us to establish Programs on Employment and Workplace Systems (PEWS), codirected by Lazes, Whyte, Donald Kane (director of management programs), and Robert Schrank (author of *Ten Thousand Working Days*). PEWS is based in the Division of Extension and Public Service of the New York State School of Industrial and Labor Relations, but we also hope to involve members of the teaching and research faculty and students in developing a program of participatory action research. Our various field experiences have encouraged us to go beyond a project-to-project focus, in order to build within the university a continuing commitment and capacity to work with labor, management, and community leaders in job creation and maintenance.

CONCLUSIONS

Max Elden commented on my rough draft (personal correspondence):

> It is only in participatory research where the people who supply the data also learn from the results of analyzing it. They learn on their own terms, in their own language, and at their own speed. I have found that describing different research approaches from the point of view of "who learns" is a useful way to distinguish between ASR-1-2-and 3.

> ASR-1 is not useful in local change because it does not help people understand their immediate world. Mostly social science aims at producing general theory of the type we find in physical and natural sciences. This type of theory does not explain a specific situation in a way that facilitates change by the people in that situation. Hence "local theory."

> For me, the major difference between ASR-2 and ASR-3 is in the goal of the research enterprise. Participatory research aims at helping people learn about their immediate context *and* mobilize to change it. ASR-3 therefore requires language and concepts *from* that context. In other words, social science "for the people" uses everyday natural language (i.e. non-technical terms and no social science jargon) as much as possible and is grounded in the experience of the people as they themselves work with and understand it. At the same time that one emphasizes everyday language one also seeks to adhere to the basis rules of sound scientific enquiry. I have often thought that if we were to call this a technical title it might be something like "Cooperatively Evolved Grounded Theory."

Social scientists may assume that people in organizations we study do not have any theories to guide them. In fact, people cannot make sense of the world around them and act in any coherent way without some theory. The problem is that local theory is seldom explicitly articulated by the practitioners. They do not tell us, "I will do X because the ABC theory tells me to do so." We have to discover the nature of the local theory from observing what people do and getting them to explain their actions and beliefs.

As Elden pointed out, in any hierarchical organization we are bound to find that the local theories of managers and workers are different though overlapping. To help the parties solve their problems, the facilitator helps them to integrate the two separate local theories into one more comprehensive theory.

This does not mean that the social scientist abandons the aim of advancing social science theory. It does mean that, if we are able to make use of social science theory in action situations, we must be able to integrate it in our own minds with local theories.

The basic researcher who carries out a social experiment in the field has opportunities to study that would not exist except for his or her intervention. However, since field experiments are very difficult to design and carry out, the literature reports few such cases. Especially in its ASR-3 form, applied social research offers much broader opportunities to study situations that would not exist except for the involvement of the researchers. Without such involvement, the changes described in the Norwegian Industrial Democracy Program, in the Sky River Project, and in Rath Packing Company would not have taken place. While it does not allow the apparent scientific rigor of a well-executed experiment, participatory action research greatly extends the variety of situations available for study. At the same time ASR-3 advances knowledge for researchers, it greatly enriches learning opportunities for organization members who work with us in designing, implementing, and evaluating research.

NOTE

1. Because the term "facilitator" implies a more passive role than Kennedy played, he prefers a term taken from French usage—"social animator"—but that sounds awkward to me in English.

11

Ethics in Field Research
and Publication

$\mathbf{F}$ield research involves us in many ethical problems. We operate in a complex and shifting field as we go about establishing relations with individuals and organizations, making (or avoiding) commitments, keeping (or breaking) those commitments.

There are several sets of relations that must be of concern to field workers:

(1) with sponsors of the project,
(2) with the subjects of the study (in general and especially with those few who serve as gatekeepers and/or collaborators), and
(3) with colleagues whose own research can be hindered or blocked if we arouse strong hostilities in the field.

When we are doing research abroad, especially in developing nations, there are special problems in developing and maintaining relations with our colleagues and students. Then there is the question underlying all field work: Do we have a right to manipulate the subjects of our research in order to advance our studies?

Out of lively debates on professional ethics, various disciplines have established their own codes of ethics (see, for example, the Code of the American Sociological Association, *Footnotes,* 1982). I find such general codes useful but of limited value. Abstract rules are hard to apply in

---

Author's Note: Some material in this chapter is adapted from Whyte (1969a).

the field. It may be more helpful to deal with ethical issues in the context of my own experience. Let me make it clear that I am not reporting on my own behavior as a model for others—except as they may be able to learn from my ethical transgressions, as well as from what seem to me the more successful ways in which I have learned to handle these problems.

RELATIONS WITH SPONSORS

In my first study on the street corners, I enjoyed the academic's ideal relationship to a sponsor. For four years I was supported at Harvard by the Society of Fellows. My only responsibility to the sponsor was to work conscientiously on research problems I chose myself.

In my first field study in industry, with Phillips Petroleum in Oklahoma in 1942 and 1943, I faced quite a different situation. To gain access to the field, I had to go to top management. In return for access, I promised that I would provide management with reports designed to aid them in improving worker-management relations. In these reports, I would not identify any workers. I did not make a similar commitment regarding management personnel. In fact, it would have been impossible to maintain anonymity for management people in studies of particular plants.

At the time worker hostility to management was directed particularly at Ed Masters, general superintendent of field operations, who had an office in the headquarters city of Bartlesville and was supposed to be the chief link between the main office and the Phillips divisions and districts. Masters was committed to cracking down on what he saw as the laxities of the previous general superintendent.

I had submitted my reports to management several weeks before I was to leave Oklahoma—which happened to be also a short time before the union representation election had been scheduled.

As I was saying my good-byes to workers and members of management in Oklahoma City, Personnel Manager Franklin called me into his office to tell me how highly he and Division Superintendent Wenzel and valued my research. I expected him to give me credit for giving local and higher management a better understanding of labor relations, but he startled me, saying, "Without your research, we could not have beaten the CIO."

I laughed, but it was a nervous laugh. My sympathies had been with the union; I was friendlier with those who supported the union than with any on the other side. How then could I have helped to produce such an outcome? Franklin explained that, a few weeks before the representation election, he and Division Superintendent Wenzel had gone to Bartlesville for a top-level strategy meeting with Vice President Rhodes, General Superintendent Masters, and the company employee relations manager. Masters was playing the dominant role in this meeting and seemed to be assuming that he would be in Oklahoma City for the last few days before election, directing the company campaign. Toward the end of the meeting, Wenzel said someting like this: "This is a local problem. We know our men, and we know how to handle them. I don't want anyone from Bartlesville around Oklahoma City between now and the election."

They all looked at Vice President Rhodes, After a brief pause, he said, "Okay, Al, we'll leave it in your hands."

If Masters had been observed by workers maneuvering around Oklahoma City in the tense days before the election, this might well have been enough to swing the few votes necessary to give the victory to the CIO in the Oklahoma City District.

No one could prove that I had changed the outcome, but I could not prove to myself that such an influence was out of the question.

If management had asked me to do a study that would help them to beat the CIO, I would, of course, have refused. This experience points to the hazards of researchers getting used in ways we did not intend. While we cannot fully control the uses to which our research may be put, at least we can try to anticipate and guard against some of the more serious misuses.

Publication presents some of the most difficult ethical problems. As a means of gaining access, I had promised that, if a book should come of this study, I would submit the manuscript to management for clearance.

What I intended to be my second book, *People in Petroleum,* went off to management as I was leaving Oklahoma for another job. Many weeks later I received a letter from the employment manager congratulating me on the book. He said that he and other management people had found it a fascinating account and that they had learned much from it. However, it was their conclusion that it would not be in the best interests of the company to allow publication, and therefore they withheld permission.

This was a severe blow, especially as it came when I was flat on my back, in the process of rehabilitation from a case of polio. I cursed myself for having volunteered to clear the book with the company. Had I not done so, perhaps management would not have demanded this commitment, because at the time they had only the vaguest understanding of my study. Furthermore, I now recognized that the commitment itself had been a violation of professional ethics. If we allow executives of an organization we study the right to veto publication, we can be justly accused of serving the interests of the organization rather than the interests of science. Still, I was stuck with the promise.

My restaurant study involved a different problem with the sponsoring organization. On my behalf, in 1943 the Committee on Human Relations in Industry at the University of Chicago had signed a contract with the National Restaurant Association committing us to submit the manuscript before publication to a sponsoring committee of NRA. The contract stated that, after considering all criticisms and suggestions, the author had the sole right to determine what should be published. Still we did have serious problems in gaining acceptance for a book that I would consider an accurate project report. Before my first meeting with the committee to discuss the first draft of the book, I received a set of written criticisms from all of the members. There were a number of detailed criticisms, but the underlying problem was most pungently expressed by one man who simply wrote: "I thought the purpose of tieing up with the University of Chicago was to raise the status of the restaurant industry. If this book is published, it will have the opposite effect. Therefore, it should not be published."

Since the status problems of restaurant employees and of the industry in general provided one important base of analysis, there was no way I could rewrite the book so as to leave out status problems. If NRA had had the right to veto publication, I believe that I could not have revised the book to satisfy both myself and the sponsoring committee. There followed a long and painful process of rewriting, mediation, and negotiation.

I was not prepared to give up on any point I considered essential, but I did have a strong interest in securing the sponsorship of the National Restaurant Association. I don't believe royalties for the book were an important consideration. I realized that sponsorship by NRA would add to sales, but several members of the sponsoring committee had already told me that "restaurant people don't buy books." I thought it important then, as I do now, to produce a book that would be useful to people in the industry studied. Obviously, the endorsement of NRA would tend to legitimate the book for restaurant people and for students of the industry.

Lloyd Warner was a most skillful mediator. He made it clear to me that the final decision was mine, that I would retain the right to publish what I believed should be published, even if the NRA eventually decided to withhold its approval.

Warner and I went over the criticisms in detail, looking for nonessential points on which I could afford to yield, and also trying to express the same ideas in ways less offensive to the leaders of the industry. We then met with the sponsoring committee. I had previously enjoyed reasonably friendly relations with some of the members, particularly in response to the talks I had given at their invitation in several cities. On these occasions I had dealt with "human elements in supervision," a section of the book that had no negative status implications. Now, the atmosphere was formal and chilly. They talked to me, but it was clear that they were appealing to Warner to rein in the irresponsible young upstart who was threatening to undermine the standing of their industry.

I found myself forced into an uncomfortable role. I resented the implication that I was too young and inexperienced to have an appropriate sense of professional responsibility. I thought I was capable of dealing with their criticisms in a reasonably understanding way. On the other hand, I realized that it was a great advantage to us to have two roles to play instead of one. As mediator, Warner could meet with key members of the sponsoring committee before and after our general meeting, to give his interpretation of my position—what I might be willing to do and what they could not expect me to do—then he could remind them that I had the right to publish what I saw fit. I presume he also helped them to understand that this was not simply a matter of personality or character, that academic freedom was so deeply imbedded in the university that he could not deny my right to publication.

After agonizing over many sentences and paragraphs, cutting here and modifying the phraseology there, I submitted a second draft. I can no longer remember whether we met to discuss the second and then the third draft, but I have a vivid memory of the final negotiating meeting. By this time, relations were somewhat less frigid, as the members of the sponsoring committee apparently recognized that they had made some progress in "improving" the manuscript, but we finally reached an impasse on one point. In a discussion of the role of waiter in continental Europe versus the United States, I quoted a waiter saying, "In the United States, you can't be a man and be a waiter too." That hurt the most. They insisted I take it out, and I insisted that the quote expressed the status problem better than anything else and therefore was essential.

At this critical point, the business school member of our committee, Charles Rovetta, proposed a compromise. Would I agree to take these quotes from waiters out of the body of the book and place them in an appendix? Looking at the expressions on the faces of the sponsoring committee members, I sensed that agreement on this point would resolve the impasse. After a moment's hesitation, I said, "I will agree to put the quotes in an appendix providing I have the right to indicate in the text of the book that such quotations are to be found in an appendix." That did it.

I have now answered the question that nobody has ever asked me: Why are there two appendixes in *Human Relations in the Restaurant Industry?* No explanation is needed for an appendix on research methods, but, since job attitudes are presented and discussed throughout the book, why have an appendix entitled "Job Attitudes"? A more accurate title would have been "Job Attitudes that the Sponsoring Committee Could Not Stomach in the Text."

Was the rewriting and compromising worth the struggle? Others could answer that question better than I, but they would need the first draft of the restaurant book, and that has been lost. All I can say is that, as I look back on it, I can't think of anything of importance that I sacrificed in the negotiating and rewriting process.

During my work with the Committee on Human Relations in Industry at the University of Chicago (1944-1948), my salary and expenses came out of contributions from the National Restaurant Association and the various companies that were supporting our program. Since I had received no salary and only $25 per month expense money from Phillips, one might assume that I was even more compromised by management sponsorship in my Chicago activities. In fact, some of our critics assumed that, if workers and union leaders knew we were financed by the companies, they would be unwilling to talk to us or would deliberately mislead us.

It did not work out that way, for several reasons. In some of the plants we studied, union-management relations were adversarial but also reasonably stable. Company managements had accepted collective bargaining and were making no efforts to drive out the unions.

Before undertaking any study, we conferred with the local union leaders as well as with local managers. We made known our sources of financing, but went on to say that we hoped our studies could contribute to the improvement of worker-management and union-management relations. Undoubtedly some of the union leaders were suspicious of us and sceptical about the value of our contribution, but all of them went along with the study, or at least imposed no barriers. In fact, in this period we had more difficulty in gaining management acceptance than we did with union leaders.

At first, many workers were suspicious of us, and a few retained those suspicions to the end. With most workers, we went through a testing process. They would tell us something that might hurt them— but not too much—if it got to management, and then wait to see what happened. When nothing adverse happened, their trust in us would increase, and some even came to look upon us as people who might help them to influence management decisions. They would say something like, "We have complained about this problem again and again, but we haven't been able to get management to listen to us. Maybe you can get them to take some action."

I also was able to arrange for official union-management joint sponsorship for projects to look at marked changes from bitter conflict to close cooperation (Whyte et al., 1946; Whyte, 1951b). This type of study posed minimal problems of mutual acceptance. The leaders of labor and management were proud of what they had accomplished, and even enjoyed telling me how they had hated each other in the bad old days.

Early in the 1950s, in Elmira, New York, I worked with several students on a study of worker-management and union-management relations in a Remington Rand typewriter plant. Here the financial sponsorhsip posed no problems, since we were supported by the New York State School of Industrial and Labor Relations. However, company and plant had a history of labor conflict, and relations were then quite tense. When it came to doing a survey of workers, we had to negotiate with management and the union separately regarding the feedback of the results. We agreed to report to management, but not to the union, our findings on worker attitudes toward the company and their supervisors. We agreed to report to the union, but not to management, on workers' attitudes toward their union. (We retained the right to publish, but without identifying company or union.)

RELATIONS WITH INFORMANTS AND COLLEAGUES

Anthropological field methods pose more complex and difficult problems of relations with informants than those generally encountered with other methods. By its very nature, the questionnaire survey is a highly impersonal instrument. It is general practice to inform respondents that they are not to sign their names and that their individual indentities will not be revealed.

Even when the surveys contain no code specifically identifying individuals, there is nevertheless a possibility of identification. In our survey of Lima Light and Power Company, a union leader responded to my promises of anonymity with the argument that the survey contained enough demographic items so that, with access to company personnel records, we could identify individuals. I had to concede the point. However, I added that this would require a major investment of time, and I could not imagine why we would want to do so. Apparently that satisfied him, and he cooperated in the survey. However, this indicates that even a survey demands some level of trust between respondents and researchers.

Anthropological field workers depend upon research subjects to provide us with data, and particularly upon certain individuals as gatekeepers and guides, so we necessarily have some special obligations toward them. We establish a reciprocity relationship with those who help us. While the study is going on, we are not likely to overlook the obligation to give a hand to those helping us, but do we forget them when we no longer need them?

This point was brought home to me most vividly in my last conversation with Frank Luongo (Mike Giovanni in *Street Corner Society.*) I had sent him a copy of the book after publication, and we had exchanged letters over a period of years, and then lost contact. Many years later I learned that Frank was with the Textile Workers Union, working out of Stuyvesant, New York. When I was planning to drive to Boston, I telephoned to see if we could get together. Frank responded cordially, but later, when I called to confirm the arrangements, his wife told me that he was in the hospital. We visited him there. It was a sad occasion; Frank had cancer and knew he would not have long to live.

After some nostalgic discussion of the good old days on the street corner, Frank filled me in on the years when he had been working regularly as a union organizer. Finally, he told me that over those years, on a number of occasions, he had been approached by students or professors for information about the union. He added, "I have had enough of that. I will never again do anything for anybody from college." I asked why he felt that way, and he responded,

> I have always taken time with them. I've gotten things out of the file for them and answered all their questions as well as I could. And I never asked anything in return except, I would say to them, "When you get through, send me a copy of what you write, will you?" They would always say yes, they would be glad to do it, but I never yet have got anything back. So to hell with them.

Social researchers have lost nothing by this rejection, since a few weeks later Frank was dead. I quote his last words to me in the hope that future researchers will try harder to keep their promises to people in the field, even after they no longer need help.

Keeping our commitments to individuals is only a minimal requirement. If some of our subjects become active participants in our project, then we need to work out a more institutionalized pattern of mutual obligations. I return to this point at the end of this chapter.

Some of the most difficult ethical problems in our relations with informants involve what and how we publish. Such problems can arise even when we have made no commitments to project sponsors regarding clearance or even regarding their right to consultation prior to publication.

The restaurant project led to an action research project in a hotel. When she had completed her year with the hotel, Edith Lentz wrote "The Tremont Hotel Study." I believed that the study, with some revisions, was worth publishing, but I recognized a problem, and, fortunately, so did Edith. She had provided pseudonyms for the hotel and all of the people she studied, so we could assume that few in the general reading public cound identify the organization or the principal actors. However, a publisher would naturally want to promote it in the hotel field, and a number of the people we studied would know that the "Tremont" was their hotel. Furthermore, I had already (1947) published a description of our project in a hotel journal, identifying the research site as the Radisson Hotel in Minneapolis.

The study contained much intimate quoted material that could be embarrassing and might even have more serious consequences for some of the hotel people. Our contract protected our right to publish, but we decided there was no way to do so without violating the confidences of many of our informants and hurting a number of the people who had spoken frankly and freely with us. We put the manuscript aside for the time being. In 1965, we used that case study along with further materials in a book on action research (Whyte and Hamilton)—my co-author was now Edith Lentz Hamilton. Probably we did not need to wait so long, but other projects had intervened. In any case, it had been almost two decades since the completion of the study, the chief executive officer was dead, the second in command was retired, and we could assume that most, if not all, of the supervisors we had studied had long since left the hotel. Still, this long wait was a high price to pay—especially for Edith, since this would have been her first publication.

My next publication problem arose after Chris Argyris, who had taken his doctorate with me, was teaching at Yale. He had written a doctoral thesis on a factory, focusing particularly on the plant manager with whom he had enjoyed sort of a love-hate relationship. He liked Tom (as I shall call him) and respected his sharp intellect and thorough command of the technical and financial side of the business. At the same time, Tom's style was far from the ideal of democratic leadership so dear to the heart of Argyris. He put great pressure on his superintendents and foremen and was able to outthink and outpush all of them while cultivating close personal relationships with them and with the rank and file workers. In our free-flowing supervisory training sessions we were particularly interested in the plant manager's handling of interdepartmental relations, as each superintendent teamed up with his foremen to blame other departments for any deficiencies that Tom might discover. In fact, the superintendents and foremen talked freely about the need "to throw the dead cat over into the other fellow's yard."

I did have reservations on the first draft of the Argyris thesis. Reflecting upon his depiction of the leadership style of the plant manager, I asked Chris, "What are you, the prosecuting attorney?" His second draft modified the hostile tone, and I gave the matter no further thought.

It was when Chris telephoned me to report that Harper & Bros. would publish a revision of his thesis under the title of *Executive Leadership* (1953) that alarm bells sounded in my brain. Of course, Chris had disguised the name of the plant manager, the company, and the location of the plant, so that no one outside the company would be able to identify the case, but it was well known within the company that we had been heavily involved with Tom at his plant.

I telephoned Chris. He was also concerned about our relationship with the company, and did not want to harm Tom. We agreed to send the manuscript to the vice president for industrial relations, who had helped to work us into the system. He would judge whether Tom should read it, and we'd see.

Several weeks later I got a very worried call from the vice president. Yes, he'd read it, Tom had read it, and Tom had risen right up through the roof. Chris agreed to come to Ithaca and he and I drove to the regional headquarters, where Tom was now managing a much larger plant than the one Chris had studied.

We met at nine o'clock the following morning in the headquarters conference room and shook hands—it struck me as a prize fight scene, with the referee saying, "Shake hands and come out fighting." Then Tom laid out the manuscript. He had red-penciled the objectionable passages, and it looked to me as if there was more red-penciling than not.

Chris handled the situation with consumate skill. Tom would read a passage and state his objections vehemently. Chris would respond with something like this, "I understand how you feel about that, but this is the point I am trying to get across. . . . Now is there some way I can reword it without sacrificing that point?" Then the four of us would grope for words to express the same idea, searching until Tom was more or less satisfied. By noon the tension had subsided. In the afternoon Tom would read over red-penciled passages, and sometimes he would laugh and say, "Well, I guess that's the way it was." At the end of the day there was a different handshake, and Tom invited us home for a drink, saying, "I haven't had a good argument in a long time." So we drove home much happier. Still, the outcome may have depended on luck as well as upon our skill in handling the situation. We were lucky that Tom was a strong enough person to accept a sometimes critical interpretation of himself.

I had no personal responsibility for the "Springdale" case, but I entered the debate as editor of *Human Organization,* presenting my own description of what had happened and a preliminary evaluation of the issues involved (Human Organization, 1958: Vol. 17, No. 2, pp. 1-2). Arthur Vidich and Joseph Bensman (in Human Organization, 1958-1959: Vol. 17, No. 4) responded at length, and the debate continued in subsequent issues (1959: Vol. 18, No. 2, pp. 49-52; 1960: Vol. 19, No. 1; see also Vidich et al., 1964: 313-349).

I opened the debate with this statement:

Freedom and Responsibility in Research:
The "Springdale" Case

A small upstate New York village has now been immortalized in anthropological literature under the name "Springdale." The local newspaper reports that the experience has not been a pleasing one. We pass on this account:

"The people of the Village [Springdale] waited quite awhile to get even with Art Vidich, who wrote a *Peyton Place*-type book about their town recently.

"The featured float of the annual Fourth of July parade followed an authentic copy of the jacket of the book, *Small Town in Mass Society*, done large-scale by Mrs. Beverly Robinson. Following the book cover came residents of [Springdale] riding masked in cars labeled with the fictitious names given them in the book.

"But the pay-off was the final scene, a manure-spreader filled with very rich barnyard fertilizer, over which was bending an effigy of 'The Author'."

The account suggests that a good time was had by all—on this particular occasion. Nevertheless, local observers report that the disturbance caused by the book in the village has not been enitrely compensated for by even such a ceremony carried out in the best anthropological traditions. We feel that it is high time that these issues be raised:

1. What obligation does the author of a community study have to the people of the community he studies, particularly when it comes to publication of his findings?

2. When the author is a member of a research team, what obligations does he have to the project director? And what obligations does the project director have to him?

Vidich spent two and a half years living in "Springdale" as field director of a Cornell project carried out in the Department of Child Development and Family Relations. The project was directed by Urie Bronfenbrenner, a social psychologist. As a result of this research experience, Vidich published several articles, but the official report in book form regarding the project did not materialize during his tenure at Cornell and is only getting into print at this writing. Some time after he left Cornell, Vidich began work on a book of his own, in collaboration with Joseph Bensman, who had had no previous association with the project.

The Vidich manuscript gave rise to considerable controversy between the author and the Springdale project director.

Before Vidich came onto the scene, Springdale people had been assured that no individuals would be identified in printed reports. While all of the Vidich characters are given pseudonyms, they were easily identified within Springdale. The author argues that, when there is only one mayor and a small number of village and town officials and school board members, it is impossible to discuss the dynamics of the community without identifying individuals. He further argues that what he has reported in the book is "public knowledge" within Springdale. Even if this be true, is there a difference between public knowledge that circulates in the village and the same stories appearing in print?

In addition to his objections regarding the anonymity pledge, Bronfenbrenner claimed that certain individuals were described in ways that could be damaging to them, submitting a long bill of particulars.

The strong reaction against the book in Springdale was not a momentary or passing phenomenon. At this writing, more than a quarter century after the publication of the Vidich-Bensman (1958) book, its memory is still very much alive in Springdale. In fact, the reaction remained so strong for many years that it was understood on the Cornell campus that there was no use in approaching Springdale for cooperation on any research project. Within the last few years, a member of my department was able to include Springdale in a larger study, but he reported with some bitterness that the effort to gain cooperation had been far more difficult in Springdale than anywhere else—because of the Vidich-Bensman book.

Vidich's initial response to public criticisms was reported in a story in the *Ithaca Journal*:

> Strictly speaking, I take the position that in the interests of the pursuit of scientific truth, no one, including research organizations, has a right to lay claims of ownership of research data.
>
> That is a violation of the entire spirit of disinterested research.
>
> Asked whether he was aware that there would be a reaction in Springdale, Vidich replied:
>
> > I was aware that there would be a reaction in the town when the book was published. While writing the book, however, it did not

occur to us to anticipate what these reactions might be, nor did it
occur to us to use such anticipations of reactions as a basis for
selecting the data or carrying out the analysis.

One can't gear social science writing to the expected reactions of any
audience, and, if one does, the writing quickly degenerates into
dishonesty, all objectivity in the sense that one can speak of objectivity
in the social sciences is lost.

In other words, Vidich based his case on academic freedom in
pursuit of scientific truth. This leaves a number of important questions
unanswered. The project director had made a commitment to community leaders not to identify individuals in publications. Furthermore, the
program did develop its own "principles of professional ethics" (Human
Organization, 1959: Vol. 18, No. 2, pp. 50-52), and Bronfenbrenner
assumed that all members of the program were committed to these
principles. At the time Vidich was serving as field director, there was no
discussion between Bronfenbrenner and Vidich regarding what eventually became *Small Town in Mass Society,* because that book only
developed some months after Vidich had left Cornell.

Vidich argued that it would be impossible to present a case study of a
village without using material that would enable the villagers to identify
particular individuals. He added that he was simply following
customary practice in "the Lynds' study of Middletown, West's study of
Plainville, Warner's study of Yankee City, Selznick's study of the T.V.A.,
Hunter's study of community power, and Whyte's study of *Street
Corner Society.* In the latter case, Doc still suffers from the recognition
he received in the book."

DECEPTIVE PRACTICES

Can the use of deception in research be justified? If one takes the
absolutist position that the ends never justify the means, then the
negative answer is automatic.

If we are willing to assume that the answer depends upon the nature
of the deception and its possible consequences, then we might ask the
following questions: Does the deception expose subjects to serious risks
of negative consequences? Could the same information be secured
without deception? If not, how important scientifically is the information? (I recognize the difficulty of applying this standard to oneself
because the information we want always seems of great importance.)

In general, I assume we should inform people in our field of study what we intend to do and why we want to do it, as fully and honestly as it is possible for us to report on our own motives. If we conceal our true motives for actions we take in the field, in my terms this amounts to deception.

For example, in my SCS study of what I called the Cornerville Social and Athletic Club, I had explained to the members that I was simply trying to understand them and the district and was trying to avoid influencing the decisions made in the club. At a critical point, I violated this understanding. The incident occurred in a meeting during which Tony Cataldo, the racketeer, was trying to persuade the members to invite an Irish candidate to meet with them, whereas most of the members felt committed to an Italian-American candidate. Tony argued that they had nothing to lose, as they weren't committing themselves to vote for his candidate, but he was vigorously opposed by the leader of one of the two factions in the club. As the argument continued, I spoke up, saying that I didn't see anything wrong with inviting the candidate. Shortly afterward the members voted to invite him.

Why did I do this? I had earlier developed a relationship with Tony that promised to lead into a substantial exploration of the social processes and the social structure of the numbers racket, but then our relationship lapsed. I supported Tony in the hope that this would revive the relationship and the research opportunities. In other words, I was manipulating the club for my own personal ends—a serious ethical violation. It served me right that the maneuver did not achieve what I had intended. From this point on, Tony paid much more attention to the leader of the opposing faction than to me.

George Strauss used questionnaires designed by Lois Dean with 500 workers he had been studying through anthropological methods. The respondents were directed not to sign their names, but the questionnaires were coded so that the researchers could identify each respondent. The purpose of this coding was to enable the researchers to compare questionnaire responses on frequency of attendance at union meetings with the observations Strauss had made at these meetings throughout the year. Since meeting attendance averaged thirty more or less regulars, Strauss was able to keep a systematic record of attendance (Whyte, 1963b).

This led to a striking finding: 29 percent of those reporting some frequency of meeting attendance had never been observed by Strauss at any union meeting. Without the identification, Dean and Strauss would have known that the survey responses greatly exaggerated meeting attendance, but they would not have been able to distinguish between the actual attenders and those who made false claims. Such distinctions turned out to be important in the analysis, for Dean found marked differences in attitudes toward union and management among those in three categories: the nonattenders who reported correctly, the attenders who reported correctly, and the "positive dissemblers" who reported attendance when none was observed. The positive dissemblers were markedly more favorable toward the union than those who correctly reported their nonattendance; it seemed they felt guilty about not attending and had difficulty in acknowledging the fact.

If a survey researcher had wished to compare attitudes of attenders and nonattenders solely on the basis of self-reports, clearly the analysis would have been seriously flawed. The information secured through this covert identification of respondents seems to me of real importance. It suggests the danger of deceiving ourselves if we assume that survey respondents' self-reports on their behavior are at least accurate enough so that distortions will cancel themselves out. Finally, the researchers' identification of survey respondents could hardly have exposed them to any negative consequences. Though the survey data were not always kept under lock and key in our files, the factory was located 100 miles away from Cornell, and no one who might have sneaked a look at the undisguised data knew anyone in the factory. Only if Strauss had reported to management the names of the regular meeting attenders would there have been a possibility of any negative consequences to the respondents. Even in that case—which, of course, did not occur—the negative impact on respondents is not obvious; in a plant of about 500 workers, managers must have a pretty good idea of who the active union members are.

For *Men Who Manage,* Melville Dalton (1959) persuaded a secretary in the payroll department to smuggle out salary figures on all the management personnel. This espionage was undetected. Still, one cannot refrain from asking some "what if" questions. Suppose the secretary had been sick on a Monday and unable to return the salary data until after their absence had been discovered? If superiors had caught her sneaking the data back into the files, probably she would have been fired. Furthermore, she would undoubtedly have been grilled to discover why she had broken the rules, and this could have led to the discharge of Dalton himself. Although we can assume that detection was unlikely, its consequences would have been drastic both for the researcher and his accomplice.

Of course, it was not just idle curiousity that lured Dalton into this maneuver. He was studying the informal influences that produced variations in individual salaries from explicitly stated company policies. However, only at one point in the book (Dalton, 1959: 175-177) did he use figures from the payroll office. Various other references to salary questions or specific salaries were drawn from personal interviews. As Dalton (1959: 175) acknowledged,

> Income data are deficient. At one point in the research at Milo, exact incomes were obtained for ninety-six officers. But while inflation progressed with the research, the timing, rapport, and hazards of my personal contacts lacked this regularity. And as the sources of my information closed, some salaries were increasing more sharply than others.

In hindsight, the smuggled salary data did not prove to be as valuable as expected.

For further background on the project in which Lieutenant Morton Sullivan posed as a recruit so as to study training of airmen, I wrote to Stuart Queen. Still going strong at age 93, Queen wrote that it was reading *Street Corner Society* that gave Sullivan the idea of such a participant observer study, and he proposed it to Queen.

> I accepted it without question. But as to whether it could be really "covert," at each post to which Mort, as a fake new recruit, was assigned, the only ones who knew what he was and sought were the commanding officer and chaplain, both sworn to secrecy. When we were nearing the end of our work, I, posing as Mort's uncle, invited him to visit me in St. Louis and have Sunday night dinner. I suggested that he bring along one of his "buddies." He brought his sergeant. After a very pleasant chat, Mort and I told the sergeant who we really were and what we were doing. He flatly refused for at least half an hour to believe what we were telling him. But finally he was convinced and quite approved.
>
> On the other hand, after publication of our article, Blank, "defender of the faith" wrote me a very scathing letter, calling it unethical and "a start toward a police state in America." Mort wrote a good reply, but still left some questions unanswered.
>
> I think that the Air Force study might have been carried through with less expense of time and money, without any "covert" operation, but

it would have missed a lot of possibly useful material about new recruits, attitudes, habits, and failures.

Given the safeguards of confidentiality and the exclusion of names and personally identifying characteristics from the written reports, the risks of negative consequences to the study subjects seem to have been very small. Of course, if the deception had been publicly uncovered, this would have been at least personally embarassing to Sullivan and Queen, but that is quite a different matter from risks to their unwitting subjects.

THE ROLE OF THE U.S. RESEARCHER IN DEVELOPING NATIONS

We encounter additional problems when the U.S. researcher engages in research in developing nations. Can we find ways of working with colleagues and students without reinforcing the dependence of a poor country upon a rich one?

Latin American universities suffer from institutional disadvantages compared to the United States, and the same general statement probably applies to developing countries in other parts of the world. Generally, professors are poorly paid in comparison with other professionals, and it has been customary for many of them to work at one or more other jobs in order to make ends meet.

If we think only of these disadvantages, we are likely to take the patronizing attitude toward Latin American social scientists that denies any possibility of full collaboration. To balance these disadvantages, we have to recognize certain important assets within the Latin American social science community. In spite of all of the material and institutional obstacles, in most countries we find at least a few enterprising individuals who have done distinguished work and won international recognition. It goes without saying that they possess a much more intimate, intuitive, and also systematic knowlege of their own countries than any outsider, but we should not consider them simply local informants and gatekeepers. They have also developed theoretical ideas and orientations which have recently had major impacts upon both theory and research in industrialized nations. For example, it was our close working relationship with Peruvian students and professors which led us to recognize the deficiencies in the modernization framework we had brought to Peru, and to turn to a much more fruitful framework integrating North American and Latin American orientations. Furthermore, there is no lack of talent among Latin American social science students. I would not hesitate to match the Peruvian students who worked on our program with any group of U.S. students of sociology or anthropology.

Given this background, are there ways in which we can contribute to the institutional development of the behavioral sciences in developing nations while we pursue our own research? First, we need to review the past pattern of intercultural research relations. The problems have been well expressed in these terms:

> The complaints go beyond the nature of the projects and methods used. Some Indians feel they are being "prostituted" by outsiders who can exploit the situation by offering temporary research employment on topics to which Indian sociologists are actually in theoretical opposition. Foreign social scientists are said to use paid local sociologists only to gather interviews and questionnaires and to serve as interpreters. Indian sociologists often do not help to design the study or process the data, which is done in the foreign country prior to coming to India. Others have charged that the Indian colleagues are not sufficiently recognized in the publication of the research. The American or other foreign social scientist takes the credit, leaving the Indian sociologist with a research stipend, but with no gain in professional status either in his own country or abroad [Clinard and Elder, 1965].

Speaking from experience in another country half a world away, the authors were describing a problem familiar to Peruvian social scientists. By the time we began our joint program with the Instituto de Estudios Peruanos, we were well aware of this pattern, which Peruvians called "academic imperialism." We therefore sought to make our IEP collaborators full partners in planning the research, analyzing the data, and publishing our findings—in Spanish as well as in English. (In fact, the program eventually yielded a larger volume of publications in Spanish by Peruvian authors than in English by us from the United States.) This strategy not only enabled us to maintain a close working relationship in Peru through eleven politically turbulent years; it also led us to rethink U.S. graduate and undergraduate education.

I began in 1964 by trying to recruit as field workers Peruvian graduate students of sociology or anthroplogy. At the time, people in this category were simply not available. Either they had positions in the government bureaucracy or else they were out of the country getting further education. I therefore had to settle for undergraduates.

In Peru the undergraduate program is five years long, the first two years being devoted to general studies and the last three to more specialized work, ending with a thesis. As we developed our program with IEP, we found ourselves working with students from the third year on—those who had completed the fifth year and were working on their theses served as field supervisors. I was delighted with the abilities and enterprising spirit displayed by most of these students.

As the following incident illustrates, I found I could learn as much from them as they could from me. José Matos, IEP director, had planned a field excursion to the highland village of Huayopampa, a little more than three hours from Lima by car. Matos, Julio Cutler, IEP coordinator, J. Oscar Alers, Cornell coordinator, and a visiting French professor went in one and I was assigned to a stationwagon with four students. I learned later that the French visitor had expressed concern about this arrangement, assuming that, in assigning me to the lower status car, Matos was signaling some friction between us. On the contrary, I suspect he made this arrangement for the same reason that I was delighted with it. In the IEP offices in Lima, I had ample opportunity to talk with Matos and other professional colleagues. This trip, I was privileged to spend more than six hours, going and coming, plus several hours spent in Huayopampa, with four able students who had recently returned to Lima after almost six months in Huayopampa. To get along with them, there was no need to think about how I should try to minimize status differences. The situation naturally cast me in the role of student and them in the role of teachers. My intial knowledge of this village was superficial and faulty, so I welcomed the opportunity to listen to the experts and to ply them with questions. It was only toward the end of our return trip to Lima that I felt I had gained enough understanding of Huayopampa to venture a few remarks in the role of teacher.

Giorgio Alberti, Oscar Alers, and Lawrence K. Williams (during his year in Peru) played the teacher role much more extensively than I, but, in all cases, the teaching revolved around the planning of projects, the gathering of data in the field, its analysis and the writing of research reports. With access to the necessary equipment in the Ministry of Health, we did most of our data processing in Peru. While he was gathering data for his own thesis in the Mantaro and Yanamarca Valleys, Alberti worked closely with three students in the Central University in Huancayo. As Alberti (with Lamonde Tullis), drove the students to the villages, dropping off each at one of the research sites, they discussed the work they were planning. As they drove back to Huancayo, they exchanged information and ideas from the day's work. Also Alberti conducted informal seminars in his home on background theoretical reading and research reports.

To make sure that, even in the surveys, the students were not limited to the role of data gatherers, I worked on a two-week seminar with Alers and Cotler. After an initial orientation in survey analysis, we asked the students to formulate one or more hypotheses that could be tested with the survey data they themselves had gathered. We then had each student process the data and present orally to the group and in writing to us the statistical tabulations and their interpretation. We did not assume that such a two-week exposure would make survey researchers of beginning students, but we did help them to understand the potential of surveys.

If we apply to Peru the conventional U.S. program in which students do not go beyond a token exposure to field research until well along in their graduate studies, the standard development strategy calls for exporting enough North American or European professors to teach the variety of sociological or anthropological courses for the bachelor's degree and further to provide staffing to begin some research in the host country. If we assume that development of a real research professional requires advanced graduate work in a U.S. university, this means travel, tuition, and support funds over many months for enough students to form a critical mass when they return to their own country. Those whose total graduate education is gained abroad are likely to have difficulties when, in competition with professionals educated entirely at home, they try to apply U.S. methods and theoretical frameworks to research in Peru.

This was, in fact, the university development strategy being pursued by USAID and U.S. foundations in the 1960s and 1970s. There are two problems with this strategy: (1) It is exceedingly costly, and (2) it does not work.

I am not arguing that the student must limit undergraduate and graduate work entirely to institutions in his own country. At least five students in our joint program with IEP went abroad for graduate work, two to Cornell and three to English universities. In all of these cases, the students arrived on the university campus with the data and a research report (in Spanish) for their master's or doctoral theses. They thus had a running start toward their degrees, compared with U.S. students who began graduate work without any field experience. Even before they left Peru, some of these students had research reports published by IEP.

So, when they returned to Peru, they could reenter the local world of social research with much less difficulty than those whose research training had been entirely outside the country.

The model we developed in our joint program in Peru is based upon a marked departure from conventional conceptions of the relation between teaching and research. If you assume that students are not equipped to do research until they have gone through 30 or 40 hours of courses and seminars, then there is no alternative to the costly and unproductive program of exporting U.S.-style college and university education.

In Peru, we learned that it is poor educational policy to confine field work to the last stage of graduate education. Students will learn much better from classroom and library work that follows or accompanies experience in the field.

While I take pride in the program we were able to develop and maintain with Peruvian colleagues and students, no account of that experience would be complete without reference to a crisis that nearly sank our program in its early stages.

In a session at an annual meeting of the American Anthropological Association, I presented some preliminary findings of our Peruvian rural research, emphasizing the potential benefits of integrating surveys with anthropological methods. Later, I received a letter from an official of the Advanced Research Projects Agency (ARPA) in the Pentagon. The writer expressed great interest in what we were doing and asked if I knew of people who wanted to do similar research in developing countries and needed financial support.

At the time (1966) I would have preferred almost any other source of support, but we had come to recognize that we needed further financing beyond NSF if we were to make this a truly joint program. Up to this point, we had kept our promise to share our findings fully with Peruvian professors and students working with us. For example, this meant reporting the marginal percentages on our surveys as soon as they were available. Furthermore, I had discussed the possibilities of survey analysis with students and professors and had invited them to suggest questions that could be answered by further data processing. They listened politely and with apparent interest, but made no suggestions. It then became apparent that unless we were able to involve Peruvian students directly in the survey analysis, they could not participate fully with us in all phases of the program. Matos and I had already agreed that ideally we should have funds to maintain two professional researchers in Peru, one representing Cornell and the other IEP. We then faced the question of how to raise the additional funds.

On my way to Peru in January 1966, I stopped at Washington to see the ARPA official. In response to my probing questions, he gave me the following assurances: (1) No secret reports would be required. We would simply provide ARPA with the progress reports and findings that we would make available to any financial sponsor. (2) We would have complete freedom to publish, without even submitting the material in advance to the funding agency, (3) no security clearances were required, and (4) ARPA would make a decision on any proposal within sixty days of its submission and very likely in a month. Except for the political-ethical questions, the terms offered by ARPA were superior to those available from any funding agency. We were promised the same freedom to conduct research and publish as we would have had with any grant from NSF, NIMH, or a private foundation. The conditions for AID support would have been much more onerous. AID would have required U.S security clearance for our two principal Peruvian collaborators, certifying that they posed no threat to the foreign policy of the United States! If such a clearance had become known in Peru, those men would have been forever professionally and politicaly discredited.

The processing time for the proposal presented a strong argument in favor of ARPA. We had reached a point where the obvious next step in developing our program was to strengthen our Lima-based organization. If we did not move quickly, our momentum would be lost. Most major foundations take nine months to a year to make a decision after a proposal is submitted. The same processing time applies to NIMH and NSF.

I laid out fully before our Peruvian associates all that I learned from my discussions with ARPA. They were very concerned about the implications of money from the Pentagon—as were Williams and I—but they finally agreed, providing it was used for people hired by Cornell and not for Peruvians. On this basis, we submitted a proposal, and in about 30 days received notification of substantial ARPA support.

Some weeks later, after our two additional professionals had begun work in Peru, the Camelot scandal broke into the news, and it received even more attention in Peru—and elsewhere in Latin America—than it did in the United States.

Apart from the practical objectives and the sponsorship, Project Camelot promised to be a bonanza for researchers interested in developing countries. To be funded at $1.5 million annually over several years, Camelot was designed to provide basic knowledge regarding the sources of social tensions and conflicts in a developing nation. More specifically, the official documents state these objectives:

> *First,* to devise procedures for assessing the potential for internal war within national societies;
>
> *Second,* to identify with increased degrees of confidence those actions which a government might take to relieve conditions which are assessed as giving rise to a potential for internal war; and
>
> *Finally,* to assess the feasibility of prescribing the characteristics of a system for obtaining and using the essential information needed for doing the above two things [Horowitz, 1967: 47-48].

The project was financed by the U.S. Army through its Special Operations Research Office (SORO) at American University, under the direction of Rex Hopper. After a preliminary research conference designed to interest social scientists in the Project, Hugo G. Nutini, a Chilean-born citizen of the United States and assistant professor of anthropology at the University of Pittsburgh, was much interested in participating. Though never employed by Camelot, he managed to persuade Hopper to pay his expenses for a trip to Chile to explore the interest of Chilean social scientists in the Project.

In his initial descriptions of the project, Nutini was reportedly vague about the source of financing and emphasized its scientific character. In Chile at the time was Johann Galtung, a Norwegian social scientist, who had been invited to attend the preliminary research conference but had declined. Along with his invitation, he had recieved a full account of the objectives and financing of Camelot. He shared this information with his Chilean colleagues.

The confrontation of the Chileans with Nutini in the office of the Vice Rector of the University of Chile produced a scandal that had diplomatic and academic repercussions throughout the world. Camelot raised the sensitivities of Latin Americans to any possible connection between U.S. supported research and U.S. intervention with "counterinsurgency" measures in developing nations.

When the Camelot scandal broke, I realized that our Peruvian program was in jeopardy. We could argue that our program was basically different from Camelot. Instead of fitting in to a research program broadly designed by the U.S. army, we and our Peruvian associates had jointly planned our own program. ARPA was simply contributing to what he had independently decided to do. Nevertheless, in this changed political/academic climate, I realized that we might not be able to retain the ARPA support.

I responded in a typical North American fashion. The Board of Directors of IEP had previously been rather inactive and therefore was not fully informed on all aspects of our joint program. I proposed that we get the board together to discuss a progress report on the research program itself, including the sources of funds. The members responded enthusiastically to the progress report but expressed great concern regarding the ARPA money. Finally, the consensus was to continue as we were, limiting the ARPA support to U.S. citizens.

When the nature of this discussion leaked to the press, this decision became untenable. To add to our problems, the revelation became entangled with a political struggle. The IEP director was supporting one of the major candidates for rector of San Marcos University, and the newspaper that blasted us was supporting the other candidate. This gave them an ideal opportunity to attack a man who had long been known as a critic of the newspaper and its political policies.

The first story reported that a mysterious Mr. White (*sic*) had secured these funds and that the newspaper had learned that this White had no connection with any U.S. university. The paper also reported that I had recently died. A few days later, having brought me back to life, the paper reported that efforts to find out more about me had been unavailing, thus adding further to the suspicious nature of the project. This, of course, was absurd. Though I was by no means a household name in Lima, the local social science community was small enough so that it would have been difficult for the reporter to avoid finding out who I was and what my connections were.

As attacks continued in this newspaper, it was no longer politically possible to use the ARPA funds. We therefore returned to ARPA more than $100,000—much to the surprise and outrage of Pentagon officials. Since we were already committed to additional professional salaries, we were now spending our NSF money at a rate that would have exhausted the funds for a three-year grant in less than two years. I was fortunate in being able to persuade program officials in NSF to allow us to bring in a proposal for a new grant to carry us beyond the two years. Since the new proposal had to go through the regular review process, we were not out of the woods yet. The definite answer to the proposal—and to a companion proposal I had submitted to NIMH— was due in December of 1966, at which time our currently available funds would run out. Finally, in early December, after I had returned from Peru and a final nostalgic discussion with José Matos about how good our experience had been and how sad it was that it had to end, I got a call from the National Science Foundation to present me with an unexpected problem. NSF had approved the proposal, but NIMH had also approved. Which source of funds would I like to receive?

Our experience with the fallout of the Camelot case illustrates how problems originating in one program can have serious negative consequences for other researchers in several countries. The Camelot scandal provoked a congressional inquiry in Chile, and for some time it appeared that the government would place such strict controls even on social research directed by Chilean citizens as to make it extremely difficult to carry out any independent research. The case also reinforced suspicions against U.S. researchers in neighboring countries. How could we prove that we were *not* secret agents for the CIA, whatever our source of funds?

The recent case of Steven Mosher illustrates this fallout problem in another part of the world. Since neither Mosher nor the university have been willing to release the report supporting the decision to expel Mosher from the Stanford doctoral program in anthropology, an outsider can hardly judge whether the alleged ethical violations were serious enough to justify this drastic step. However, some of the facts in the case are not in dispute.

> One act by Mosher damaged his credibility with Americans concerned with the issue. Using a pseudonym, he published an article in a Taiwan journal exposing the use of coercion in rural China to force women to submit even to third-trimester abortions as part of the official birth control program. This article included unmasked photographs of women undergoing such abortions. When . . . asked why he had not followed accepted procedures to protect the identities of the women in the photographs and why he would allow his research to be put to such political use in Taiwan, Mosher initially denied authorship. Only subsequently did he acknowledge the article as his [M. K. Whyte, forthcoming].

Mosher could claim he was only exercising his academic freedom, but that claim seems compromised by his initial attempt to disavow authorship. And academic freedom hardly justifies his use of the photographs when masking the faces in the pictures would have protected the identities of the women without altering the facts.

Finally, academic freedom does not tell one where to publish the truth. If Mosher had published the same information in an academic journal in the United States or Europe, probably some Chinese social scientist would have seen it, and the word would have got back to Peking, but such publication would not have created the fire storm provoked by publication in the popular press of Taiwan.

Mosher charges (and Stanford denies) that his expulsion from the doctoral program was caused by Chinese government pressures upon the University. In any case, it is known that the Chinese government did lodge very vigorous protests.

In 1981 Chinese authorities imposed a "moratorium" on field work by foreigners, and that ban remains in effect to this writing. Since other foreign scholars had been having difficulties gaining field access before the Mosher case, the role of that case in bringing about the moratorium can be debated. However, there can be no doubt that Mosher has made access of his colleagues to social research in China more difficult.

CONCLUSIONS

I doubt the value of trying to lay down specific and detailed rules of ethical behavior, but I will venture to suggest some general guidelines drawn from the experience I have described.

(1) Integrating ethical considerations into the planning process. If we do not try to think through in advance the ethical implications of commitments we make, we are bound to get trapped into actions dictated by expediency. In this way, we can lose the trust of people in the field and even come to mistrust ourselves. This means avoiding commitments that we will be unwilling or unable to honor later. We owe it to those we study to make our commitments regarding the protection of human subjects in the early stages of the project—and then to honor those commitments even when it is inconvenient to do so.

(2) Obligations in publication. Allowing sponsors of a project the right of veto over publication is an unwise abandonment of academic freedom. However, that does not mean that we are ethically justified in publishing whatever we please. Even had I not granted the Phillips management the right of veto, I would have had to wrestle with the protection of human subjects problem in what I did publish. As it was, I handled the book veto problem and the human subjects problem by publishing much of my Phillips material, in disguised form, in an article

(1944b) and, many years later, in textbooks (1961, 1969). Now, more than forty years after I left the field, there seems no need any longer to disguise the identity of the company.

In the restaurant study, I got around the human subjects problem not only by using pseudonyms and drawing illustrative cases from a number of different restaurants. When I wanted to use a number of cases from the same restaurant, I made up several different names for that restaurant.

When we want to publish a case study of a single organization or community, the protection problem is more difficult. In the Radisson Hotel case, we waited almost 20 years before publishing—hardly an ideal solution. In the case of the Argyris book, we solved the problem belatedly in the feedback session with the plant manager, but it would have been much better if we had begun this process long before publication. In the Springdale case, no feedback was undertaken—with the consequences described. Since feedback involves broader questions of field relations, I will return to this point at the end of this chapter.

(3) Balancing rights and obligations. The ethics of field work pose difficult problems because rights often conflict with obligations. If we insist that academic freedom is absolute and that we need not consider the effects of what we write on our subjects, on our colleagues, and on governments that control access to field work, then we are likely to stir up popular opposition to social research and to block access of our colleagues to important field sites. On the other hand, if we go to the other extreme in avoiding any publication that could possibly hurt any individual or organization or make access more difficult for other social researchers, we can end up by undermining the scientific validity of our work. I know of no rule to guide us in walking the fine line between the two extremes. The best we can do is weigh and balance rights and obligations as we go along.

(4) Studying social conflicts. It is not *inherently* unethical to use your research to advance the interests of one party in a conflict situation—if you do so openly. It is unethical if you pose as a neutral scientist but allow your research to be used by one party against the other. In the Phillips case, I should not have submitted my reports until after the union representation election. On the other hand, if you wish to have access to both parties in a conflict situation, it is sometimes possible (as in the Elmira case) to negotiate an agreement as to which data are to be revealed to each party.

(5) Passive subjects or active collaborators? I am not claiming that deception can never be justified in social research, but you do not deceive those with whom you are collaborating. To the extent that we develop field relations in which the subjects of study participate actively in the research process, we resolve the deception question, along with some other ethical problems of field relations. There are still ethical problems to face, but we share them with our subjects/collaborators instead of having to resolve them solely in our own consciences.

In this context, research feedback before publication is not simply an obligation we owe our subjects/collaborators. The process can strengthen the scientific basis of our research. In his contribution to the Springdale debates (in a letter quoted in my editorial, *Human Organization*, 1959: Vol. 18, No. 2, p. 49), L.H. Bell wrote:

> Personally, I have come to the conclusion that responsibility to the community does *not* conflict with responsiblity to science. As a matter of fact, I have found frequently that attempting to state material coolly and objectively, rather than in terms of personalities and anecdotes, sharpens my understanding of sociological processes.
>
> After writing the first draft of the Haskell County, Kansas Study, I took the manuscript to the community and went over it with my major informants. In many ways, this was the most productive part of the field work. It enabled the informants for the first time, to understand what I was attempting to accomplish. This broader understanding brought to mind many things which they had not told me, largely because I did not have the knowledge of the culture and social system to formulate some significant questions. They also pointed out numerous errors of both fact and interpretation and thus saved me personal embarrassment and scientific error.
>
> Douglas Harring also involved key informants in the review and criticism of draft copies of articles growing out of his field work in the Ryukyu Islands. He reports experiences similar to mine.
>
> Ralph Linton used to say that we never would know the great errors in ethnological studies because non-literate people were not able to "talk back."
>
> In summary, it seems evident to me that conscientiously fulfilling our responsibility to the community need not weaken our scientific integrity. Indeed, it may improve the scientific quality of our final product.

Diane Vaughan (1983) came to the same general conclusion after the feedback session on her study of a pharmacy chain's unlawful reimbursements by a state agency. Investigation of the case involved collaboration among several agencies that had not previously worked closely together. As the gathering of evidence was completed and the case was turned over to the attorney general's office, communication among the agencies lapsed, and some of those involved in the earlier stages did not understand or approve of the way in which the case was finally settled. Reading and discussion of the report by the actors in the case helped to clear up misunderstandings and fill in information-al gaps, and thus had a favorable effect upon interagency relations. Vaughan (1983: 130-131) concludes with this interpretation:

> When the research was completed. I felt conveying the research findings to others was a promise I was obliged to keep. A dilemma surfaces in the necessary trade-off with professional mandates that this activity brings. As sociologists, we are not rewarded for dis-seminating information to those in the real world who can apply it. We are rewarded instead for publication in scholarly journals. Time spent in one direction is time taken from the other. How do we meet our obligations to disseminate our research findings to audiences beyond our discipline and at the same satisfy our need for professional self-perpetuation?

> Since this now-fateful meeting, I no longer see this as a dilemma of mutually exclusive choice; I have recast it, in fact, as a nondilemma. The pursuit of professional goals can be enhanced by time spent disseminating information to those whom it directly affects. The meet-ing with the network organization members, which, at the most, required two days of arrangements and preparation, directly enriched my own professional interests in several ways. The immediate feed-back was invaluable. The conversation confirmed the research con-clusions, as well as generated ideas for additional work. In addition, I received the latest information from these experts on new legislation, political activities, and prosecution efforts that affected their work on Medicaid provider fraud. Having withdrawn from day-to-day contact with these organizations some nine months earlier, I was unaware of the consequences of these new developments for the network.

> The outcome of this meeting was so overwhelmingly favorable that I followed through on my original promise with no second thoughts. After an initial inquiry on my part was followed up by HEW, I agreed to meet with officials responsible for control of Medicaid fraud and abuse in Washington. Though no money was to change hands, I knew the exchange would be professionally valuable: there would be new ideas, and perhaps a foundation laid for a broader study of networks

as a device for social control. Tangible benefits to one's own research and research interests can come from sharing information with people outside the profession who find it relevant. However, there is another factor to support such activity: the more relevant our work is to the practical problems of the organizations we study, the more agreeable those organizations will be to researchers who might later want their cooperation.

This fits my experience from my first field study. Throughout the SCS period, I had innumerable discussions with Doc on both factual matters and problems of interpretation. We worked so closely together that I can not be sure now which ideas were mine and which his. Before I left the North End of Boston, Doc had read every word of the first draft of my book and had given me extensive criticism. At some points, he would say, "This will embarrass me if the boys read the book—but let it ride." When the book did come out, and the book jacket (by Kathleen) was displayed on the bulletin board of the library, he told the fellows not to read it because it was written in very academic jargon! Through me, Doc met some people at Harvard and Wellesley and for several years seemed to revel in being invited to talk to college classes. Then he tired of it and asked me not to identify him. We did eventually drift apart, but—contrary to Vidich's claim—I am not aware of any way in which I hurt Doc.

In later studies, I have also found the feedback process essential to good research. On various occasions, people I was studying have pointed out factual errors, and they have also offered important new data and interpretations of events that were as persuasive to me as my own preliminary conclusions.

12

Focusing the Study
and Analyzing the Data

Good field methods are necessary, but not sufficient, for good research. You may be a skilled and diligent observer and interviewer and gather "rich data," but, unless you have good ideas about how to focus the study and analyze those data, your project will yield little of value.

Finding the focus for a study using anthropological field methods is a different process than finding a focus for a survey. By its very nature, the survey must be focused—that is, the problems defined and the variables specified—before beginning the data gathering process.

At this point we leave behind discussion about gathering data to consider the more elusive problem of *how to think about the thinking process.* In other words, how do you use data to generate ideas, and how do those ideas lead you to reexamine existing data or to gather new data?

Anthropological field methods have the advantage of flexibility, allowing us to explore the field, to refine or change the initial problem focus, and to adapt the data gathering process to ideas that occur to us even in late stages of our exploration. On the other hand, as you immerse yourself in the field situation, you may find so many interesting things to study that you are at a loss as to how to delimit the scope of the project and focus on specific problems. As I reported in SCS, I had been in the field eighteen months before I discovered what I was really studying.

In my case, the process was especially long because I was not only learning how to adjust to a new role in a community completely different from anything I had experienced, but I was at the same time moving from an undergraduate degree in economics to study methods, theory, and substantive contents in sociology and social anthropology. Throughout this time, I was gathering rich data, much of which were ultimately put to good use, but it took me that long to discover patterns in what I was learning and to recognize the significance of those patterns. Without suggesting that it should take that long for other field workers, I would argue against premature closure, that is, against striving for a sharp focus on your problems before you have had a chance to explore the territory.

DEPTH VERSUS BREADTH

Let us assume that now you have completed at least the first stages of your social exploration, how do you focus on the problems to study? I find it useful to think in terms of two issues: breadth versus depth and description versus analysis.

The difficulty of resolving the depth versus breadth question depends in part upon the time one has to devote to field work. In his excellent study of the West End of Boston, Herbert Gans (1982) knew that he would only be able to be there eight months. In my earlier study of the adjoining district, I knew at the outset that I would have at least four times that length of time, and, as it turned out, my total time in the field was about forty months. Given his time constraints, Gans recognized that if he was to achieve any breadth in his view of the West End, he would not be able to become so deeply involved as I with small groups.

However, he had a compensating advantage in being able to focus on a major public policy question: urban renewal and its effects upon the "urban villagers." In my study the public policy implications were more scattered and indirect.

Even with so much time I found myself constantly wrestling with the problem of breadth versus depth. I was enjoying my membership among the corner boys I called the Nortons and among the college boys of the Italian Community Club, but I kept reminding myself that I was coming to know fairly intimately only about 25 people in a district with approximately 20,000 population. As I was well into my second year of a three-year fellowship and thought then that I would need at least three more years, I faced the necessity of writing a report that the senior fellows would consider strong enough to warrant reappointment.

Forced to fall back upon my only solid bodies of data, I wrote case studies of the Nortons and the Italian Community Club. In this process I at last discovered what it was that I was studying. I recognized that the Nortons were similar to other street corner groups throughout the neighborhood. I could not undertake equally intensive studies of other street corner groups, but, with the collaboration of Doc, my chief informant and guide, and Sam Franco, I managed to get enough data on other groups to generalize about group structures and leadership.

There was no other group of college boys in the district at that time. However, I learned that just a few years earlier there had been a similar group, also meeting in the settlement house, and this helped to put the Italian Community Club in a broader perspective.

To extend my study, I joined State Senator George Ravello's campaign when he was running for Congress. Since the only middle-level racketeer I had met belonged to the Cornerville S&A Club, I joined that organization myself.

As I look upon this first field experience, it seems to me that I achieved considerable depth in description and analysis of corner gangs, of college boys' groups, of the rackets, and of the political organizations. However, I could not claim to have produced a full and well-rounded community study. I gathered fragmentary information about family life, relations between the generations, the roles of girls and women, and the Catholic church, but, since I did not have systematic information on any of these topics, I preferred not to deal with them in my book. In other words, even if your time for field work is far longer than is usually possible, you must choose between breadth and depth.

In the project leading to *Human Relations in the Restaurant Industry* (1948), I faced the same issue under considerably more time pressure. Within fifteen months I was expected to produce a book describing human relations with an analysis of potential value to restaurant operators. I worked with three research assistants. However, I was determined to do a substantial part of the field work myself. I began in a large and busy restaurant, Stouffers on State Street in Chicago's Loop. I spent three months there and another three months writing up the case. Assuming that I would need at least three months to write the book after completing the field work, I had already spent half of my own time on just one restaurant.

As time went by, I worried more and more about the breadth I seemed to be sacrificing. As I look back on the project, I am convinced that the six months was well spent. Two of the five parts of the book

("From Kitchen to Customer" and "Human Elements in Supervision") were based very largely on data and ideas generated in the Stouffer study. That study, plus the information and ideas from different restaurants studied by my research assistants enabled us to identify the main gaps in our data and plan the last six months of field work much more systematically. For example, Stouffers did not employ checkers to total the customer slips for waitresses. Since this position is frequently found in large and busy restaurants, it was important to study at least one restaurant having checkers. Similarly, since Stouffers then employed no minority people, it was important to find a restaurant that did, so that we could examine race relations on the job. Also, since Stouffers employed only waitresses, it was important to study a restaurant that used waiters. Since Stouffers was not unionized, we wanted to look at restaurants where the workers were represented by a union. When we got interested in the effects of tipping, we needed a comparison with a restaurant using a flat service charge, and were fortunate in finding one quite comparable to Stouffers in every other respect.

This is not to say that most of the ideas presented in the book came out of the Stouffers study. For example, Edith Lentz's study of what we call Chandler's Restaurant provided valuable data and ideas, not only upon the waitresses' reaction to service charges, but also on the relations between waitresses and countermen. Since women served in the service pantry or counter positions in Stouffers, the comparison between Stouffers and Chandler's highlighted the importance of sex differences in interaction. It was also Edith Lentz who discovered the technological elements involved in smoothing relations between these two positions—a point to which I will return later. However, the field work at Stouffers and organizing that report provided me with an overall pattern of the book I hoped to write.

HOW DO YOU ANALYZE A CASE?

Once, in handing back a student's paper, I said, "You have given me a description. I asked for an analysis."

The student asked, "What do you mean by 'analysis'?"

I found that a difficult question to answer when I first faced it years ago, and I still find it difficult, but also fundamental. Rather than attempting a general answer here, I shall describe the ways in which I have gone about analyzing data and working toward theoretical conclusions.

I see myself using a general conceptual scheme or orienting theory to guide the gathering of data and the selection of particular items for analysis. In the analysis process, I am practicing what has been called "grounded theory" (Glaser and Strauss, 1967), the building of generalizations out of a particular body of data. In the final chapter, I shall discuss the relationship between conceptual scheme and grounded theory.

In what follows, I will review my experience in three approaches to analysis:

(1) following the orienting theory and methodological strategy to theoretical conclusions
(2) case analysis through asking questions and challenging your answers
(3) learning theory through action

I am not claiming I have discovered the one best way or the three best ways to move from description to analysis to theory. I simply claim that if more experienced researchers undertook to explain in detail their own strategies and tactics in thinking about data, this would help to demystify the theory building process.

FROM METHODS AND ORIENTING THEORY
TO PROBLEM DEFINITION

When in the SCS study I finally discovered what it was that I was studying, I also recognized that the research methods and orienting theory I had been using had been leading me to problem definition and also to problem analysis. In the Society of Fellows, I was fortunate in having a friend and mentor in social anthropologist Conrad M. Arensberg. It was he who persuaded me that it was important to make a detailed record of my observations and interviews even before I knew what I was studying. At the time, Eliot D. Chapple and Arensberg had recently worked out their interaction framework for studying interpersonal events. That framework linked methodology with theory. In methodology, they measured the frequency and duration of interactions among people observed and the initiation of changes in group activities. The theoretical assumption was that interactions are not random events, that each individual has a characteristic pattern of interaction, and that interactions within a group also tend to form a pattern. This suggested that changes in interactions experienced by individuals would have social and emotional consequences.

When I had to face the senior fellows, I discovered that I had solid systematic data on interactions within groups and on group structure. As I continued my association with the Nortons, I discovered the relation between position in the group structure and athletic performance, and also how major changes in an individual's position in the group, and changes in the group structure itself, could have negative effects upon mental health. If I had not used the interaction methodology, I could not have arrived at the analyses of group structures and interactional changes that led me to the conclusions set forth in SCS.

In Chapters 8 and 9 I described how, in our Peruvian program, we found the data from surveys, anthropological methods, and historical research complementing and reinforcing each other. Now I will show how the utilization of those methods led me to a theoretical advance concerning the relation between conflict and cooperation. I lay the case out in some detail because it is not often that it is possible to chart one's own thought processes step by step with such precision.[1]

In both the anthropological studies and in the surveys, we were interested in evidence of cooperation and conflict in our villages. We were familiar with the anthropological debates regarding whether the peasant community was typically a harmonious social unit or one fraught with friction and conflict. Early in our program, we had enough data to show that our villages reflected a great range in the apparent prevalence of conflict or cooperation, so it made no sense to argue about what was typical. Instead we should be looking for the variables that affect the prevalence of conflict or cooperation from village to village.

The next steps did not come until 1973, when a sudden insight triggered a reformulation of the relations between conflict and cooperation in communities. I had first read the anthropology student's report on the village of Mito when I had no immediate writing plans. Now I reread it as I set about writing a chapter comparing the three Mantaro Valley villages. Based solely on his anthropological study, the student described Mito as low in both conflict and cooperation. That apparent paradox caught my attention.

I asked myself: Could it really be so? If I had only had the anthropological report to go by, probably I would have just assumed that the student was mistaken and not have pursued the matter further. To check his interpretation, I pulled out a set of marginals for the 1969 survey to examine responses to two questions:

> When it comes to cooperating on some project for the community, how well do the people cooperate? Would you say the cooperation is good, fair, or poor?

Is there much conflict or division among the people of this village? (much, some, little, none)

To my mounting excitement, I found that respondents in Mito perceived the level of both conflict and cooperation lower than did respondents in the two other Mantaro Valley communities.

Now I asked myself: Why was I surprised to find a community that was low in both conflict and cooperation? I suddenly realized that, while Lewis (1951) and Foster (1966) differed sharply with Redfield (1930) on the amount of conflict and cooperation in the peasant community, all three saw cooperation and conflict as opposite ends of a single continuum. They were implicitly assuming that, if a peasant community was high in cooperation, it must be low in conflict, and vice versa.

Suppose we made a different assumption: that conflict and cooperation were two separate dimensions, unrelated to each other. That assumption could be checked against the survey data. Lawrence K. Williams and Larry French ran the correlations between the two items for the 1964 and the 1969 surveys and found that for both years the correlations were about as close to zero as one could possibly get without cooking the data. Here we had an unusual case where a zero correlation was theoretically significant. The statistical operations confirmed the fact that the two dimensions were completely independent of each other.

The next step was to represent this finding graphically. For the single-continuum model, I simply drew a straight line and wrote "cooperation" at one end and "conflict" at the other. To represent the two-continua model, first I drew two parallel lines, labeled one "cooperation" and the other "conflict," and wrote "high" at one end of each and "low" at the other. No sooner did I have the two parallel lines before me than I realized that, if I placed one perpendicular to the other, I had the makings of a figure that would enable me to place the cooperation and conflict scores for each community at a single point on the page. In other words, I was moving toward a four-box framework that could be represented roughly as shown in Figure 1.

To see if this conceptualization made sense at the level of the individual village, we had to do some additional but simple figuring. To avoid giving extra weight to the larger communities, where our sample sizes were larger, we simply added the mean scores of cooperation and conflict for each community and divided by twelve in order to get a mean score for the total sample on each dimension. The total commu-

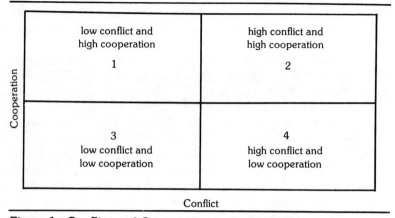

Figure 1: Conflict and Cooperation in Twelve Villages

nity mean scores gave us the dividing lines among the four boxes. Thus, for example, in 1964 Huayopampa was above average in cooperation and below average in conflict, which placed it in box 1. Similarly, Mito was below average in both dimensions, which placed it in box 3.

To visualize the overall pattern, I located each community in the four box framework for 1964 and then did the same operation for the 1969 figures. (To simplify the representation, I used two points only for the five villages that had shifted from one box to another in this five year period.) Then I asked myself whether this four way division was just a statistical aberration or whether villages falling in the same box had important characteristics in common.

As I reviewed the anthropological reports, it seemed to me that a rather consistent pattern emerged. The villages in box 1 (low conflict/ high cooperation) seemed to be highly cohesive, moving ahead on projects for which there was general agreement regarding sharing of costs and benefits. Box 2 (high/high) communities appeared to be those characterized by factional strife and widespread complaints about the equity of distribution of costs and benefits but where nevertheless some projects were moving forward. Box 4 (high conflict/low coopera-tion) villages had divisions too sharp to permit much progress, and yet the factional leaders were still struggling. Box 3 (low/low) com-munities seemed to be those that were going nowhere in terms of common village projects, and where potential leaders had given up the struggle.

Next I turned my attention to those five villages that had shifted from one box to another between 1964 and 1969. Four had moved from box 4 (high conflict/low cooperation) to box 3 (low/low), which seemed a natural move. If the community is divided into rival factions but with neither faction making progress toward its objectives, the factional leaders might eventually just give up the struggle and settle for the stagnation of Mito.

The most interesting shift was that of Huayopampa, which had not only been in box 1 in 1964 but had showed a much higher level of perceived cooperation than any other village. By 1969, Huayopampa had dropped sharply in perceived cooperation (though still remaining above the mean for that year) and showed the second highest level of conflict of all the villages.

Following the 1969 survey, I had scanned the marginals for all villages on both surveys, noting some of the marked changes. At the time, I noted the conflict/cooperation changes in Huayopampa, and they did look interesting. However, since at that time I had no framework within which to assess the significance of such changes, I gave no further thought to Huayopampa. Now placing the Huayopampa shift within the four-box framework highlighted the importance of the case and impelled us to undertake a review and further analysis of the problems and processes of change that village from 1964 to 1969.

When I had grouped high conflict villages together, this led me to compare them in terms of the sources of conflict. We did find some which fit the Marxist framework, divisions being based on social class and control over resources, but there were many others which did not fit that pattern. Lampián had split along lines of age grading, and there were other villages where generational conflict was less dramatic but important. In other cases, we found cleavages based upon neighborhoods, religious organizations, and political party membership. Recognizing the variety of possible sources of conflict may help others to go beyond ideologies and ideal models to advance knowledge of the dynamics of conflict and cooperation in peasant communities.

ANALYZING ANTHROPOLOGICAL CASE STUDIES

It was a ten-day doctoral examination question given me by W. Lloyd Warner in 1942 that stimulated me to clarify and make explicit my ideas of how to go about analyzing anthropological case studies. The problem was to explain why certain tribes gave high emphasis to age grading in their social structures. Since I had only the vaguest idea about age grading in primitive societies, there was a lot of reading to do, and, as I read, I began to formulate questions, pose tentative answers, challenge those answers with more pointed questions, and continue with further questioning and challenging of answers. I started with two general questions: (1) What are the conditions that lead to a high emphasis on age grading? (2) What are the conditions that tend to minimize age grading in shaping the social structure? Beginning at this general level, as I read and reflected on cases, I sharpened the questions and the answers step by step until (after some later revisions) I had a publishable article (Whyte, 1944a).

I then went on to utilize this case analysis strategy in my field work, as the following two examples will illustrate.

Who Goes Union and Why?

While I was doing my field work (1942-1943) in the Oklahoma City area, the CIO was pushing to drive to organize Phillips's workers.[2] I was especially interested in the organization drive, trying to figure out what factors would influence the eventual outcome. My contacts were largely limited to four groups of workers, those in the Capok control room, who were managing the process of turning natural gas into iso-octane, the principal component of aviation gasoline; the catalyst plant, where workers produced the material used in the Capok processes; the engine operators who were responsible for maintaining the motive power for the Capok processes, and the engine repairmen. The first three sets of workers were under the same foreman, while the engine repairmen reported up another line of authority.

Over a period of months, I got to know most of these men well enough so that, either in response to my questions or from volunteered statements, I could record their pro- or anti-union sentiments.

Early on, I abandoned any attempt to generalize on why men joined unions. Since I was studying workers who were more or less evenly divided for or against the union, an attempt at such a broad generalization would obviously be fruitless.

A narrower question proved more productive: Why was pro-union sentiment much stronger than in earlier years? The answer suggested one obvious factor, external to the company. It was not many years after the passage of the Wagner Act, which greatly facilitated union organizing drives, and the Oil Workers International Union had been making headway in other companies. Unions were coming into the oil fields, so the Phillips workers faced a real question that had not seemed salient before.

Then there were important factors within the company itself. The company had been founded only about 25 years earlier by Frank Phillips and had been growing rapidly. Besides this rapid growth, the substitution of Ed Masters for his widely admired predecessor as general superintendent of field operations had destroyed the previously open channel of upward communication between the workers and the main office.

At about this time, top management announced that no one would be promoted into supervision without a college degree. As the company expanded, men had frequently moved up from top worker positions into supervision, but now an educational ceiling was imposed. Some of the most strongly pro-union men were those who had reached the top operating positions just before the educational barrier was thrown up against them.

Workers in the Capok control room and the catalyst plant had recently suffered through very painful experiences under two successive college-educated foremen, Bill Jones and Tom Fitch, and told me that these foremen did not trust the workers and were always trying to surprise them in some infraction, and that they dictated how the work should be done, although they had very incomplete and faulty knowledge of practical operating conditions. They also spoke of the ways the foremen expressed their disrespect for the men. For example, Fitch had once called the operators in the catalyst plant "a bunch of WPA workers."

These external and internal changes seemed sufficient to answer the question, "Why now and not before?" But they did not answer the question, "Why some men and not others?" To answer that, I looked first at the job situation. While the engine operators were officially part of the Capok plant, they were isolated from the control room, spending their eight-hour days in the engine room about a hundred yards away. They had served under Jones and Fitch, but they commented that those foremen hadn't "bothered" them. They added that the foremen were chemical engineers, did not claim to know anything about engine operation, and mainly just left them alone. With one exception, the engine operators were all anti-union.

The engine repairmen, responsible to another line of authority, had not experienced the oppressive supervision of Jones and Fitch. They served under a foreman who had come up through the ranks and was on a friendly and informal basis with them. When I observed them discussing problems, it was hard to distinguish foreman from workers. Furthermore, the nature of the work militated against autocratic supervision. When a major piece of equipment broke down, it was usually not obvious what the problem was. Since efficiency depended first upon a correct diagnosis, it would have been folly for any supervisor to make a quick decision and issue orders to the men. In fact, sometimes I observed the foreman and repairmen standing around the machine for twenty minutes or half an hour discussing what might be wrong and what should be done.

I found all of the repairmen were anti-union. Having suffered under Jones and Fitch, with a single exception, all the catalyst plant workers were pro-union.

In the Capok control room, I found the sentiments running predominantly in favor of the union, but there were a few exceptions. Those most strongly pro-union told me that currently they were getting along very well with their recently appointed foreman, Tom Lloyd, but said that Ed Masters was still running things from the main office, "and that old company heart is beating in Bartlesville."

This examination of a range of job situations provided a partial answer to the question, "Why some and not others?" But in the case of every set of jobs except those of engine repairmen, I had encountered one or more exceptions. The challenge to explain these exceptions led me into checking the early backgrounds of the men. I looked at the social experience of these men and, more specifically, their early interaction with peers or authority figures.

The strongest anti-union men in general came from farm backgrounds—hardly a discovery. Still, I wanted to know what it was about growing up on a farm which predisposed men to identify with the company in comparison with men who had grown up in cities and towns. Oklahoma farm life was rather isolated. These former farm boys lived on relatively large extensions of land with little interaction outside of the family. In farm work, the young boy was constantly under his father's supervision. When he went to town, he was with his parents. When he went to school, he interacted with children his own age, but under the direction of an adult, and he did not have time to stay and play with his age mates after school. Similarly, when he went to church and Sunday School with his age mates, it was always under the guidance and direction of adults.

With such a background, when the farm boy went to work in industry, he naturally looked to his supervisors as he had to adult members of his family. This was not a deep interpretation requiring sociological analysis. The men from city and town backgrounds commented freely upon the peculiar tendency of former farm boys to regard the foreman as if he were their father. One former farm boy told me that when he had come to work, he "looked on the foreman just like he was my father." Years earlier, a clash with a foreman had led to his discharge. The management vision of "one happy family" was no longer so appealing to him, and he had begun to take an interest in the union, but he was much less committed to the union cause than men who had grown up in cities and towns. I found Mark Walling particularly susceptible to changes in his personal relations with management.

The boys from town and city had grown up with much more peer group experience. They seemed to enter the work situation predisposed to view fellow workers as companions who shared the same fate, and members of management as authorities whose legitimacy was not conferred by analogy to the family.

These early background experiences also tended to sort workers into the various job categories. The engine room and the engine repair crews were manned by workers who had grown up on farms. Several men in the control room told me that they could not stand working in the engine room because of the isolation and the constant noise of the enormous engines. The engine operators told me that the isolation did not bother them, nor did they complain about working conditions, although one man did say that working constantly among the thundering engines had affected his hearing. There was only one engine operator who was interested in bidding into higher classifications in the control room. While he had been brought up on the farm, his family had left it long before he had reached maturity. He was the only one of the engine operators who had ever attended a union meeting.

Those who had grown up in towns or cities generally gravitated into jobs in the catalyst plant or the control room.

As I looked further at the exceptions to the general pattern, I concluded that I would also have to factor in individual workers' differential experiences with management.

I was particularly interested in the cases of Martin Shockley, a chief operator of the catalyst plant, and Andy Taylor and Mark Walling in the control room.

Shockley was strongly anti-union when I talked with him, yet he had not grown up on a farm. He gave the description of his personal background:

> Of course, my case may be a little different from the rest of the men. My mother has always taught me to believe that Phillips Petroleum Company was the only company in the world. My father worked for the company when I was about four years old. That was when Frank Phillips was just getting started. My father knew him pretty good then. He had just worked for Phillips for a few months when a fire broke out in the plant. In fighting that fire, my father got pneumonia and died. After that my mother got a check every month. It wasn't from the company. It was from Frank Phillips' personal account. That check kept coming until my oldest brother was able to go to work for the company. Then the check was cut down some, and when I was able to go to work so that the two of us together could carry the load the check was cut out. In those early days we used to spend some time on Frank Phillips' estate. That hasn't happened for years, but he still remembers my mother every year with a Christmas card and a birthday card.

This early experience did not entirely insulate Shockley from labor organization. In an earlier CIO drive, when he was in the midst of a conflict with foreman Jones, Shockley signed a union pledge card. Then the popular foreman, Tom Lloyd, succeeded Jones, and Shockley was elected a company union representative, a position that involved frequent conferences with management. It was this change, together with his early background, that made Shockley so strongly anti-union.

To understand the cases of control room workers Mark Walling and Andy Taylor, we must examine events during the union organizing campaign. I had the impression that among those initially strongly committed for or against the CIO no votes were changed, but certain key events during the course of the campaign did appear to affect those less strongly committed, and probably determined the outcome in what turned out to be a close election.

The pro-union and the anti-union workers seemed to have two quite different cognitive maps representing Phillips Petroleum Company. The anti-union men visualized the company in vertical terms. Without actually referring to "one happy family" they seemed to visualize the company as an integrated organization in which some people had superior positions but where they were all benefiting from the progress of the organization. Some of the pro-union workers told me that "this has been a good company to work for," yet they viewed the company in terms of sharp divisions between two segments, labor and management. The key events during the campaign were those which reinforced one or the other of these competing cognitive maps.

Years earlier, at the time of the first CIO campaign, management organized the company union and built it a clubhouse. According to those on both sides of the CIO issue, it was local management that had killed the company union. After the earlier CIO campaign had failed, some of the local management people became irritated when officers of the company union took their positions seriously. Several of these men were advised by local management people that spending so much time on union matters might jeopardize their chances to get ahead in the company. That advice had interred the company union until management needed it once again. I happened to be in the office of General Superintendent Al Wenzel when he telephoned the company union president, to urge him to write a letter demanding that management meet with the company union to negotiate a new contract. Wenzel instructed the president to insist that the new contract be more comprehensive than the existing contract, which made no mention of wages, hours, or working conditions.

When top management expressed its willingness to begin negotiations in Oklahoma City, local management had to take steps to revive the company union. At the time, there was no company union representative for the Capok control room and engine room, so foreman Tom Lloyd had to arrange an election. In the first ballot, the top vote getters were Jesus Christ and Joseph Stalin, followed by a number of obscenities, and no one then working in the plants was named by anyone.

Jesus Christ and Joseph Stalin being ineligible, foreman Lloyd arranged for a second ballot. In his conversations with the men, Lloyd told them that he was not trying to sell them the company union, but there would be representatives from other units negotiating with top management. If the Capok people did not have their own representative there, decisions might be made that would be unfavorable to their plant. If the CIO won the coming election, they would have lost nothing by having one of their own in these negotiations.

The second time, the ballot box remained empty for two days before two operators, as a joke, and without his knowledge, filled it with votes for Andy Taylor. A number three operator in the control room, Taylor had grown up in a town, was the son of a blue-collar worker, had started work at an early age in industry, and had previously expressed himself strongly in favor of the CIO. Upon his election, he told me that this did not change his views, but that he had reluctantly agreed to serve.

For some days, frequent meetings of company union representatives with the top management negotiating team deflected interest among the men away from the CIO. But then the leader of the management team, Ed Masters, said something that would have won the contest for the CIO if the election had been held at that time.

Andy Taylor was pushing the claim for the number one operators that they deserved an extra increase in pay for the skills required in directing the work. Following one negotiating meeting, Taylor reported,

> Did you hear what Masters said about us? He told us that we were only watchmen. He said, "Down there in the plant you've got automatic controls and charts. If anything goes wrong with the meters, you just call a meterman. If anything goes wrong with the engines, you call a repairman. If anything goes wrong with operations, you call an engineer, and he tells you what to do. There is no skill in that work, you just have to watch the charts."

In all my years in the field, I have never encountered any management statement that caused such an explosive reaction among the workers.

Even though the remark was directed at only one position in one small part of Oklahoma City operations, it came to symbolize management's low regard for its workers. One of the union activists told me that he got fifty men to sign pledge cards in the days immediately following the watchmen statement. The attitude seemed to be, "If that's what management thinks of us, then we need the protection of a union."

The representation election was still some months off, and negotiations resumed without Masters making any more explosive statements. The negotiations proceeded reasonably harmoniously for several weeks, and this had an effect at least upon the representative from the control room. Andy Taylor, whom I had identified earlier as one of the staunchest supporters of the CIO, had this to say:

> I used to think that the company was just out to get whatever it could from us. Now, I have been meeting with those men, and I have been studying them. I have come to the conclusion that they are really sincere. You can't be with a group of men for days like I was if they are hypocrites without you seeing that. I think they mean to be good to

the men right now. If the company union wins this election I think they will do their level best to make things nice for the men—for a while. I think we would be better off in the company union right now but the thing is, is it always going to be that way? I wish I knew.

When I asked him how he planned to vote, he replied, "I don't know. I am still on the fence."

In the meantime, management made a decision which, though apparently unconnected with the unionization drive, may have had an influence upon the outcome. This was a period of rapid wartime expansion, and Phillips had completed a new plant in Borger, Texas. Following the announcement of job opportunities at Borger, management sent a team from the main office to interview those workers interested in transfers. For some days discussion of the union campaign faded out, and conversation focused on the advantages or disadvantages of going or staying.

Shortly before the transfers were to take place, it occurred to Mark Walling that they should not allow their fellow workers to leave without a farewell party. He made several telephone calls to personnel man Jess Franklin and division superintendent Al Wenzel urging them to support his idea. Wenzel finally agreed that management would furnish beer and pretzels for a party in the clubhouse. Walling then organized a collection among fellow workers and supervisors to buy parting gifts.

This was a lively party, with crap games and poker played by mixed groups of management and workers. When Al Wenzel joined in the crap game, he immediately became the center of attention, talking loudly with the men and joking about his prowess with the dice. During the evening he circulated around the hall, radiating good fellowship. I noted that he talked with Walling more than with anyone else.

The farewell party dramatized for the men the conception of the company as one big happy family—with management in the parental role. The speeches sounded a note of fellowship, and, although the party had been organized by Walling, the ceremonies were dominated by management. One of the superintendents presented the gifts and all of the management men were called upon to speak, with the final talk reserved for the division superintendent himself. After expressing his high regard for the men who were leaving, he paid tribute to Mark Walling for his persistence in persuading management that this event must take place.

I assumed that Mark Walling himself was the man most likely to have been influenced by the farewell party. Was Walling now putting the one happy family picture back together? Until he had begun organizing the farewell party, Walling had spoken firmly of his decision to vote for the CIO. A day or two after the party, he said he was on the fence.

A week after the representation election, he commented, "There are lots of crooked things about unions." He had never raised such a concern before. I asked him if he knew anything crooked about the Oil Workers International. "No, but you read a lot of things in the newspaper about that sort of thing." In the daily newspaper in Oklahoma City, syndicated columnist Westbrook Pegler had been hammering at this theme for a long time. Why did Walling suddenly become seriously concerned about union corruption?

In this case, the strategy of asking questions and challenging answers and repeating the process had enabled me to connect major changes in the external environment and within the organization over the years with the early interactional experience of the men, with their previous experience with Phillips management people, with the effect of the nature of their jobs on their interactions and attitudes so that I could establish their predispositions to vote for or against the CIO. Observing the organizing campaign then enabled me to account for shifts in union sentiments in terms of changes in the relations of individuals with management people. I had also encountered some striking cases of verbal symbols that had important effects upon the union attitudes of workers—for example, foreman Fitch's comparing the catalyst plant men to WPA (relief) workers and Masters's watchman statement.

Why Do Waitresses Cry?

I was studying Stouffers Restaurant in the summer and early fall of 1944 at a time of enormous business pressure on the employees.[3] The restaurant was doing a record volume of business, and, at the height of the lunch rush hour, turnovers (the time elapsed between when a customer sits down at the table and when he or she finishes the meal and picks up the check to leave) were as short as twenty minutes. Waitresses had to get the orders from several tables of customers coming in at different times, wait in line at the service pantry and bar, pick up the orders and serve the customers (with one trip to the service pantry for each course), and make out the checks. The restaurant was generally shorthanded in the rush hour, which added to the pressures, and young inexperienced waitresses made up a much higher proportion of the work force than in less hectic times.

The waitresses talked freely about the nervous strain in their job. To understand this strain, I had to solve two problems: (1) how to measure or estimate the stresses of the job and the nervous strain experienced by waitresses, and (2) how to explain the differential reactions of various waitresses to those stresses.

Ideally, the researcher would have physiological data on the strain experienced by waitresses, but such measures were obviously out of the question. Waitresses talked freely about job stresses and strains, but these reports did not lend themselves to comparative analysis because they all agreed that they were working in a stressful situation and were under some nervous strain. Therefore, I looked for some more objective manifestation. Every now and then a waitress would burst into tears and retreat to the locker room until she could compose herself and get back on the job. This happened fairly often, but it involved only a minority of the waitresses. What was the difference between those who broke down and cried and those who did not? As in the Phillips Petroleum Company study, I was again asking the question, "Why some and not others?"

Part of the answer came from the differential stresses provided by different work locations. The waitresses chose stations, as they became open, according to seniority. This meant that they began work where the pace was most hectic and gradually worked their way to rooms characterized by a slower pace, larger checks, larger tips, and a much higher percentage of steady customers.

I found it was rare indeed for a high-seniority waitress to break down and cry. In part this can be explained simply by attrition: One would naturally expect those most vulnerable to the stresses of the job to drop out. Also, experienced waitresses were able to move to locations where the stresses were reduced and the rewards were increased—it is easier to "take it" when the pace is slower and the financial rewards greater. And the difficult customer you know is easier to handle than the difficult and unpredictable stranger. I found that the experienced waitresses were more aggressive in handling their relations with other waitresses, with pantry women, and with bartenders. They seemed to ease the pressures of work by getting other people to respond to them more readily than did the less experienced waitresses.

So far this analysis had accounted for the absence of crying among the more experienced waitresses, but this conclusion naturally led me to rephrase the "why some and not others" question, focusing it upon the younger, low-seniority waitresses.

The observation that the experienced waitresses were more inclined to take the initiative in handling their interactions on the job led me to conceptualize skill in waitress work in interactional terms. My interviews and observations led me to recognize that the skillful waitress—the one who handles the job efficiently and does not break down—takes initiative in handling customers. When customers are seated before she is ready to take their order, she finds a moment to pass by the table, to greet them, and tell them that she will be with them in a moment. This avoids the stressful situations when customers feel that the waitress does not know they are there and try to get her attention by waving arms, clinking glasses, and so on. Especially when she is hard pressed, she looks for openings to sell a customer on the item she knows she can get most readily out of the service pantry. When the customer insists on something that will be difficult, she warns that this order will take additional time. She also organizes waitresses in neighboring stations in an informal mutual aid society so that, if she is particularly hard pressed, others will give her a hand. Even when the aid is small, the waitress feels more secure knowing she is not alone in handling difficult relations with customers or with the service pantry.

This led me to see the differential reactions of the younger waitresses in terms of leadership or followership. Since I had already been convinced by previous research and reading that individuals develop characteristic patterns of interaction over the years, and act out these patterns in the job situation as well as in home, family, and community life, I began to interview some of the waitresses about their social experience before coming to work at Stouffers. Here the relationship between interaction patterns and reactions to stress on the job emerged clearly. I found in a growing number of cases that those who did not break down under the strain had characteristically developed a pattern of relations with other people in which they took considerable initiative and others followed them, whereas those who broke down had been more submissive and dependent on others. This conclusion was supported most strongly as I examined the cases of two pairs of twins. Here I could hold more or less constant the status of the family, and the whole nature of the family and community situation. In both pairs, one of the waitresses occasionally broke down and cried, whereas the other never did. As I interviewed them and observed the pairs together, it became obvious that one was dominant, the other dependent, and it was the dependent one who cried. In fact, in one case the dependent one did not break down when she was working at a station adjoining that of her twin sister but did become subject to crying spells when she was transferred to another location where her sister could no longer help her to manage her work and the interpersonal interactions.

FROM ACTION TO THEORY

Behavioral scientists tend to think of a one-way relationship between theory and action. If theory enters into the action processes at all, it is in the sense that a good theory can help one to devise effective actions. I suggest that causation can also go the other way: the taking of actions may lead us to ideas that contribute to theory.

Over the years, I have had a number of experiences where my involvement in action projects seemed to help me generate theoretical ideas. In most cases the influences were so diffuse that it would be hard to prove the direction of learning, but in one case I can make the point in very specific terms.

The idea came to me as I was working with Congress on employee ownership legislation. The success of this project depended upon building what I called an academic/activist network and linking it to a growing network of congressional staffers. As we were learning about both the problems and potentialities of saving jobs through employee buyouts, I began thinking about what the federal government could do to facilitate such a program (Whyte and Blasi, 1980). Shouldn't there be legislation providing government support and guidance for employee buyouts? I talked first with Congressman Matthew F. McHugh from Ithaca, and he suggested that I consult also Stanley Lundine, congressman from Jamestown.

This was not a conventional lobbying operation. I said something like this: "With the network of people that are exchanging ideas and information, I have been learning about the possibilities of saving jobs through employee ownership. We think that the federal government could do much more than has been done. We're not at all sure just what kinds of provisions should be put into law, but we think there is promise here of working out some useful legislation. Would you participate with us in a joint study and action project, and assign to us one of your staff assistants as a contact person, to be personally responsible for liaison between the academic/activist network and Congress." They accepted this idea somewhat tentatively.

We began work in January 1977. Things moved rather slowly until June when I happened to meet Joseph Blasi, who was playing a unique role in Congress. He is Director of the Project for Kibbutz Studies at Harvard.

Congressman Peter Kostmayer had offered Blasi a full-time job. Blasi turned it down, but made a counterproposal: "I'll work for you four to five days a month, providing I have no routine assignments. No fire-fighting either. My responsibilities will be only to provide you with information and ideas on social policy." Kostmayer was at first taken aback, but he thought it over and agreed. Even though he was only part-time in Washington, Blasi became the key person in what developed into a network on employee ownership within Congress.

The first draft of the Voluntary Job Preservation and Community Stabilization Act was written in November 1977, during a congressional recess, by people in our congressional network. I joined them for a couple of days. After revisions, in March 1978, the three congressmen, Kostmayer, Lundine, and McHugh, introduced the bill. Our legislation gave the Economic Development Administration the major responsibility for financing, technical assistance, and providing information on employee ownership.

We had no big organization lobbying for us, but we had something perhaps more important: Network, an organization of Catholic nuns who call themselves "a religious lobby for social justice." Sisters around the country provide funds to maintain four or five young, energetic, and able women to lobby members of Congress, senators, and their staff people on a variety of issues of social concern. Sister Madaleva Roarke, whom I had met at Cornell, was enthusiastic about our idea.

There are thousands of bills introduced into Congress every year, and most of them die—not because of opposition, but because they're simply lost in the shuffle. To make headway with a bill introduced by three junior members of Congress, you have to get fellow representatives to sign as cosponsors. By the end of the 95th Congress, about seven months after the bill was introduced, one out of six members of Congress was a cosponsor. We estimate that at least half of them were provided by the sisters of Network.

As this was going on in the House, interest began to percolate up to the Senate. Senator Russell Long had been a key power in employee ownership legislation before we came on the scene, but his first bill in 1974 was aimed in a different direction, getting successful corporations to cut the employees in on some share of ownership, so that they would be more favorable to the private enterprise system. Jack Curtis, staff aide to Senator Long, learned of our bill and expressed great interest in it. Even more important than Curtis was Corey Rosen, who was working on the Small Business Committee under Senator Gaylord Nelson. A former Congressional Fellow and a Ph.D. in government from Cornell (where we had not met), Rosen was perusing the *Congressional Record* when he came upon the statement in support of our bill which I had written at Congressman Kostmayer's invitation. Rosen had been casting about for more creative things to do beyond the established routines of his committee assignment. As he told me later, "It is great to have something to work on that is intellectually challenging and that you really believe in."

Rosen sought out Blasi, and Blasi turned over his files on employee ownership, which were largely what had been photocopied at Cornell. Rosen photocopied them again and took them over to the Senate, where he drafted the Small Business Employee Ownership Act. This is the first and only piece of legislation so far to come out of our initiative. It was passed by Congress and signed by President Carter in July 1980. It lacks some of the provisions of our earlier bill, but it was a very important step in the general movement.

Our interlocking networks also had major impacts on two other government actions: inclusion of employee ownership in the Chrysler bailout legislation (which has given workers about 20 percent of the stock of that corporation), and approval by the Department of Housing and Urban Development of the Urban Development Action Grant (UDAG), which made it possible for Rath Packing Company workers to gain control of that struggling enterprise.

These results were achieved without setting up our own lobbying organization and with a minimum expenditure of personal funds. My responsibilities with the American Sociological Association and the National Institute of Mental Health paid my expenses for about six trips a year to Washington from 1977 to 1981. I was able to get up to Capitol Hill regularly the day before such meetings. Then I discovered that, since the employee ownership legislation was a direct outgrowth of research being supported by an NIMH grant, I could legitimately charge them for an additional trip or two, as necessary. I did not keep a detailed accounting, but I estimate that my personal spending to facilitate this work was hardly more than $25 over a four-year period.

Somewhat awed by what we had achieved, I found myself reflecting upon what it was that had made our strategy so extraordinarily cost-effective. My associates and I were thinking in terms of "networks" and "networking." Since I realized that the study of networks has become a very popular subfield in sociology and anthropology, I began reading in this literature.

In *Friends of Friends*, I was startled to find Jeremy Boissevain (1974) using my case of the Norton Street Gang in *Street Corner Society* as an example of a network. Ordinarily when I find another author giving prominent and favorable attention to something I have written, I take this as evidence of high quality work. But not in this case. I asked myself, "What is added when we call a gang (or clique or informal group) a network—other than confusion?"

To answer that question, I compared the Nortons with the interlocking employee ownership networks in which I had participated. The Nortons consisted of thirteen men, many or all of whom usually were interacting many hours a day over a period of many months. The members of my interlocking networks have never all been together at any place or any time.

Then I considered the motivational base supporting what I claim are two quite distinct sets of human relations. The Nortons were linked by the intrinsic satisfactions of sociability and by what I call positive exchange or reciprocity (Whyte, 1969). That is, member A did a favor for B and later B reciprocated. For the employee ownership networks, the motivational base was what I call joint payoff (Whyte, 1969). That is, we sought and got our rewards, not directly from each other, but from the external environment, from the sense of making progress toward a mutually shared objective. To be sure, participation in these networks led to friendships, and Joseph Blasi, Corey Rosen, and I have occasionally done favors for each other, but it was not positive exchange that brought us together or that maintains our relationships. And, since we see each other only once or twice a year, we hardly resemble the Nortons.

As I read further in the network literature (for example, Wellman, 1980), I recognized the source of the confusion. The writers lump the Nortons together with our interlocking employee ownership networks and then differentiate between sets of relations of high "density" (involving individuals interacting with the same people with a high frequency) and low density, in which the contacts are much less frequent and spread out in space as well as in time. However, this simply means they are calling *all sets of social relations* networks, thus blurring the distinctions among different sets of social relations.

Here one should distinguish between the methodology of network measurement and analysis and the use of a blanket term which lumps together what seem to me quite different phenomena. I find the methodology of measurement and analysis of substantial scientific interest, whereas the all encompassing definition of network seems to me only a source of confusion.

There is a further reason to avoid calling informal groups or organizations networks. When laymen speak of "networks" or "networking," they apply those terms to the kind of phenomenon I have been describing: a set of individuals who do not belong to the same group or organization and rarely if ever all get together at the same place, but who nevertheless initiate action for each other in pursuit of a shared objective. To be sure, a social scientist has a right to give any familiar term his or her own special meaning, but it seems unwise to do so when the commonly understood meaning avoids scientific confusion and facilitates communication between laymen and social scientists.

My involvement in an action project led me to a fundamental theoretical distinction between two types of sets of social relations. Perhaps, if I had read the Boissevain book without that experience, I would have recognized the theoretical confusion. But it was the action experience that got me thinking theoretically about networks, led me to the book, and sharpened in my mind the theoretical and practical distinctions between networks and what I shall continue to call informal groups.

It is not hard to find examples of action-to-theory in the works of others. Chester I. Barnard, when president of New Jersey Bell Telephone Company, wrote an early classic in the organizational behavior literature, *The Functions of the Executive* (1938), out of what he had learned as an executive. Like José Moreno writing on the uprising in the Dominican Republic or Tom Germano writing on the post office strike, Barnard was acting first and then, upon reflection, interpreting what he had learned through action.

CONCLUSIONS

There are many different ways of generating useful theoretical ideas. I have simply described some of the ways that have worked for me.

Creation does not have to be limited by formal rules of theory building. As I have illustrated through my experience in working with Congress, reflection on our own action experience can produce insights that lead us to rethink some aspects of methodology and theory.

I see no general answer to the breadth versus depth question, but in general I lean toward depth. To be sure, at first we need to reconnoiter the social terrain so as to focus on a case or problem worth studying, but then I think it better to spend time on intensive work on that part of the terrain than to continue studying all of the terrain. As I found in the study of Stouffer's Restaurant, when you have achieved some depth in a study of one part of the terrain, you have then enhanced your ability to judge what other parts of the social field are most worth studying. If you emphasize breadth throughout the project, you are likely to end the field work with the same preconceptions as when you began.

The first requirement for useful field work and theorizing is to get yourself a good orienting theory. Such a framework guides you toward data that will prove useful in later analysis without focusing the study so narrowly as to exclude data whose importance you do not recognize at the start of your project. The interaction framework has met these requirements for me, but I do not claim it is the only potentially fruitful framework.

The research methods you use tend to lead you toward certain lines of theorizing—and away from others. My interaction focus led me to theoretical ideas regarding informal group structure and the relations among structure, athletic performance, and mental health. Our integration of research methods not only provided the triangulation that strengthened confidence in our conclusions. It was the integration of surveys with anthropological studies that led me to recognize that, at the community level, perceived cooperation and conflict are two independent dimensions. Since previous writers had implicitly assumed that cooperation and conflict were simply opposite ends of a single dimension, this reconceptualization seems to me of some importance. Here I have tried to demonstrate how the four-box framework enabled us to advance our analysis far beyond what would have been possible if we had stuck with the single dimension assumption.

NOTES

1. The following discussion is adapted from Whyte (1976).

2. For a full discussion of this case, see Whyte (1961: 237-279).

3. For a full discussion of this case, see Whyte (1946: 123-147) or Whyte (1948: 104-130).

13

From Data Analysis to
Reshaping Conceptual Schemes

$\mathbf{A}$s we go on from project to project, answering each question as it comes up, we may get an uneasy sense that the theoretical framework that guides us to questions and answers is no longer providing a good sense of direction. What is needed is not simply better questions or better answers but a different framework within which to raise questions and challenge our answers. In *The Structure of Scientific Revolutions,* Thomas Kuhn (1962) examines what he calls "shifts" from an old scientific paradigm to a new and better paradigm. Something of this nature took place in my experience over the years. A major reorientation in my thinking envolved from 1964 to 1975 or perhaps later. This was not a case of concentrating on a particular problem during a limited time period, but rather of picking up ideas and discovering new leads as I moved from one project to another.

THE MYTH OF THE PASSIVE PEASANT

This shift involved moving from a modernization framework to a focus on structural change. Although some modernization theorists did take structural factors into account, the predominant emphasis was on the changing of psychological orientations from traditional to modern views of the world.

Through the Peruvian program, I changed my views on the nature of peasants—in Peru and elsewhere. I began with the then common view that peasants are, by their very nature, tradition bound, locked into their native culture, and therefore resistant to change. In these terms, the problem for action is defined as that of *overcoming resistance to change*. This view stimulated an enormous body of research on the diffusion of innovations, tracing the pathways through which innovations passed from early adopters to the late adopters, and so on, in order to discover how to overcome this resistance. Sociologists and social psychologists got research grants, published papers, gained tenure in universities and prestige among their colleagues pursuing a line of work which I now consider a waste of time and money. Perhaps it would not be too harsh to call this type of research worse than useless because it led us down a blind alley and delayed coming to grips with the real problems.

I now believe that, when peasants resist changes recommended to them by agricultural extension agents or other change agents, it is generally because (a) they know from experience that the recommended innovation will not work in their particular situation, and/or (b) they lack the money to buy the needed inputs or are unable to get those inputs in a timely fashion. This does not mean that peasants never resist change. It simply means that this is not a characteristic of peasants that sets them apart from agricultural professionals or other categories of people. If we understand the farming system practiced by the peasant and the situation of the peasant family in the community, we can find explanations of behavior having much greater practical implications than any posited resistance to change.

Starting our village studies in 1964, in conformity with the modernization framework, we asked questions designed to elicit attitudes of adherence to traditions or openness to change. (I would still use items of this nature in any survey dealing with attitudes and beliefs, but I would phrase the items differently.) Then, in the ensuing months, I encountered field data that began to undermine the modernization framework.

My shift was caused in part by my association with Peruvian colleagues who emphasized structural factors in change and development, but, also, I was affected by our concrete field experience. I had initiated the program on the assumption that the Belaunde government would intervene to stimulate progessive change in the rural areas. Within about a year of the beginning of our field work, it had become apparent that the Belaunde program had broken down, leaving the small farmers and the Indians in the position of standing still or instituting changes themselves. We did find some stagnant communities, but we were in the field during a period of rapid change in a number of rural areas. These people did not act like the passive peasants about whom we had been reading.

Then, as I got acquainted with people in the International Potato Center (CIP) in Peru, and, somewhat later, with the International Maize and Wheat Improvement Center (CIMMYT) in Mexico, I began to hear of cases in which small farmers had adopted professional recommendations with disastrous results. When I first heard of such a case, I asked myself, "How much of this had been going on?" As I talked with plant scientists I picked up case after case where the small farmers had implemented the recommendations and failed to get the results promised.

This conclusion led me to recognize the falsity of one of the major implicit assumptions accepted by those who had been studying peasant resistance to change. *The assumption was that the recommendation given by the agricultural professional to the peasant, if applied, would yield favorable results.* If the farmer did not implement the recommendation, his behavior was not economically rational, and therefore must be due to some cultural force, commonly known as "resistance to change."

As I pondered the question of why agricultural professionals were so often wrong in their recommendations and discussed this problem with my Cornell colleagues, I came to recognize some of the major causative factors. This was not simply a question of poor training or incompetence on the part of the professionals, though these were contributing factors. The underlying problem was the very structure of the agricultural research and development system.

Until well into the 1970s, in most countries, agricultural research was carried out only on experiment stations under optimum physical and economic conditions. Recommendations based on experiment station conditions often did not fit the physical and economic conditions of peasant agriculture. Nor was it simply that small farmers were handicapped in regard to the fertility of their land and access to water. Professionals had failed to recognize the enormous variability of soil conditions affecting small farmers. This means that no recommendation from an experiment station can be accepted with confidence until it has been tested under the conditions characteristic of peasant farming. Peasants themselves, with many years of experience in farming a particular plot, have far more intimate knowledge of the land and its problems and potentialities than the professionals from the experiment station. It should be obvious that any agricultural research and development system based upon unilateral initiation of changes from the professionals to the small farmers is bound to yield poor results. This conclusion is gaining ground among agricultural scientists, but its organizational implications call for drastic changes that run up against the barrier of the professionals' resistance to change.

My most striking field experience along this line occurred in 1975 when I spent two weeks at CIMMYT in Mexico. By the early 1970s, the leaders of CIMMYT had recognized that, while mayor yield gains had been achieved in the large expanses of land devoted to wheat, corn had not shown such a response to CIMMYT research. Since in Mexico corn is chiefly grown by small farmers, CIMMYT designed an intervention program, working with small farmers in one part of the state of Puebla. At the outset, this was more a demonstration than a research project. The experts thought they knew how to teach the small farmers to grow more corn. They did recognize an economic barrier and so, along with the instructional and promotional program, helped the small farmers get credit to finance fertilizers and other inputs.

By the time I arrived at CIMMYT, the Puebla Project was thought to have achieved moderate success, yet it had not lived up to the expectations of its planners. They documented a 30 percent yield increase among those small farmers cooperating with the program, significant but far short of the increases that had been achieved by the high yielding wheat varieties. They also noted that, after an initial period in which increasing numbers of small farmers entered the progam, the percentage adopting the Puebla recommendations had leveled off at about 30 percent of corn farmers in the project area (CIMMYT, 1975).

Concerned about the lack of further progress, Mexican project leaders took the radical step of going out into the field to interview and observe some of those who had declined to participate. This led them to the startling discovery that some of the more successful farmers were growing crops of twice the value they would have had if they had adopted project recommendations.

The explanation was simple. The project was designed for a monocultural strategy, maximizing the yield of a single crop, corn. The more successful nonadopters were intercropping, planting beans between the rows of corn and thus making a much more intensive use of land. (In fact, intercropping is commonly practiced by most peasant farmers in developing countries.)

When the Mexican professionals made this discovery, they began asking themselves why they had been insisting upon a monocultural strategy. When all other answers had been found wanting, they hit upon the correct one: "That is how they raise corn in the Iowa Corn Belt."

In Iowa, the cropping practices they were trying to introduce to Puebla made economic sense. Compared with Puebla, land and capital were plentiful and labor was scarce and expensive. There the farmers could afford to mechanize, and their tractors required open spaces between the corn rows. The CIMMYT planners had not made the mistake of trying to introduce tractors on the small holdings of the poor Mexican farmers, but they had failed to recognize that the Iowa system made sense only on the assumption that farmers had to leave open space for the wheels of the tractor. Since the small farmers in Puebla were short of land and capital but had ample family labor, it made sense to use the land and labor intensively, which required an interplanting strategy.

This discovery naturally raised the question: Who were resistant to change in this case, the small farmers of Puebla or the Puebla Project planners?

Mauro Gomez, general coordinator of Project Puebla (1970-1973), reinforced this new way of thinking:

> In Mexico we had been mentally deformed by our professional education. Without realizing what was happening to us, in the classroom and in the laboratories we were learning that scientists knew all that so far had been learned about agriculture and that the small farmers did not know anything. Finally we had to realize that there was much we could learn from the small farmers.

As I reflected upon this reorientation in my thinking about rural development and change, I recognized a parallel with what had been happening in industry. Reviewing the history of professionalization of management, with particular emphasis upon "scientific management" (Clawson, 1980), I realized that the movement spearheaded by Frederick W. Taylor was not simply a system to make industrial work more efficient. Taylor and his associates devised methods to shift the power and control over work from the workers themselves and their immediate supervisors, thus concentrating control in the hands of an emerging group of engineers and professional managers.

Under the system practiced earlier, efficiency depended upon the knowledge, skills, and diligence of workers. By studying jobs and subdividing the work into its simplest elements, which were then put together according to management's plan rather than workers' skill and intelligence, Taylor aimed to separate thinking from working. Thinking was to be done by managers; workers were directed to do the job in the "one best way" specified by management. In fact, a worker who experienced the introduction of the Taylor system quotes the creator of scientific management as telling him, "You're not supposed to think" (Copley, 1923: 188).

I could now see more clearly that much of my work over the years had focused on worker and union efforts to resist not only the leadership styles of particular managers but also the very system of power and control that supported autocratic and dehumanizing management.

This reflection enabled me to recognize a close parallel between agriculture in developing countries and industry in highly industrialized nations. Attempts by professional experts to establish tight control over the work of peasant farmers or industrial workers often fail to yield gains in production and inevitably produce serious frustrations and frictions.

This conclusion is no longer regarded as a radical view of the current industrial scene. Since the end of World War II, we have witnessed a clear shift in the position and prestige of U.S. management in the industrial world.

Now U.S. business leaders are increasingly looking abroad for models to follow. Recognizing that Japan's extraordinary industrial advance has been partly based upon much fuller use of all the human resources of Japanese companies—including the brains of workers—leaders of U.S. companies have been struggling to develop their own system of worker participation in decision making.

Reducing social conflict and increasing productivity depend upon finding better ways of integrating the knowledge and skills of professional experts with the skills and knowledge gained through experience by workers, small farmers, and peasants. This integration can only be achieved if working people are active participants in the campaign to increase productivity.

This sweeping generalization may be suspect because it fits so well with my personal values. However, mounting evidence in agriculture and in industry amply confirms what I would like to believe.

A book focused primarily upon field methods is not the place to document such a general conclusion. I offer it simply to illustrate the development of my own thinking, from the initial field observations and interviews in peasant communities. This case illustrates the importance of checking initial field data against the frame of reference we carry in our heads in the early stages of research program. As we encounter data that appear not to fit this framework, we need to search for other information which we hope will resolve the apparent contradiction between data and theory. This process may lead us to a reformulation enabling us to analyze old and new data in a framework that promises greater scientific and human progress.

INTEGRATING TECHNOLOGY AND WORK WITH HUMAN RELATIONS

Consolidating this new framework led me to renewed efforts to integrate technology and the nature of work with human relations. I have come to feel that sociology has been held back by our common tendency to deal with social relations as if they occurred in an economic and technological vacuum. Of course, we have been aware that economic factors are important, and that technology has impacts on behavior, but those elements tended to stay in the background of our studies, not really integrated into our conceptual schemes. This separation prevailed until in the 1950s, Eric Trist and his associates began developing their conceptions of sociotechnical systems (Trist, 1981).

As I look back on my own research career, I recognize that as early as the restaurant studies (1944-1945), I was gathering data that should have enabled me to put together a sociotechnical systems framework, even before Trist laid claim to this theoretical territory. Since many of the workers were involved in serving customers, obviously I had to factor in the worker-customer relations. This led me to follow the rest of the work flow from the waitress to the service pantry and so on.

As I examined these work flow relations, I could not help noticing the impact of the technology and physical arrangements in Stouffers. Customers were served on two floors, and the kitchen was located below the first floor. This meant that efficient service depended upon a rapid and smooth flow of food from the kitchen to the service pantries on the two upper floors and a flow of information from the service pantries to the kitchen.

There were three means of communication between service pantries and kitchen: the teleautograph (which would reproduce in the kitchen messages written in the service pantries), the telephone, and face-to-face communication. At the height of the rush hour, I would sometimes observe people running up and down the stairs to try to take a more direct hand in speeding up the work flow.

In the service pantries, we found that it made a difference in work flow and in human relations whether the counter was low enough to permit interaction between waitresses and service counter people or whether it was high enough to make it difficult for waitresses to call in their orders and urge counter people to speed things up.

Edith Lentz discovered what seems to have become one of the best known pieces of technology in the organizational behavioral literature: the spindle. This was a simple spike set in a wooden or metal base, on which the waitresses placed their order slips. Each waitress, as she reached the counter, would put her order slip on the spike, and the service counter people would pull order slips off the bottom of the spike. This simple queueing device automatically established the order in which the waitresses should be served, thus eliminating the arguments we had observed in other restaurants over who had got the order in before whom.

To some extent I used such data on technology and the nature of work in our book on the project, and I even worked that material more systematically into what was probably one of the best articles I have ever written, "The Social Structure of the Restaurant" (1949). But I did not try to integrate technology and the nature of work with human relations at that time.

Since I had all of the pieces of the puzzle necessary to fit together a sociotechnical systems framework, why did I not capitalize on my theoretical opportunities? I think there were two main factors influencing me. In the first place, at the time I was preoccupied with the urge to find ways of democratizing management and regarded technology as an extraneous factor, rather than as an element that would have to be fitted into the democratization process. In the second place, I looked upon my restaurant study as a sideline to work in industry. Therefore, I wanted to get into factory studies as soon as possible. To be sure, when the opportunity presented itself to do an action research project in a large hotel (Whyte and Hamilton, 1965), a direct outgrowth of the restaurant studies, I pursued it, but otherwise for some years I focused my attention on factories.

I did not bring to factory studies any coherent sociotechnical framework. In my first attempt at a textbook (1961), I titled two major parts of the book "The Social and Economic Environment" and "The Technological and Physical Environment." However, these discussions simply involved tracing the impact of economic and technological factors in a series of cases, rather than developing a general framework.

At the same time, these field observations led me to recognize the need to gain more systematic understanding of technology and work processes than was available simply through reading the sociological literature. Until the 1970s, perhaps my most systematic work along this line grew out of bringing together a variety of studies on worker reactions to piece rate systems (*Money and Motivation,* 1955). To understand these reactions, it did not seem necessary to learn how to do the jobs that the workers were performing nor to learn how to do a time and motion study, but my co-authors and I had to learn a good deal about the nature of different jobs and the problems they presented to workers and to those measuring work. I had to understand the logic used by industrial engineers in time and motion study and rate setting, and the technical and human problems involved in arriving at rates.

The best integration of technology and work with social relations I have so far achieved is in studies of the agricultural research and development process. As I have pointed out, the voluminous body of research on peasant resistance to change depended upon a false assumption: that the recommendations given by the professional to the peasant were always scientifically sound and practical. To challenge this assumption, it was not necessary to learn how to do research in the biological sciences and work in agricultural extension. But it was essential that I gain some background in the plant, animal, and soil sciences and agricultural engineering and understand how agricultural research and extension were typically carried out. This learning led me to recognize, not only that the recommendations of the extension agent were in fact often unsound, but also the causes of these errors. It was this analysis that led to the recognition of the importance of integrating peasant knowledge and experience with the laboratory and experiment station-based knowledge of the professionals. Given that insight, it was obvious that such integration could only be achieved if peasants (or small farmers) participated actively in decision making in the agricultural research and development process.

This theoretical integration was not a one-man job. I was able to take advantage of the structure and culture of Cornell University, which facilitates collaboration across college, departmental, and disciplinary lines. Visitors are surprised to find that at Cornell social scientists and biological scientists in agriculture actually get together to talk about their work, and sometimes even work on joint projects. To be sure, it is only a small minority in each camp that is interested in such a range of interdisciplinary communication and collaboration, but they constitute a critical mass which makes Cornell an exciting place for someone with my interests.

By 1977 I had found a number of biological scientists and social scientists who had also become aware of the inability of conventional agricultural research and development programs to meet the needs and interests of small farmers. We were approaching a common diagnosis of the problem and beginning to agree on the broad outlines of a new action strategy. However, the information and ideas necessary to develop this strategy were scattered about on our own campus and among a few of our colleagues working on research and development in the Third World. This material was only just beginning to penetrate the scholarly literature, and only in fragments here and there.

It seemed to me the time had come to consolidate what we knew and, as we established this base, to use it to accelerate our learning. Through the Center for International Studies, I circulated a memo proposing that we join together to write a book on this emerging framework for the study and practice of agricultural research and development. With the enthusiastic support and participation of Norman Uphoff and Center Director Milton Esman, I formed a working group that met irregularly, but fairly frequently, over a five-year period, for reporting, discussion, and planning sessions. In the early stages, at the suggestion of Uphoff, I was able to recruit as co-coordinator Damon Boynton, a retired professor in the plant sciences, who had long experience in research and development in the Third World. Without such shared leadership between a social scientist and a plant scientist, this project could not have been successful. It was not only that we shared the work and that Boynton could check me for technical errors and help me to communicate in language understandable to biological scientists. While I was on friendly terms with the biological scientists in the group, the partnership with Boynton served to assure them that this was really a joint project, rather than one in which social scientists were simply using them.

The project culminated in publication of *Higher-Yielding Human Systems for Agriculture* (Whyte and Boynton, 1983). The book had twelve co-authors: a horticulturist, a soil scientist, an animal scientist, two agricultural engineers, two political scientists, two sociologists, two economists, and one social psychologist. Ten of us were Cornellians and two were colleagues based elsewhere with whom we had worked. Readers have commented that for a book written by people of such diverse disciplinary backgrounds, it is extraordinarily well integrated.

There are two explanations. First, we did not simply ask a wide range of people each to write a chapter. We worked closely together throughout the five-year period. Second, Kathleen King Whyte did extensive copy editing to make sure that we avoided our various technical jargons and wrote in clear and simple English.

This project not only reinforced my belief in the importance of sociotechnical integration. It also demonstrated the possibility of achieving this objective through a participatory strategy in which we work together across disciplinary lines.

When social scientists think of interdisciplinary collaboration, we ordinarily have in mind linking disciplines within the social sciences. (for an important exception, see Fox and Swazey, 1974). For me, *Higher Yielding Human Systems* suggested the importance of bridging much wider gaps in bodies of knowledge and ways of thinking.

CONCLUSIONS

This experience suggests to me that social research is not simply a matter of applying a good orienting theory, using good research methods, and then analyzing our data. Pursuing well-accepted methods and theories, we may be imprisoned unwittingly within a currently popular view of the world. As long as we remain within that world view, refinements in methods and theory will leave us in the same old rut. To get out of that rut, we need from time to time to look beyond particular elements of methods and theory in order to reexamine the fundamental bases of our thinking.

Doing field work in a wide variety of settings and trying to integrate economic and technical data into our thinking can help us to keep our minds open to the theoretical reformulations essential for social and scientific progress.

14

Science and
Styles of Social Research

Should I worry whether the kind of work I am doing—and encouraging you to do—is really scientific? Sometimes I think this is a foolish issue. Why not just do the best we can and not worry about how our critics classify us? Although today one seldom hears arguments over whether sociology is really a science, nevertheless that question still hangs over us.

In his Appendix to *Urban Villagers,* Herbert J. Gans (1962: 409) wrote, "This, then, is not a scientific study, for it does not provide what Merton has called compelling evidence for a series of hypotheses." In the edition published twenty years later, Gans (1982: 414) had changed his mind:

> If I could rewrite my Appendix today, I would, however, expunge its apologetic conclusion that the study was an unscientific reconnaissance which produced hypotheses rather than valid sociological findings.

He then went on to reflect upon why he had originally made the disclaimer:

> I was writing in a period when science was still worshiped and social scientists, like others, believed that the idealized scientific method they also worshiped could be achieved in the real world. . . .

> At the time, I was mainly aware of the limitations of participant observation, but today I know that all research methods and studies,

even of the multimillion-dollar variety, fail to live up to the ideals to which I was paying respect.

In other words, Gans is now telling us that the more widely practiced survey research model is no more scientific than participant observation, but that conclusion still leaves up in the air the judgment of how scientific we sociologists really are, whatever methods we use. I ran up against this question in 1941 when Lloyd Warner nominated me for membership in Sigma Xi, the scientific honorary society. Later he was embarrassed to inform me that I would not be so honored because I was getting my degree in sociology, which Sigma Xi did not include among the sciences! Even if I had been doing surveys, that would not have got me in.

I must have been aware of this issue earlier, but I had to face it when, following graduation from Swarthmore, I was a junior fellow at Harvard (1936-1940). The dominant figure among the senior fellows was Chairman Lawrence J. Henderson, a physiologist who had made important contributions to studies of the chemistry of the blood. Henderson did not hestitate to express his domatic views on topics ranging from politics to the nature of science, and seemed to take special pleasure in attacking the sentimentality and general muddleheadedness of social scientists in general and sociologists in particular. I reacted against Henderson's extreme conservative political views and, of course, against his attacks on social scientists, but at the same time I felt the need to justify what I was doing as truly scientific. That sent me off on a long search not yet concluded.

When I was in the Society of Fellows, physics was commonly thought to provide *the* model of a true science. At the time, *The Logic of Modern Physics* (Bridgman, 1927) appeared to be the last word on defining the nature of science. I did not read it until many years later, but the ideas of the book were so much discussed among the junior fellows that I thought I knew it almost by heart. Indeed, the record indicates that this was an influential book. The library copy I recently consulted was from the seventh edition, printed in 1954.

I recently learned that it was not only sociologists and other social scientists who felt inferior to physicists. In an earlier period, many biologists felt this same sense of inferiority and therefore a need to ape the physicists (Mayr, 1983). The extraordinary advances of biology in recent decades have eliminated any question regarding the scientific legitimacy of work in that field. Nevertheless, it is important to recognize the long dominance of physics as *the* model of science in the minds of many social scientists.

> Most general histories of "science" have been written by historians of physics who have never quite gotten over the parochial attitude that anything that is not applicable to physics is not science. Physical scientists tend to rate biologists on a scale of values depending on the extent to which each biologist has used "laws," measurements, experiments, and other aspects of scientific research that are rated highly in the physical sciences. As a result, the judgments on fields of biology made by certain historians of the physical sciences that one may find in that literature are so ludicrous that one can only smile [Mayr, 1983: 14].

Mayr adds,

> Most historians of science display an extraordinary ignorance when discussing methods other than the experimental one [p. 30].

In the intellectual atmosphere of the Society of Fellows in the late 1930s, logical positivism was the dominant doctrine on the nature of science. This required applying certain rules to social research:

(1) The research design should be value neutral. That is, independent of any values the researcher may hold.

(2) To avoid contaminating the results, as much as possible the researcher should avoid influencing the subjects of the study—except when carrying out an experiment, in which case the researcher tries to establish maximum control over the behavior of the subjects. (Since I did not expect to do experiments, I assumed I should be committed to the noninfluence principle.)

(3) Concepts should be based upon operational definitions.

> *In general, we mean by any concept nothing more than a set of operations; the concept is synonymous with the corresponding set of operations* [Bridgman, 1927: 3; emphasis in original].

(4) Operations must be subject to measurement. Quantification is the basic requirement of science.

(5) The basic aim of science is to arrive at *laws* governing the behavior of the phenomena under study.

At the time, my reaction to those rules was ambivalent. I had the urge to do things that violated the rules, and yet I wanted my work to be regarded as scientific. For years I lived with this ambivalence, feeling alternately guilty for violating the rules and happy over what I was learning through my transgressions.

Today few sociologists would accept such a bald statement of scientific principles, and yet I believe the physics model has had a deep and continuing influence upon our ways of thinking and teaching. This influence has produced what I call "the standard model of social research taught to our graduate students" (Whyte, 1982: 10).

According to that standard model, to do research, you should take the following steps. You review the literature and consult with colleagues regarding a problem you would like to study. Then you select hypotheses to test, arming yourself with a combination of reasonably well-supported hypotheses to reinforce, hypotheses that involve conflicting evidence from past research, and perhaps a novel hypothesis or two that you can think up yourself. With this theoretical armament in place, you pick out a target population for study—and with this research style, the "target population" is well named. You then move in to persuade the gatekeepers controlling access to this target population that, if they let you do the study, somehow the information you gather will be useful to them as well as to you. Having done the study, if you aren't too busy writing research papers and proposals for new research, you may return to the gatekeepers to report what you have learned.

This standard model is less appropriate to sociology than to physics. Compared to social phenomena, in physics, the phenomena under study are relatively fixed, at least in the sense that, although they are in constant movement, they follow a reasonably standard orbit. The physicist is experimenting on the basis of a highly developed and coherent body of theory. And finally, since the phenomena are partly under the control of the investigator, there is no possibility of them taking an active part in the experiment.

In sociology or organizational behavior, the phenomena we study are in movement, and new combinations are constantly emerging. Our theory base is much less firm, and our links from data to theory are often exceedingly shaky. Furthermore, we are dealing with active human beings, who can contribute to our study if we allow them to participate. Under these conditions, before adopting the standard model we should at least ask ourselves: Do we really know the territory we are investigating? Or are we just mechanically applying a given research instrument?

One of the problems of graduate education in sociology today is the complete physical separation of many investigators from the field they are studying. The development of survey research and modern data processing made this possible. Many years ago, as editor of *Human Organization* (1960-1961), I attacked this separation in an editorial entitled "The Card Shuffling Method of Graduate Education." I had discovered an increasingly popular method for doing doctoral theses. If students could just get hold of a set of data cards from an earlier survey research project, they could devise a set of hypotheses different from those posed by the original investigators, run the cards through the machines, inspect the results, and write up their "findings" for the thesis.

That editorial is now technologically dated because we have moved on from data cards to computer tapes, but the principle remains the same. I recently learned from a colleague that, in one of our most prestigious sociology departments, the common method for doing the doctoral thesis follows the model I had earlier described. My informant added that this strategy was so widely practiced that any student who wanted to go out into the field to do research was looked upon by fellow students and faculty members as rather peculiar.

In a talk before the Southern Sociological Society, I attacked what now should be called "the tape spinning method of graduate education" (Whyte, 1981). After my talk, one chairman told me about his experience in recruiting for a tenure track position in his department. The department invited nine candidates to come and speak on their doctoral thesis research. Eight of the nine conformed perfectly to the model I have described. When they were asked questions about what might have been going on in the field from which the data had originally been drawn, they were unable to answer. Furthermore, they seemed to consider such questions illegitimate. It was as if they were saying, "If I have command of the numbers, how can you expect anything else of me?"

BIOLOGY AS AN ALTERNATIVE MODEL

Each discipline must find its own way of doing research and advancing theory. However, if we have been misled in the past into assuming that physics is *the* model of science, it may liberate our thinking to consider biology as an alternative model. The need to pull together my thoughts on the nature of the behavioral sciences led me to *The Growth of Biological Thought* by the distinguished biologist and historian of science, Ernst Mayr (1983). That book did not make a sociobiologist of me— in fact Mayr devotes little attention to sociobiology—but it did provide a welcome escape from the physics model.

Should we aim to discover *laws* of human behavior? Mayr (1983: 43) argues that the search for laws is useful in some branches of biology and fruitless in others:

> Instead of formulating laws, biologists usually organize their generalizations into a framework of concepts. The claim has been made that laws versus concepts is only a formal difference, since every concept can be translated into one or several laws. Even if this were formally true, of which I am not at all sure, such a translation would not be helpful in the actual performance of biological research. Laws lack the flexibility and heuristic usefulness of concepts.

> Progress in biological science is, perhaps, largely a matter of the development of these concepts or principles. The progress of systematics was characterized by the crystallization and refinement of such concepts as classification, species, category, taxon, and so on; evolutionary science by such concepts as descent, selection, and fitness. Similar key concepts could be listed for every branch of biology.

Mayr makes a fundamental distinction between functional and evolutionary biology. In functional biology, the scientist is studying the behavior of biological organisms. In this pursuit, it is possible to proceed like the physicist to observe, to experiment, to predict, to quantify, and to arrive at laws of biological behavior. In evolutionary biology, which involves the study of growth and transformations, such a model cannot be applied.

> The physical world is a world of quantification (Newton's movements and forces) and of mass actions. By contrast, the world of life can be designated as a world of qualities. Individual differences, communication systems, stored information, properties of the macromolecules, interactions in ecosystems, and many other aspects of living organisms are prevailingly qualitative in nature. One can translate these qualitative aspects into quantitative ones, but one loses thereby the real significance of the respective biological phenomena, exactly as if one would describe a painting of Rembrandt in terms of the wave

lengths of the prevailing color reflected by each square millimeter of the painting.

In a like manner, many times in the history of biology, brave efforts to translate qualitative biological phenomena into mathematical terms have ultimately proved complete failures because they lost touch with reality. Early efforts to emphasize the importance of quality, like those of Galen, Paracelsus, and van Helmont, were likewise failures owing to the choice of wrong parameters, but they were the first steps in the right direction. The champions of quantification tend to consider the recognition of quality as something unscientific or at best as something purely descriptive and classificatory. They reveal by this bias how little they understand the nature of biological phenomena. Quantification is important in many fields of biology, but not to the exclusion of all qualitative aspects.

These are particularly important in relational phenomena, which are precisely the phenomena that dominate living nature. Species, classification, ecosystems, communicatory behavior, regulation, and just about every other biological process deals with relational properties. These can be expressed, in most cases, only qualitatively, not quantitatively [Mayr, 1983: 54-55].

In biology, it is critically important to devise a scheme of classification useful for ordering the phenomena under study. Mayr devotes 150 pages to the history of the struggle of biologists, from Aristotle forward, to overcome arbitrary or "common sense" classifications in order to establish systems appropriate for scientific advance. He points out that Darwin's historic breakthrough to the theory of evolution was based upon classification in terms of "descendants from a common ancestor" (p. 239).

Mayr (1983: 239) also emphasizes the importance of studying change through time:

Indeed it is impossible to arrive at meaningful classifications of items that are the product of a developmental history unless the historical processes responsible for their origin are duly taken into consideration.

ON THE IMPORTANCE OF CLASSIFICATION

As Mayr (1983) has argued, advances in the biological sciences have depended in large measure upon improvements in systems of classifications. These advances have depended particularly upon shifting from conventional or common sense classifications to systems more useful for scientific research. Furthermore, classificatory schemes in biology have been based primarily upon qualities rather than upon quantities. The same general conclusions should apply to the behavioral sciences.

This does not mean that quantification is unimportant. It means that enormous time, effort, and money can be wasted if we lump together for counting phenomena that properly belong in different categories. The behavioral science literature is oversupplied with such futile efforts to quantify. Before we decide upon the method or combination of methods to use, we need to resolve the problem of classification.

In the literature of organizational behavior, there have been two main sources of such errors: the normative doctrines of "scientific management" and exclusive reliance upon one method of research.

In undertaking to state laws of organizational behavior, exponents of scientific management assumed that there was no problem of classification. For example, in 1927 Mary Parker Follet wrote:

> Whatever the purpose towards which human endeavor is directed, the principles of that direction are nevertheless the same [cited in Woodward, 1965: 55].

British sociologist Joan Woodward (1965) directed a study of 203 manufacturing firms to determine the factors influencing the structure of industrial organizations and patterns of staff-line relations. She found much variability and no clear patterns. For example, she found little relationship between the size of the workforce and the numbers of levels of authority in the firm.

Woodward then decided to focus on technology. This involved first setting up types of technology so as to have objective standards for the categories in which she would sort her cases. She classified into three types: unit or small batch, mass production, and continuous process operations. She now found systematic relationships between type of technology and certain aspects of formal organization structure on the one hand and staff-line relations on the other.

I am not arguing that Woodward has said the last word on classification in studies of technology and organization structure. I am simply pointing out that her advance in classification made it possible to draw general conclusions which could not be arrived at when all organizations were lumped together.

For years, studies of supervisory leadership enjoyed great popularity among researchers. That interest has faded recently, perhaps in response to the recognition that solid findings lagged far behind the enormous volume of research. It seems to me that this lag has been due primarily to the exclusive reliance on the survey by most students in the field. The nature of the methodology has led researchers to focus particularly upon the relationships between workers and first-line supervisors. For purposes of statistical analysis of findings, this focus has one important but illusory advantage. In any large organization, there are large numbers of workers and first-line supervisors, thus aiding the researcher to arrive at statistically significant findings.

We need to distinguish between statistical significance and theoretical or scientific significance. Statistical significance simply means that a given finding could not have occurred more than one time (or five times) out of a hundred on a chance basis, but this does not tell us whether what we are measuring is worth measuring.

The implicit assumption behind this survey approach is that all first-line supervisory roles are sufficiently alike so that they can be lumped together. It took many years of number crunching before survey researchers were forced to recognize, out of the problems in their own data, that there are important differences among supervisory roles and that these tend to be related to the nature of the technology and the work tasks being supervised (Schein, 1980).

This does not mean that each supervisory role is unique—a conclusion which would rule out any possibility of generalization. It does mean that studies of supervisory leadership must be based first upon a system of classification which groups together those supervisors with apparently similar roles and directing apparently similar work processes. The supervisors who then can be compared with each other are greatly reduced in number, thus making it more difficult to arrive at statistically significant conclusions. However, if researchers were willing to combine anthropological field methods with surveys, this limitation could be overcome.

The importance of such triangulation becomes evident if we review the efforts of survey researchers to relate the attitudes and perceptions of workers to supervisory behavior. Basically this involved correlating worker perceptions of supervisory behavior with worker attitudes. Researchers in the Ohio State Group used worker perceptions to rank supervisors in two dimensions: consideration (people oriented) and initiating structure (task oriented). University of Michigan researchers in the same period were using similar dimensions which they labeled *employee centered* and *production centered*. Others also devised similar ways of sorting out supervisors according to worker perceptions.

After forty years or more of such research, the scientific yield has been disappointingly small. According to the evaluation of Edgar H. Schein (1980: 131):

> Researchers continue to differ in two crucial and as yet unresolved ways. . . . (1) whether task concern and people concern are two ends of a single continuum or two independent dimensions such that one could be high or low in both; and (2) whether the dimensions refer to inner attitudes and values or only to overt behavior.

I would shift the emphasis of Schein's critique to argue that the *survey researchers had no data on the overt behavior of supervisors*. The researchers only secured data on *worker perceptions* of such behavior. In reporting on supervisory behavior, based on such extrapolation, survey researchers were practicing a respectable fraud—respectable because this was the style of research practiced by some of the leading behavioral scientists but nevertheless fraudulent because it enabled them to report measures of behavior that had been neither observed nor measured.

I am not arguing that it is useless to measure worker attitudes and worker perceptions of supervisors. Such survey measures could be scientifically important if they were combined with systematic observation of supervisory behavior and intensive interviews with workers and supervisors. Such triangulation was not attempted by any of the leading survey researchers, and I only came to recognize the value of surveys long after I had moved away from studies of supervisory leadership.

The same argument regarding classification applies to the rapidly expanding field of network studies. In the last chapter, I argued against lumping together as networks an informal group such as the Norton Street Gang and a set of relations established in the effort to move Congress toward employee ownership legislation. Of course, those specializing in network studies recognize *quantitative* differences in interactions between informal groups such as I have studied and the academic/activist and congressional employee ownership networks. However, if we apply the lessons learned in biology to social research, by itself quantification is not a sound basis for scientific advance. Again I am not questioning the value of quantitative studies. I am simply arguing that progress in network analysis will be retarded until researchers recognize the prior importance of classification. With improvement in classification, quantitative studies within a given category will be more fruitful than quantitative studies that are *not* channeled within a classificatory system.

Advances in studies of the nature of the agricultural research and development process also depended upon coming to grips with the problem of classification. In the long and fruitless history of studies of the diffusion of innovation, behavioral scientists were imposing their own implicit system of classification upon phenomena which did not lend themselves to such treatment. Here again convenience in research design misled researchers. To simplify the design problem, it was convenient to focus on a single item of behavior change: the acceptance or rejection of a particular innovation promoted by agricultural professionals. This specification of the dependent variable greatly facilitated measurement, but it also reinforced an orienting theory in which the diffusion of innovation depended upon overcoming peasant resistance to change.

Plant scientists and social scientists also were mistakenly imposing their own scheme of classification upon the farms and farming practices of peasant farmers. At the most basic level, professionals tended to think in terms of *monoculture* whereas peasant farmers think in terms of *polyculture*. For decades agricultural scientists have been in trying to achieve the highest yields and the best overall performance of particular commodities, whether corn, beans, potatoes, or rice, and so on. Peasant farmers almost universally think and act in terms of polyculture, attempting to arrive at the best combination of a variety of commodities grown in association with each other or in rotation. Furthermore, in most cases the peasant farmers also raise animals and therefore must act in terms of the complementarity between animals and crops. For example, consider a new variety of corn with stalks that are tougher so as to resist the corn borer and shorter so as to channel the growth of the plant more into the ears of corn. This variety will be valuable to a farmer specializing in corn but of no interest to the small farmer who has cattle which have difficulty chewing and digesting the tougher stalks and need a more ample supply of stalks for fodder.

This shift in classification from monoculture to polyculture and farming systems helps us to understand a further problem in the study of diffusion of innovations. The implicit assumption of that line of research is that a single innovation, if adopted, would provide significant benefits for the farmer. In fact, farming systems are so complex that it is rare indeed for any single innovation to produce the results anticipated by experts.

The research problem in this field may also be stated in terms of Max Elden's concept of "local theory." Implicit in this local theory is a system of classification in the minds of peasant farmers. Until researchers come to understand this local theory and the associations and sequences and rotations of various crops, along with animals, the application of agricultural sciences to the practical problems of small farmers will be severely limited.

Again I am not ruling out quantification but simply arguing that classification is a prior step. We must begin by learning to think in terms of farming systems. Of course, that is only a very general concept. We need to focus on the farming system practiced within the given geographical and cultural area, for researchers have found important common elements in such local farming systems. When the researcher has got his classificatory system straight for a given farming area, then he also has the basis for fruitful quantification. At this point, quantitative studies may be as important as further qualitative research.

Some time ago I surprised those planning to start a journal to be called *Qualitative Sociology* by declining to serve on its board of editors. I recognize that I am generally thought to be on that side of the conventional quantitative-qualitative dichotomy, but I object strongly to that very dichotomy. To use measurement for scientific progress we need to ask

(1) what to measure (subjective states and/or overt behavior),
(2) within the context of what qualitative classificatory system we intend to measure, and
(3) how to integrate quantitative and qualitative data.

ON THE EVOLUTION OF MY WORK

Since I am only now becoming acquainted with the philosophy of the biological sciences, I cannot claim that this guided my work over the years. From the street corner onward, I have been involved in a fumbling and searching effort to develop methods that advance theory and theory that advances methods. Now I find that what I am learning about biology is helping me to see a pattern in what I have been learning from the field over the years.

It is impossible to do research without theory because, at the outset of any project, theory indicates what phenomena are important to study. I call the type needed to plan a project *orienting theory*—orienting in the sense that it indicates what phenomena deserve particular attention and what other phenomena can be disregarded or be accorded less attention. Glaser and Strauss (1967) propose two categories of theory: *substantive* (derived from and applied to the phenomena being studied) and *formal* (more abstract generalizations built upon substantive theory). I think it important to recognize *orienting theory* as logically prior to *substantive* and *formal* because we first need to determine about what we wish to generalize.

A colleague once gave me this backhanded compliment:

> I think it is extraordinary how much mileage Bill Whyte has been able to get out of such a simple-minded conceptual scheme.

Since I see no inherent virtue in complexity, I make no apology for this simple-mindedness—on the level of orienting theory. My orienting theory tells me that interpersonal interactions and the activities people engage in are (1) observable, (2) quantifiable, and (3) important. About observability and quantifiability there can be no question. The importance of such data depends upon what we can do with them—theoretically and practically. For building theory and discovering practical implications, we must go beyond the simple-minded guidance of our orienting theory, but at least we will be building on a firm foundation, as we strive to understand how interactions and activities relate to mental health, athletic performance, interorganizational relations, and the functioning of bureaucracies.

From the beginning I have tried to study the relations of individuals to groups, of groups to each other, building up to studies of large organizations and interorganizational relations. It was the work of Eliot D. Chapple and Conrad M. Arensberg (1940) that originally led me to the focus on interactions. From this early formulation, Chapple (1949) went on to carry out highly quantitative observational studies of what I call micro-interaction, measuring the speaking and gestural actions of subjects.

I believe that the interaction chronograph, the methodology developed for such measures of micro-interaction, represents an important scientific advance in objective and quantitative measures of important aspects of human personality, but the methodology is not readily adapted for use in field situations. For field purposes, I have adapted the methodology so as to focus on the initiation of changes in activities (the things people do). In contrast to the methodology used with the interaction chronograph, for this purpose we have to give some attention to the meaning of the words spoken, but only to interpret them in terms of objective behavioral changes. For example, we hear A say to B and C, "Let's go to that show at the Orpheum." We then observe A, B, and C moving out of their stationary position on the corner and walking up to a theatre which has over its marquee the title of Orpheum. If we did not understand the words spoken, we would not be sure that A had indeed initiated action (or activity change) for B and C. However, this interpretation requires no subtle content analysis. Furthermore, if other observers had been present, or if we had been able to put the particular interaction on videotape, we could readily check the reliability of the observation that A did in fact initiate action for B and C.

In the past it was often assumed that this focus on interaction simply involved a study of communication, as if we were trying to interpret behavior in terms of good or bad communication or trying to change behavior through improving communication. "Communication" is a term applied to a wide range of phenomena that have distinctively different outcomes. To study patterns of leadership, influence, and informal and formal hierarchies, it is important to concentrate on the words (or gestures) that precipitate changes in activities.

I began by building on patterns of interaction and activities but this left up in the air the question of how to deal with the subjective side of behavior (attitudes and sentiments, beliefs and values). At first I was inclined to treat the subjective states as simply products of interaction and activities, assuming that, as interactions and activities change, we can expect to find changes in subjective states. Then I realized that such an assumption, while pointing in the right direction for interpreting changes in subjective states, did not account for the fact that these subjective states are influential in determining whether particular individuals will enter into interaction with other persons or engage in particular activities. This recognition led me to think in terms of mutual dependence—the assumption that changes in interactions, activities, and subjective states were mutually dependent upon each other.

If we want to study the attitudes, beliefs, and values of an aggregate of subjects, then clearly the questionnaire or survey is the method of choice. We can go beyond subjective states by asking respondents to report on certain behaviors, but then we must recognize that in certain cases—as in the question on attendance at union meetings—answers may be subject to considerable distortion.

Only as we interview and observe the same people over a period of time in a group or organizational situation can we get at the dynamics of attitude change. On the other hand, when we combine anthropological methods with a survey of a small community or small organization this triangulation gives us the advantage of measures of responses to standardized items combined with a documentation of the behavior to which the respondents are reacting. I cannot state how small the organization or community studied should be in order to gain the advantages of such triangulation but am simply pointing out that if we are sampling respondents in an organization or community of some thousands of individuals, then these large social units are composed of distinctively different elements so that we cannot assume that any set of respondents is responding to rougly the same experiences.

Having allowed subjective states into my framework, I still realized there was something missing. I had to recognize that, while human beings do need some sociability, generally we do not come together simply for the sake of interaction. There are some objectives that we seek to obtain through the group, and interactions and activities in which we are engaged lead to consequences that we find rewarding or punishing. Here I deal with what psychologists call positive or negative reinforcements.

I was initially attracted to the basic assumption of B. F. Skinner and his notions of operant conditioning: the idea that behavior is shaped by its consequences, which means that future behavior is shaped by the consequences earlier experienced with similar behaviors in the past. This seems plausible, but there are a number of obvious problems with this formulation when we move from pigeons to people.

Earlier (1972) I discussed these deficiencies in some detail, but here I limit myself to one point. The basic problem is that most of the rewards and penalties shaping our behavior are not the immediate consequences of the actions we take. A pigeon pecks and immediately is rewarded by a pellet of food. Not so with human beings, who find rewarding a wide range of consequences, many of which we expect or hope to experience a considerable time in the future. I assume that human beings tend to interpret potential rewards or penalties in terms of a cognitive map that has arisen out of our past experiences. Therefore, we have to assume that differential past experiences will lead to differential interpretations of what is rewarding or punishing, within certain obvious limits. We should not be surprised that the opportunity to join a union will seem to some to promise potential rewards and to others only potential penalties, as I have sought to explain in the analysis of who goes union and why.

Over the years, I have found that I have to deal with two additional elements: symbols and the physical/technical requirements of activities. Behavioral scientists have long recognized that the physical settings of offices and other workplaces tend to indicate to actors the expected relations among people and the appropriate behavior for a given setting. Verbal symbols can reinforce or disrupt existing relations. In my study of Phillips Petroleum, I noted the dramatic effect of the watchman statement upon relations between workers and management. On the other hand, I also observed that when subsequent interactions and activities between workers and management people did not conform to the demeaning pattern suggested by the watchman statement, the cleavage between workers and management was at least partially bridged. This suggests that in any social situation we may encounter verbal symbols that have the immediate effect of stirring hostile or friendly sentiments and thus lead to changes in activities and interactions. However, unless this change in activities and interactions is reinforced by future experience, the effect of such potent symbols will gradually fade out.

From the restaurant studies on to studies of agricultural research and development, I was groping for a way to integrate technology and work requirements with human relations. While I have yet to work out a systematic theoretical statement on such an integration, at least I am now clear as to the dangers inherent in dealing with human relations as if they occurred in a technological and physical vacuum.

FROM ORIENTING THEORY TO SUBSTANTIVE AND FORMAL THEORY

In building from data to theory, we should recognize that the logic of analysis in survey research is quite different from the analysis appropriate to anthropological case studies. As Martin King Whyte (personal communication) comments:

> With a case study approach, you are more likely to look in detail at deviant cases, and perhaps come up with new ideas and hypotheses.

In quantitative analysis there will always be lots of cases deviating from the tested hypotheses, and these are simply assumed to be due to other variables considered, variables not considered, and random error. Typically such analysts are happy if they explain 20 to 40 percent of the variance, and rarely do they inspect the "outliers" that do not fit their regression equations to see if they can think of new factors to explain them.

Whyte goes on to consider the problem of small numbers in case studies:

Typically, you end up case study research such as you describe here with results that are "overdetermined"—you have a set of factors that together seem to you to explain all of the cases, or almost all of them, but you can't be sure of the relative strength of the various factors, since you don't have enough cases to control for all of the factors to test any single one. With quantitative analysis, on the other hand, you can measure the relative strengths of various factors with some precision, but there will be many deviant cases that are not explained by the factors considered—so the apparatus may not help if you want to explain what happens for any single case, but only in explaining the general tendencies in a population of such cases.

I would add that how many numbers you have to analyze depends upon whether you are counting indivisuals, groups or units of behavior of individuals or groups. For example, in theorizing about Long John's mental health problems and poor bowling performance, I was focusing on a single individual but examining drastic *quantitative* changes in his interactions with the Nortons. To be sure, I had no precise measurements of these interactional changes, but I had observed (or learned from other observers) that, prior to the onset of his problems, Long John was interacting six to seven days a week for several hours a day with his fellow Nortons, that, during his problem period, he was interacting with greatly reduced frequency with those few who remained on that corner, and that, during the recovery period, he had reestablished in another group the sort of interaction pattern he had enjoyed earlier.

I shall use my observations of the Norton Street Gang to illustrate further the process of moving from orienting to substantive and to formal theory. It was orienting theory that led me to focus on the interactions and activities of the Nortons. This led to the recognition of an informal but stable structure of hierarchical relationships. The charting of this structure represented the first stage of substantive theorizing.

When we bowled for money on the last night of my first season with the Nortons, I was struck with the close correspondence between the ranking of the members in the final scores and their ranking in the informal group structure. I could now state a substantive proposition regarding the relationship between performance and ranking for this particular group. In a later publication, I built upon this to derive a formal theory:

> There tends to be a correlation between the *performance* of the members and their *ranking* in the informal group structure when the following conditions obtain:
> 1. The members *interact frequently* together.
> 2. The group *participates frequently* in some kind of competitive activity.
> 3. The activity contains an important element of *skill*.
> 4. The activity is *highly valued* (considered important) by the group.
>
> . . . I assume first a relationship between frequency of interaction and fixity of individual rankings in the group structure. If members seldom interact, their relative positions are likely to be unclear and unstable. As members increase their frequency of interaction, a more definite patterning of positions tends to emerge.
>
> The competitive activity must also be frequent for us to expect a pattern to emerge here. Skill is important, for a game of pure chance would yield chance rankings of individual members.
>
> If the activity is thought of little consequence, then it is unimportant how the members perform. Only in a *highly valued* activity is it important how the members score and do we expect to find the ranking-performance relationship [Whyte, 1964: 258-259].

Note that the general conclusions proposed are subject to quantitative testing—and have been tested experimentally (Harvey and Sherif, 1953). However, it was participant observation that led me to ideas worth testing.

As I followed the remnants of the Nortons through to the end of the next bowling season, I came upon Long John's mental health problems and the deterioration of his bowling scores as he lost the support of the leadership subgroup. Then, when Doc took steps to support Long John's social position, I witnessed his dramatic comeback at the bowling alleys—and learned that his mental health problems were now behind him. Such observations could provide the basis for building a formal theory of the relations between mental health and certain types of changes in the interaction patterns of individuals.

The mental health case also underlines the importance of studying phenomena through time—as in some branches of biology. In my study of "who goes union and why," I was studying current and recent history for two aspects of the problem. Orienting theory told me that, in the course of growing up in family, home, school, and community, each individual develops a characteristic interaction pattern. Discovering the fit or lack of fit between this preexisting pattern and the interactions and activities the individual experiences on the job should provide a partial explanation for the inclination to accept or reject the union. I also recognized the importance of the history of worker-management relations before I came on the scene and the changes taking place during my period of observation. Such data provided the basis for a substantive theory on the pro- and anti-union inclinations of Phillips workers and could have been the basis of a tentative formal theory.

Similarly, the crying waitress study followed the same orienting theory in relating the interactional experience of the women before coming to work at Stouffer's with their tendencies to break under the strain of waitress work.

In those early studies, I followed current history through observation only for several months to several years, supplementing these observations through interviews on company history and the earlier life experiences of my subjects. In the Peruvian research program, I eventually recognized the importance of extending the study of changes back through decades and, in one area, for centuries. I do not claim to have integrated such historical data into my conceptual scheme, yet I have become convinced that the advance of the behavioral sciences will be seriously retarded until we can integrate data from past and current history with our observations, interviews, and surveys.

Shifting the focus from small groups to large organizations and interorganizational relations, I have found gathering data on changes in patterns of interaction and initiation of activities essential for understanding both (1) changes from conflict to cooperation in union-management relations (Whyte, 1949) and (2) changes in attitudes and productivity of industrial workers (Whyte, 1961, 1969) and of peasant farmers (Whyte and Boynton, 1983).

SOCIAL INVENTIONS AS THE NEXT FRONTIER

I conclude this personal exploration by linking together reflections on my beginnings as a social scientist with some ideas as to where we should go from here.

As I have noted, during my period in the Society of Fellows and for years thereafter, physics provided *the* model for a *real* science. Although Chairman Lawrence J. Henderson had no use for most of academic sociology, at least he was not trying to impose the physics model on me.

By the time I entered the Society of Fellows, Henderson had left the laboratory behind him and established himself as a self-taught sociologist. He had discovered Vilfredo Pareto and was fascinated with his theoretical work—and also, I suspect, with Pareto's conservative political orientation. Every year Henderson offered a seminar on Pareto. There were no official course requirements for junior fellows, but social scientists among us assumed that this course was a must, and some of the natural scientists also enrolled.

I found some of Pareto interesting reading but never could find a way to use his theoretical formulations. Henderson's other teaching assignment, a course in "concrete sociology" had more of an impact upon me. This course provided no theoretical framework, but rather a series of cases in which the researchers or practitioners presented accounts of particular social and organizational problem situations. There was no textbook, but Henderson distributed the introductory lectures in mimeographed form (Henderson, 1938). One passage has stayed with me over the years. Henderson proposed these requirements for progress in the scientific study of society:

> The sociologist, like the physician, should have first, intimate, habitual, intuitive familiarity with things; secondly, systematic knowledge of things; and thirdly, an effective way of thinking about things.

Whether that statement has guided me or simply encouraged me to follow my natural inclinations, I cannot say, but I do find myself applying Henderson's standard to my work and that of others. For example, in a review of a colleague's book on human relations in complex organizations, I commented that it appeared to have been written by someone who had never set foot inside of a factory. This provoked a long and indignant letter from the author—but he never did state whether he had ever been inside any of the organizations he was analyzing.

In 1944 when I began work at the University of Chicago with the Committee on Human Relations in Industry, I shared an office with Burleigh B. Gardner, so I could listen when students came in from the field to report to him. I remember how impressed I was because, whatever incident or problem the student reported, Gardner could pick out parallels from his own field experience and thus put the case in a broader framework. In other words, Gardner could see the pattern in the fragments of data the students brought him.

As I broadened my field experience from Phillips Petroleum to restaurants and a hotel, a plastics fabricating plant, a steel fabricating plant, a glass works, and aluminum plants, I found myself increasingly able to put fragments into general patterns. At first I enjoyed the experience. As the students came in to report from their field studies, I could say, "That's interesting. Now, I saw something like that in the XYZ company. What happened there suggests something else you ought to be looking for."

This seemed helpful to students, and, up to a point, I took pride in my increasing ability to see patterns in organizational behavior. But then the patterns became all too familiar to me.

As this went on and on, I found myself getting bored. It was as if I was asking, "Is this all there is? Why can't I find something different?" I am not suggesting that scientific work comes to a conclusion with the perception of patterns. A perceived pattern can be an illusion, and so it needs to be tested again and again. Furthermore, perception of a general pattern, even if correct, requires more systematic description and measurement than I had been able to do. However, I had to consider where my talents lay and what my weaknesses were. I decided that I was good at perceiving patterns and had limited ability to establish the validity of those patterns. That latter task would have to be the responsibility of other social scientists.

I now see the need to add a fourth requirement that has guided my work in recent years. When Henderson spoke of "an effective way of thinking about things," implicit in the statement was the additional phrase, *as they currently exist.* Why not study things *as they might be?*

This suggested the importance of advancing my own learning through trying to produce behavior changes. In the period of my street corner study, this was not a legitimate type of behavior for a social scientist. Unless you could control the behavior you were studying (through an experiment) you were not supposed to get involved in the action at all. Not without some anxieties about breaking this rule, I did nevertheless get involved in the action on at least three occasions. From the protest march on city hall I organized, I learned practical pointers on such marches but nothing of theoretical significance. The other two interventions seemed to me more fruitful. Through discussions with Doc on Long John's mental health problem and through Doc's subsequent actions, I was confirming ideas regarding the relation between certain kinds of interactional changes and mental health. Through persuading the settlement house director to put a corner boy leader in charge of one of the three storefront recreation centers, I provided a limited test to the notion that such an indigenous leader would be more successful than outsiders with social work credentials.

The street corner interventions were more or less ad hoc. Later I stopped worrying about the legitimacy of mixing action with research and looked for opportunities to try out more systematic and far-reaching interventions—first in a large hotel and later with the Jamestown Area Labor-Management Committee, Rath Packing Company and Local 46 of the United Food and Commercial Workers Union, and the Congress of the United States.

In recent years, I have also come to recognize the importance of learning from the innovations created by others. By the time I gave my Presidential Address before the American Sociological Association (1982), I had formulated this new approach in terms of a strategy focusing on the discovery, analysis, and practical and theoretical interpretation of social inventions.

As I see it, a social intention can be

- a new element in organizational structure or interorganizational relations;
- new sets of procedures for shaping human interactions and the relations of humans to the natural and social environment;
- a new policy in action (that is, not just on paper); or
- a new role or a new set of roles.

This leads me in quite a different direction from that indicated by the conventional approach to establishing research priorities. So as to be able to generalize the conclusions of any case study to a large number of organizations in the same field of activity, researchers have been inclined to concentrate on studies of what I call "standard organizations." In any long practiced field of human activity, there arises a more or less standard way of doing things and of managing the way things are done. There also arises a set of beliefs on how things should be done. My experience in industry and community studies suggested that the standard ways of doing things and the standard ways of defining problems and dealing with them were not resolving those problems.

More and more research on these "standard organizations" could produce more and more refined measures of attitudes, behavior, productivity, and so on, but would not tell us how an organization that was structured and managed in radically different ways would function. At best, further research on "standard organizations" would yield only theoretical and practical implications regarding how marginal improvements in performance might be achieved.

Bored with the study of standard organizations, I began casting about for situations in industry and in agriculture where people had arrived at different definitions of problems, were doing things in markedly different ways, and were getting results that at least appeared promising. This led me to studies of employee ownership and worker cooperatives in industry and new patterns of participatory agricultural research and development.

This focus on social inventions means that, in any field of activity, we can find very few cases for study and therefore the universe to which we generalize the findings of any case study is extremely small. For example as my colleagues and I looked in Latin America, Africa, and Asia for cases of agricultural research and development in which small farmers were active participants, we could not find more than three to five cases that seemed to fit this specification. Nevertheless, the organizational principles underlying these cases were strikingly similar, and the results in both participation and productivity seemed so promising as to lead us to announce the discovery of an emerging new model of agricultural research and development (Whyte and Boynton, 1983).

My research on worker cooperatives has been limited to a single case—or set of cases—the Mondragón cooperative complex (Gutiérrez-Johnson and Whyte, 1977; Whyte, 1982). However, even before we made our first trip to Mondragón in 1975, it was obvious that this was a critical case for practical and theoretical purposes. The extraordinary economic, social, and technological success achieved up to that data (and continuing to the present) indicated that the designers and leaders of the Mondragón organizations had overcome problems that had previously doomed worker cooperatives to failure or to an exceedingly precarious existence. I therefore felt it was vital to discover the social inventions that might account for the success of Mondragón. We were not the first but among the earliest foreign visitors to Mondragón. Since 1975 there has been an accelerating flow of social scientists and practitioners to that small Basque city in search of the secrets of Mondragón. As Mondragón has become more widely known, we find increasing numbers of people, especially in England and the United States, trying to apply some adaptation of the Basque cooperative model to the building of worker cooperatives in other countries.

While most people most of the time do things in standard ways, there is enough creativity in the human species so that in any field of activity we can find people who are doing things in new and promising ways. To grasp the nature and significance of these social inventions, we must learn to understand the technical as well as the social problems they are intended to solve. If we can then describe these social inventions systematically and place them within a conceptual scheme that permits us to suggest their applicability to similar problem situations elsewhere, we can contribute both to the advance of science and to the enhancement of human welfare.

REFERENCES

Anderson, E.
1978 A Place on the Corner. Chicago: University of Chicago Press.
Argyris, C.
1953 Executive Leadership. New York: Harper & Row.
Bales, R. F.
1950 Interaction Process Analysis: A Method for the Study of Small Groups. Reading, MA: Addison-Wesley.
Barnard, C.
1938 The Functions of the Executive. Cambridge: Harvard University Press.
Berreman, G. D.
1961 Behind Many Masks: Ethnography and Impression Management in a Himalayan Village. Society for Applied Anthropology, Monograph 4.
Blau, P.
1964 "The dynamics of bureaucracy," in P. Hammond (ed.) Sociologists at Work. New York: Basic Books.
Blumberg, P.
1968 Industrial Democracy: The Sociology of Participation. New York: Schocken.
Boissevain, J.
1974 Friends of Friends. New York: St. Martin's.
Bridgman, P. W.
1927 The Logic of Modern Physics. New York: Macmillan.
Burawoy, M.
1979 Manufacturing Consent. Chicago: University of Chicago Press.
Cancian, F.
1955 Economics and Prestige in a Maya Community: The Religious Cargo System in Zinacantan. Palo Alto, CA: Stanford University Press.
Chapple, E. D.
1949 "The interaction chronograph: its evolution and present application." Bulletin of the American Management Association.
Chapple, E. D. and C. M. Arensberg
1940 Measuring Human Relations: An Introduction to the Study of Interaction of Individuals. Provincetown, MA: Journal Press.
CIMMYT
1975 The Puebla Project: Seven Years of Experience, 1967-1973. El Batán, Mexico: CIMMYT.

Clawson, D.
1980 Bureaucracy and the Labor Process: The Transformation of American Industry, 1860-1920. New York: Monthly Review Press.

Clinard, M. B. and J. W. Elder
1965 "Sociology in India." American Sociological Review 30 (August): 581-587.

Cole, R.
1981 Work, Mobility and Participation. Berkeley: University of California Press.

Collier, J.
1957 "Anthropology: a report on two experiments." American Anthropologist 59: 843-859.

Copley, F. B.
1923 Frederick W. Taylor: Father of Scientific Management. New York: Harper & Row.

Craig, W.
1969 "The peasant movement of La Convención: dynamics of rural labor organization," in H. A. Landsberger (ed.) Latin American Peasant Movements. Ithaca, NY: Cornell University Press.

Dalton, M.
1959 Men Who Manage. New York: John Wiley.

Davis, A., B. B. Gardner, and M. R. Gardner
1941 Deep South: A Social Anthropological Study of Caste and Class. Chicago: University of Chicago Press.

Denzin, N.
1970 The Research Act in Sociology. Chicago: Aldine.

Doughty, P. L.
1978 "Review of *Power, Politics and Progress.*" American Anthropologist 80, 3.

Elden, M.
1979a "Three generations of work-democracy research in Norway: beyond classical socio-technical systems analysis," pp. 226-257 in C. L. Cooper and E. Mumford (eds.) The Quality of Working Life in Europe. London: Associated Business Press.
1979b "Participatory research leads to employee-managed change: some experience from a Norwegian bank," pp. 239-250 in International Council for the Quality of Working Life, Developments in Europe. Boston: Martinus Nijhoff.

Elden, M. and J. C. Taylor
1983 "Participatory research at work: an introduction." Journal of Occupational Behavior 4: 1-8.

Espinosa, W.
1973 Los Huancas, Aliados de la Conquista. Lima: Casa de la Cultura.

Fioravanti, E.
1974 Latifundio y Sindicalismo en el Perú: Estudio del Caso de los Valles de la Convención y Lares. Lima: Instituto de Estudios Peruanos.

Foster, G.
1966 "Peasant society and the image of the limited good." American Anthropologist 67, 4.

Fox, R. C. and J. P. Swazey
  1974   The Courage to Fail: A Social View of Organ Transplants and Dialysis. Chicago: University of Chicago Press.
Freeman, D.
  1973   Margaret Mead and Samoa: The Making and Unmaking of an Anthropological Myth. Cambridge, MA: Harvard University Press.
Freeman, H. E., R. R. Dynes, P. H. Rossi, and W. F. Whyte (eds.)
  1983   Applied Sociology: Roles and Activities of Sociologists in Diverse Settings. San Francisco: Jossey-Bass.
Fuenzalida, F., T. Valiente, J. L. Villaran, J. Golte, C. I. Degregori, and J. Casaverde
  1982   El Desafio de Huayopampa: Comuneros y Empresarios. Lima: Instituto de Estudios Peruanos. (Originally published 1968)
Gans, H. J.
  1982   Urban Villagers: Group and Class in the Life of Italian-Americans. New York: Free Press. (Originally published 1962)
Garfield, S. and W. F. Whyte
  1950-1951   "The collective bargaining process: a human relations analysis." Human Organization (4 parts; Winter 1950 to Spring 1951).
Geertz, C.
  1973   The Interpretation of Cultures. New York: Basic Books.
Glaser, B. G. and A. L. Strauss
  1967   The Discovery of Grounded Theory: Strategies for Qualitative Research. Chicago: Aldine.
Gostyla, L. and W. F. Whyte
  1980   ICTA in Guatemala: The Evolution of a New Model for Agricultural Research and Development. Ithaca, NY: Cornell University, Center for International Studies.
Greenwood, D.
  1976   Unrewarding Wealth. New York: Cambridge University Press.
Gutierrez-Johnson, A. and W. F. Whyte
  1977   "The Mondragon system of worker production cooperatives." Industrial and Labor Relations Review 31 (October): 18-30.
Hammond, P. (ed.)
  1964   Sociologists at Work. New York: Basic Books.
Harvey, O. J. and M. Sherif
  1953   "An experimental approach to the study of status relations in informal groups." American Sociological Review 18, 4: 357-367.
Henderson, L. J.
  1938   "Sociology 23: introductory lectures," 2nd ed. (mimeo)
Horowitz, I. L.
  1967   The Rise and Fall of Project Camelot. Cambridge: MIT Press.
Horowitz, R.
  1983   Honor and the American Dream. New Brunswick, NJ: Rutgers University Press.
Ianni, F.
  1972   A Family Business: Kinship and Social Control in Organized Crime. New York: Russell Sage Foundation.

Jacobs, J.
    1977   Stateville: The Penitentiary in Mass Society. Chicago: University of
            Chicago Press.
Jick, T.
    1983   "Mixing qualitative and quantitative methods: triangulation in action," in J.
            Van Maanen (ed.) Qualitative Methodology. Beverly Hills, CA: Sage.
Katz, H. C., T. A. Kochan, and K. R. Gobeille
    1983   "Industrial relations performance, economic performance, and QWL pro-
            grams: an interplant analysis." Industrial and Labor Relations Review 37
            (October): 3-17.
Kennedy, T.
    1982   "Beyond advocacy: a facilitative approach to public participation." Journal
            of the University Film and Video Association 34, 3: 33-46.
Kornblum, W.
    1974   Blue Collar Community. Chicago: University of Chicago Press.
Kuhn, T. S.
    1962   The Structure of Scientific Revolutions. Chicago: University of Chicago
            Press.
Lawrence, P. and J. Clark
    1958   The Changing of Organizational Behavior Patterns. Boston: Harvard
            Graduate School of Business Administration.
Lazes, P. and T. Costanza
    1983   "Cutting costs without layoffs through union-management collaboration."
            National Productivity Review (Autumn): 362-370.
Lévi-Strauss, C.
    1967   "Four Winnebago myths: a structural sketch," pp. 15-26 in J. Middleton
            (ed.) Myth and Cosmos: Readings in Mythology and Symbolism. Garden
            City, NY: Natural History Press.
Lewis, O.
    1951   Life in a Mexican Village: Tepoztlán Restudied. Urbana: University of
            Illinois Press.
Liebow, E.
    1967   Tally's Corner. Boston: Little, Brown.
Lynd, R. S. and H. M. Lynd
    1929   Middletown: A Study in Contemporary American Culture. New York: Har-
            court Brace Jovanovich.
    1937   Middletown in Transition: A Study of Cultural Conflicts. New York: Har-
            court Brace Jovanovich.
Malinowski, B.
    1922   Argonauts of the Western Pacific. London: Routledge & Kegan Paul.
Matos Mar, J. and W. F. Whyte
    1966   Proyecto de Estudios de Cambios en Pueblos Peruanos. Lima: Instituto de
            Estudios Peruanos.
Mayr, E.
    1983   The Growth of Biological Thought. Cambridge, MA: Harvard University
            Press.
Mead, M.
    1973   Coming of Age in Samoa. New York: Morrow. (Originally published 1928)

Moreno, J.
1970   Barrios in Arms. Pittsburgh: University of Pittsburgh Press.
Pace, D.
1983   Claude Lévi-Strauss: The Bearer of the Ashes. London: Kegan Paul International.
Parish, W. L. and M. K. Whyte
1978   Village and Family in Contemporary China. Chicago: University of Chicago Press.
Read, K.
1965   The High Valley. New York: Scribners.
Redfield, R.
1930   Tepoztlán: A Mexican Village. Chicago: University of Chicago Press.
Reinharz, S.
1979   On Becoming a Social Scientist: From Survey Research and Participant Observation to Experiential Analysis. San Francisco: Jossey-Bass.
Richardson, S. A., B. S. Dohrenwend, and D. Klein
1965   Interviewing: Its Forms and Functions. New York: Basic Books.
Roethlisberger, F. J. and W. J. Dickson
1939   Management and the Worker. Cambridge, MA: Harvard University Press.
Rossi, P. H. and W. F. Whyte
1983   "The applied side of sociology," pp. 5-31 in H. Freeman et al., Applied Sociology: Roles and Activities of Sociologists in Diverse Settings. San Francisco: Jossey-Bass.
Roth, J.
1975   "Hired hand research," in G. Lewis (ed.) Fist-Fights in the Kitchen. Pacific Palisades, CA: Goodyear.
Roy, D.
1953   "Work satisfaction and social rewards in quota achievement." American Sociological Review 18 (October).
1964   " 'Banana Time'—job satisfaction and informal interaction," in W. G. Bennis et al. (eds.) Interpersonal Dynamics: Essays and Readings on Human Interaction. Homewood, IL: Dorsey.
Sayles, L.
1954   "Field use of projective methods: a case example." Sociology and Social Research 38, 3: 168-173.
1958   Behavior of Industrial Work Groups. New York: John Wiley.
Schein, E. H.
1980   Organizational Psychology. Englewood Cliffs, NJ: Prentice-Hall.
Schleper-Hughes, N.
1983   "The Margaret Mead controversy: culture, biology and anthropological inquiry." Human Organization 43, 1.
Servan-Schreiber, J. J.
1968   The American Challenge. New York: Harper & Row.
Stern, R. N. and T. H. Hammer
1978   "Buying your job: factors affecting the success or failure of employee acquisition attempts." Human Relations 31: 1101-1117.
Strauss, G.
1952   "Direct observation as a source of quasi-sociometric observation." Sociometry (February/May): 141-145.

Sullivan, M., Jr., S. Queen, and R. C. Patrick, Jr.
　　1958　"Participant observation as employed in a military training program."
　　　　　American Sociological Review 23: 660-676.
Thomas, R.
　　1984　Citizenship, Gender and Work: A Study in the Social Organization of
　　　　　Industrial Agriculture. Berkeley: University of California Press.
Thorsrud, E.
　　1977　"Democracy at work: Norwegian experiences with nonbureaucratic forms
　　　　　of organization." Applied Behavioral Science 13, 3: 410-421.
Tilly, C.
　　1981　As Sociology Meets History. New York: Academic.
Trist, E.
　　1981　The Evolution of Socio-Technical Systems: A Conceptual Framework and
　　　　　an Action Research Program. Toronto: Ontario Ministry of Labor.
Vaughan, D.
　　1983　Controlling Unlawful Organizational Behavior: Social Structure and Cor-
　　　　　porate Misconduct. Chicago: University of Chicago Press.
Vidich, A. J. and J. Bensman
　　1958　Small Town in Mass Society. Princeton, NJ: Princeton University Press.
Vidich, A. J., J. Bensman, and M. Stein
　　1964　Reflections on Community Studies. New York: John Wiley.
Warner, W. L.
　　1958　Black Civilization. New York: Harper & Row. (Originally published 1937)
Warner, W. L. and P. S. Lunt
　　1941　The Social Life of a Modern Community. New Haven, CT: Yale University
　　　　　Press.
Warner, W. L. et al.
　　1941-1957　Yankee City Series. New Haven, CT: Yale University Press.
Wax, R. H.
　　1971　Doing Field Work: Warnings and Advice. Chicago: University of Chicago
　　　　　Press.
Weiner, A. B.
　　1983　"Ethnographic determinism: Samoa and the Margaret Mead controversy."
　　　　　American Anthropologist 85 (December): 909-919.
Wellman, B.
　　1980　"A guide to network analysis." Working Paper 1A, Structural Analysis
　　　　　Programme, Department of Sociology, University of Toronto.
Whyte, M. K.
　　1983　"On studying China at a distance," pp. 63-80 in A. F. Thurston and B.
　　　　　Pasternak (eds.) The Social Sciences and Field Work in China. Boulder,
　　　　　CO: Westview.
forthcoming　"Review of Broken Earth: The Rural Chinese by Steven W. Mosher."
　　　　　Peasant Studies.
Whyte, M. K. and W. P. Parish
　　1984　Urban Life in Contemporary China. Chicago: University of Chicago Press.

Whyte, W. F.
    1931   "Bill Whyte visits the elementary school." Bronxville Schools Bulletin 18.
    1935   "Financing New York City." Bulletin 2, American Academy of Political and Social Science.
    1944a   "Age-grading of the Plains Indians." Man 44 (May/June): 53-70, 68-72.
    1944b   "Who goes union and why." Personnel Journal 23 (December): 215-230.
    1946 (ed.)   Industry and Society. New York: McGraw-Hill.
    1947   "Solving the hotel's human problems." Hotel Monthly (June).
    1948   Human Relations in the Restaurant Industry. New York: McGraw-Hill.
    1949a   "Patterns of interaction in union management relations." Human Organization 8 (Fall): 13-19.
    1949b   "The social structure of the restaurant." American Journal of Sociology 54 (January): 302-310.
    1951a   Pattern for Industrial Peace. New York: Harper & Row.
    1951b   "Observational field work methods," in G. Jahoda et al. (eds.) Research Methods in Social Relations, Vol. 2. New York: Dryden.
    1955   Money and Motivation. New York: Harper & Row.
    1956   "On asking indirect questions." Human Organization 15 (Winter): 21-23.
    1960   "Interviewing," pp. 352-374 in R. C. Adams and J. J. Preiss (eds.) Human Organization Research. Homewood, IL: Dorsey.
    1960-1961   "The card shuffling method of graduate education." Human Organization 19, 4: 169.
    1961   Men at Work. Homewood, IL: Irwin-Dorsey.
    1963a   "Toward an integrated approach for research in organizational behavior." Presidential Address, Industrial Relations Research Association, IRRA Proceedings.
    1963b   "Culture, industrial relations, and economic development: the case of Peru." Industrial and Labor Relations Review 16, 4: 583-594.
    1964   "On *Street Corner Society*," pp. 256-268 in E. W. Burgess and D. Bogue (eds.) Contributions to Urban Sociology. Chicago: University of Chicago Press.
    1969a   "The role of the U.S. professor abroad." American Sociologist 4 (February): 19-28.
    1969b   "Rural Peru: peasants as activists." Transaction (November): 39-47.
    1972   "Pigeons, persons and piece rates." Psychology Today (April): 67-68, 96-100.
    1975   "Conflict and cooperation in Andean communities." American Ethnologist 2 (May): 373-392.
    1976   "Research methods for the study of conflict and cooperation." American Sociologist 11 (November): 208-216.
    1981   Street Corner Society. Chicago: University of Chicago Press. (Originally published 1943)
    1982   "Social inventions for solving human problems." American Sociological Review 47, 1: 1-13.
    1983   "Worker participation: international and historical perspectives." Journal of Applied Behavioral Science 19, 3: 395-407.

Whyte, W. F. and G. Alberti
  1976   Power, Politics and Progress: Social Change in Rural Peru. New York: Elsevier.
Whyte, W. F. and J. Blasi
  1980   "From research to legislation on employee ownership." Economic and Industrial Democracy 1, 3: 395-415.
Whyte, W. F. and D. Boynton (eds.)
  1983   Higher-Yielding Human Systems for Agriculture. Ithaca, NY: Cornell University Press.
Whyte, W. F. and R. R. Braun
  1966   "Heroes, homework and industrial growth." Columbia Journal of World Business 1 (Spring): 51-57.
  1968   "On language and culture," pp. 119-138 in H. S. Becker (ed.) Institutions and the Person. Chicago: Aldine.
Whyte, W. F., B. B. Gardner, and A. Whiteford (eds.)
  1946   "From conflict to cooperation: the Buchsbaum case." Applied Anthropology (Fall): special issue.
Whyte, W. F. and E. L. Hamilton
  1965   Action Research for Management. Homewood, IL: Irwin-Dorsey.
Whyte, W. F., T. H. Hammer, C. Meek, R. Nelson, and R. N. Stern
  1983   Worker Participation and Ownership: Cooperative Strategies for Strengthening Local Economies. Ithaca, NY: ILR.
Whyte, W. F. and L. K. Williams
  1963   "Supervisory leadership: an international comparison," pp. 1-8 in Symposium B3, C.I.O.S. International Management Congress XIII.
  1968   Toward an Integrated Theory of Development: Economic and Non-Economic Variables in Rural Development. Ithaca: New York State School of Industrial and Labor Relations, Cornell University.
Woodward, J.
  1965   Industrial Organization: Theory and Practice. London: Oxford University Press.